Newfoundland

The Traveller's Canada

Newfoundland

Harold Horwood

Toronto / Macmillan of Canada

First published 1969
First paperback 1977

ISBN 0-7705-1614-9

Some sections of this book are based on articles by the author that appeared originally in *Maclean's* Magazine, the *Star Weekly, The Canadian* Magazine, *Weekend* Magazine, the *Imperial Oil Review,* and Maclean-Hunter's *Canada: Portrait of a Nation,* and on scripts written for the Canadian Broadcasting Cor-poration. The author wishes to thank the editors of these publications and the CBC for permission to use the material in revised form in this volume.

Printed in Canada for
The Macmillan Company of Canada Limited,
70 Bond Street, Toronto, Ontario   M5B 1X3

Dedicated to

Andrew Horwood, my father,
Captain John Horwood, master mariner, my grandfather,
Captain Cyril Horwood, master mariner, my great-uncle,
Captain Mark Burke, master mariner, my great-uncle,
Skipper Sam Horwood, master mariner, my great-uncle,
Captain Hugh Horwood, master mariner, my great-grandfather,
all of whom sailed out of Carbonear,
and to six earlier generations of sailors, shipbuilders,
and fishermen, our ancestors in this great island of
Newfoundland.

Contents

Illustrations

Map

Newfoundland (*centre pages of photograph section*)

Photographs (*between pages 84 and 85*)

Newfoundland

1. The Camper's Wilderness

In north-central Newfoundland, about eighty miles from the city of Corner Brook, is the popular fishing and camping ground of Birchy Lake, a narrow ribbon of water winding between mountains for thirteen miles and emptying into the greatest lake system in the island: the Sandy Lake–Grand Lake chain that almost cuts Newfoundland in two.

At the eastern end of this beautiful lake is the old portage trail to Lake Seymour, and near by rises the hill that used to be known to the trappers as the Teapot Dome. I climbed the Teapot Dome when I was a boy just out of school, on my first trip through the Newfoundland interior, and there, about two miles to the north, I saw a river flowing eastward into the sunrise. This was my first view of Indian River, the old canoe route that connected the eastern and western hunting grounds of the Beothuck Indians.

I mentally filed the river for future reference, followed the trail westward to Sandy Lake; and fifteen years passed before I saw it again. By that time, a road had been cut through the wilderness where I had formerly tramped on foot with so much labour, and, since you could now traverse the whole of central Newfoundland by car, a canoe trip along this ancient route had become nothing more than a sporting proposition.

But that autumn, having quit my newspaper job for freelance writing with enough money to see me through three or four months, I headed for the interior again, parked my car near the end of Hall's Bay, and started up Indian River in a fifteen-foot canvas canoe.

It proved to be one of the best rivers in Newfoundland for this kind of travel – big enough to give ample water under your keel, small enough to be free of dangers, with a steady, gentle current and few obstructions, falling at the rate of about five feet to the mile, with long stretches of still water.

So I pushed my little red canoe up-stream all day along the placid surface of Indian River, pausing as I wished, to cook a meal or to explore the country on either side. Even though the highroad was often only a mile or two away, it was as though the world were without human inhabitants. And then, on the third day, as I headed into the red and gold of the sunset, I came to an old camp-ground, a small plateau in the forest, set high on a wooded bank.

The river forked above, and there was a whisper of a rapids below – a 'chute' leading to a 'rattle', as our woodsmen describe it. Beyond, glimmering in the afterglow, was the wide sweep of the caribou barrens.

This point that I had reached had once been a meeting-place for Indian bands, a summer staging-point for the mysterious Beothuck people, a tribe without known antecedents or relations, that vanished like smoke into the Newfoundland forests a hundred and fifty years ago. Here they pitched their *meoticks* – dwellings falling somewhere between a tent and a house – and built their fires and laughed and loved and sorrowed, and passed from the eye of man, leaving no trace of their passage except for a few chipped flints and bone ornaments half buried in the sand.

Upon an old raised camp mound, with a little moat still faintly visible through three centuries of moss, I pitched my canvas tent, as they had pitched their *meoticks* of bark or skin for uncounted generations. As the last light faded from the sky, I built a little fire of dry spruce branches, and the blue-white disc of the moon floated above the trees, turning Indian River to a sheet of ghostly silver.

The voices of the night came out around me. The eyes of a mouse peeped from a thicket of Labrador Tea. On the far bank, a prowling lynx, catching, perhaps, the scent of my fire, screamed as though in anguish, and went bounding off through clumps of alder and balsam fir.

Time melted and flowed like the river, and it was easy to imagine a fleet of birch canoes, built in the curious double crescent of an earlier age, slipping down through the up-stream forks, grey and wraith-like in the moonlight, to ground with a gentle murmur upon the gravel far below. Listening, I could fancy the sound of voices in a tongue now long forgotten, the beginning of a chant in a barbaric key strange to our ears, transplanted, perhaps, from the steppes of far Siberia – and the thudding of a hundred feet in the ritual of the dance.

No change had come upon this land in the even flow of the five centuries since white men came to stay – no change except that the tall, handsome Beothucks had gone, and I had come to take their place, and the last wolf was slain – a big, dark beast without a mate, alone in all that vast land, turned scavenger at the end, and shot seeking scraps around the ashes of a human fire.

Sitting beside the fragrant coals of native spruce, gazing back along a stream of time foreshortened by the ageless earth and moon, I felt that this was holy ground, a fitting memorial to a vanished race. Here on this deserted lookout they had watched for the caribou herds in the green light of autumn dawns, or scanned the rapids of the river for the first salmon in the cool, bright days of spring. The white hunters who followed them have also gone, and the sportsman has come in their place, seeking, in his turn, the red salmon and the grey caribou, until he, too, vanishes into the endless flux of nature.

I sat most of the night upon the old camp-ground, until the moon set, and the river became a murmur in the dark. I may have dozed, for the fire burned down to a handful of glowing embers, wrapped in white ash, and my thoughts drifted into the sequence of a dream, with visions of tall men fleeing across the sea in bark canoes – fleeing an unknown terror that pressed hard upon their backs, of women digging in the clay of Ochre Pit Cove for the magic red pigment that brought success to the hunters and peace to the dead, of naked children, sun-browned and lithe and beautiful, playing tag along the sands of Red Indian Lake, their laughter faint and timeless, as it was in the beginning, is now, and shall be when the stars have left their courses to form new constellations of a shape we do not know.

Morning found me curled in my sleeping-bag, at peace in my little domed world of green canvas, with the river lapping gently at the butt of my canoe below the door. I slept while the sun rose, until the heat inside the tent drove me outdoors. Then I went swimming from the little sand beach, wondering whether any man had done so since the last of the Indian hunters – all of whom were expert swimmers – took his morning dip in the clear, cool water, and then headed up-stream toward the Armageddon of his race. Everything I did seemed to have this eerie quality of being a re-enactment from a forgotten time and a vanished people.

I took my canoe up-stream to the forks, thrusting the blade with all the strength of my shoulders. Then I lay back in the sun and let the wonderful little shell of a boat drift with the current slowly past the high banks, past the plateau of the campsite, and into the chute leading to the rattle. There I dipped the paddle once more, and guided the canoe into the dark vee of the current, exulting as it bounced joyously past the white water into the still and foam-flecked steady below, thinking all the while how this had been done thousands of times by men who exulted, like me, in the agility of their light river craft, back in the pre-Columbian centuries when my own ancestors were building clumsy tubs of ships to serve the tyrant kings of Europe.

I tracked the canoe up-stream, past the rapids, and paddled back to the landing. There I boiled tea, and made a breakfast of biscuit and cheese. And as I lay, soaking up the late summer sun on the sand, the familiar urge that every writer knows so well came over me, and out of my meagre camping supplies I dug the paper and pencil necessary for translating dreams into the equally fragile world of words.

There on the Indian campsite, in the heart of Newfoundland, this book was born. I remained for five days, repeating an unchanging pattern: swimming from the sand-bar, paddling on the river, eking out sparse meals with fat trout from the pool below and berries from the barrens above, more swimming and lying in the sun, and short bouts of writing, an hour or so at a time, with endless rereading and revision. Each day was like the others, warm and perfect and almost cloudless, with the golden sunshine and the blue haze that make the Newfoundland Indian summer one of the most beautiful seasons with which any part of the earth is blessed.

Then I packed and returned, enjoying almost a free ride — slipping rapidly down-stream where I had worked my way upward so much more slowly the week before, gliding along the smooth highway of the lower river to the roadside landing where my car was waiting, and driving back through the star-studded night toward the paper town of Grand Falls with a song flowing through my mind and the smooth road flowing blackly under my wheels.

2. The First-comers

Archaeologists have uncovered a Norse settlement at L'Anse-aux-Meadows, near St. Anthony, on the northern tip of Newfoundland, that has been dated by radio-carbon at approximately A.D. 1000. It is the first authenticated Norse settlement west of Greenland.

The Norse (or 'Vikings' as they are often called) were great voyagers, but their colonizing effort in North America was a failure. They got into bloody fights with the Indians or Eskimos or both, and the only colony of which we have any written record, that founded by Thorfinn Karlsefni, in the first decade of the eleventh century, was abandoned after three years. Some of the remains at L'Anse-aux-Meadows may date from the Karlsefni expedition.

They continued making voyages at least as far as Labrador, for timber, during the next three or four hundred years, however, and long before the failure of their Greenland colony the Basques had penetrated into Greenland waters and the Labrador Sea, hunting whales. There was, in fact, no 'discovery' of North America by Europeans later than the Norse. The New World was known at least to a few whalers and fishermen right through the centuries between Leif Ericsson and John Cabot.

The Basques were hunting whales in Greenland and off the Labrador coast before 1450. They had established whaling factories in the Strait of Belle Isle (near the old Norse settlement, then long forgotten) by the early 1500s, but how long they had been there before that, nobody knows, for they were great but illiterate seamen, and left no written records, so that the intermediate chapter that they occupy between the Norse and the English remains a mystery.

The next discoverers were the men of Bristol, among whom John Cabot was a late-comer. Bristol customs records (only lately examined with any care) show that the fishermen of that English port began fishing at Iceland and trading in Icelandic products in the early 1400s. They probably learned of the New World from the Icelanders, but their first recorded voyage in search of new land and new fisheries on this side of the Atlantic took place in 1480. The first expedition – in search of a legendary land somewhere west of Ireland called 'the Island of Brasil' – produced no results, but the next year, 1481, they sent two ships, the *George* and the *Trinity*, into the western Atlantic, with eighty bushels of fishery salt. They were apparently successful, and there was a subsequent lawsuit based on the belief that the salt was being used for trade. There is no record of their return to England, but the *Trinity* was back in an English port two years later, and some historians believe that she probably spent one winter in the New World.

A number of English chronicles of the sixteenth century say quite specifically that Newfoundland was discovered by the Bristol traders in 1494, but this does not necessarily mean that other Bristolmen had not been there before. In those days, whenever a man made a first voyage to a new land he was said to have 'discovered' it.

The voyage of 1494 was made by two fish merchants named Robert Thorne and Hughe Elliot, and Robert Thorne, Jr., writing in 1527, claimed that his father was the true discoverer of the New Found Land.

This claim is given much substance by the John Day letter, discovered in the Spanish archives in 1956, where it had lain undetected for more than four and a half centuries because it was wrongly filed under 'Brazil'. After describing the Cabot voyage at length, this document of 1498 adds: 'It is considered certain that the cape of the said land [that reached by Cabot] was found and discovered in the past by the men from Bristol who found Brasil, as your lordship knows. It was called the Island of Brasil, and it is assumed and believed to be the mainland that the men from Bristol found.'

Add to this another document from the Spanish ambassador to England, also dated 1498, stating that for seven years past the Bristol merchants had been sending two, three, and four ships into the western Atlantic, and we begin to see the Cabot voyage in its true perspective, as an official follow-up to earlier discoveries by the Bristol merchants.

All this is further confirmed by a curious fact from the first Cabot voyage: John Cabot brought back from the New World, among other artefacts that he picked up on shore, a carved wooden net needle. For centuries this was assumed by all historians to have been an Indian artefact. But no Indian ever made or used anything that a European would call a net needle. It could only have been a relic of an earlier fishing voyage.

Cabot sailed from Bristol in 1497 with the stated object of proving that the 'Island of Brasil' was part of Asia, or that the Asian mainland lay close behind it.

From his New World landfall, wherever it was (and the old belief that it was in Newfoundland has been disproved by recent research), he coasted for nine hundred miles in a generally easterly direction before taking his departure for Bristol. On the way home he sighted two islands which may, indeed, have been two of the southern capes of Newfoundland. But if we assume this, then the latitudes given by the chroniclers are wrong. No possible theory can make all the facts fit together, but the most likely one seems to be that he sailed south of Newfoundland deliberately, guided by Bristol crewmen who had fished in this region before, trying to find the Asian mainland; that he landed somewhere in New England, coasted eastward to some cape in Nova Scotia, and thence took his departure for home.

On his second voyage, in 1498, he vanished without a trace.

Sebastian Cabot did not sail with his father, as used to be assumed by historians. He certainly was not on the second voyage, and, if he was on the first, then it was as a boy of fourteen. His one major voyage was in 1508-9, and was a search for a Northwest Passage in the region of Greenland, Baffin Island, or northern Labrador.

Gaspar Corte Real, the first Portuguese 'discoverer' whose voyage has any documentary support, sailed to Greenland in 1500 looking for a Northwest Passage, returned the following year, and coasted all the way down Labrador and along eastern Newfoundland to Cape Race. From that point two of his ships returned to Portugal (with loads of Indian or Eskimo slaves) while the third, commanded by Corte Real himself, turned westward toward the Canadian mainland and was never seen again.

His voyage is honoured by a heroic statue in front of the provincial building on Confederation Hill in St. John's.

Next year, Miguel Corte Real set out to find his brother. Again, two of the three ships arrived home, but the one with Corte Real himself disappeared. Portuguese fishing ships promptly followed the Corte Reals to the Grand Banks and Newfoundland, however, and they have been coming to St. John's harbour every year since then. The arrival of the Portuguese 'White Fleet' every spring is still one of the cardinal points of the year in the Newfoundland capital.

After the discoverers came the colonists. Nobody knows just when or where. The first royal patent for the founding of a colony in Newfoundland was issued to the Bristol Company Adventurers to the New Found Land in 1502. They made their first attempt at colonization in 1503. They brought out a priest (probably the first to sail to the New World) in 1504. There are indications that the colony survived until 1506, but it must have failed thereafter. Nothing about it, indeed, is certain, except that the attempt to plant a colony was made. There is also a document of 1504 referring to an English 'settlement' in Newfoundland, though this does not necessarily mean a permanent colony.

At the tail end of all this discovery, commerce, and colonization came Jacques Cartier in 1534, looking for a Northwest Passage. He made his landfall on Funk Island, forty miles out in the Atlantic to the north-east of Newfoundland (and now a major sea-bird sanctuary), where he killed boatloads of birds, then went on to the Strait of Belle Isle, sailed into the gulf, and up the St. Lawrence to 'discover' Canada.

So much for the 'discoverers'. More than four centuries later Newfoundland was discovered once again, first by the Canadian government, and then by the tourists. They found in the island a strange, insular breed of humans who had somehow managed to survive there for almost half a millennium, and to develop into a people with unique qualities.

3. By Road across the Island

I'm the number one Newfoundland tourist myself. Though I was born in the island, and though my ancestors (not including Eskimos) have lived there for the past three hundred years, I never grow tired of 'visiting' it. I have crossed the island forty-seven times by car, sailed around it in big ships and small boats, traversed its interior again and again by train, on foot, and by canoe, sailed up and down the coast of Labrador, and flown across it in every possible direction time and again. Still I have not seen it all, for Newfoundland is a huge province, more than six hundred miles from east to west, and more than a thousand miles from north to south.

Three-quarters of this territory lies on the mainland, and is known as Labrador, but even the one-quarter that lies within the island of Newfoundland is much larger than any of the other Atlantic provinces, only slightly smaller than Great Britain, and ranks tenth among the islands of the world.

There are two ways to see it today – by ship and by car (for you can drive into Labrador now, with the aid of ferries) – but if you want to get even a fair sample of the province, you have to use both.

The Trans-Canada Highway in Newfoundland is a rough semi-circle 550 miles long, linking the capital, St. John's, with the rail and ferry terminal, Port-aux-Basques, at the south-west corner. From St. John's it curves northward, westward, and southward, skirting all the great bays of the east, north, and west coasts. Except for the south coast and the Great Northern Peninsula, it is only a few miles by road from the Trans-Canada to any settlement on the island.

On a typical morning in early April I leave St. John's by Route

9

One, joining it at the cloverleaf intersection with Route Three, just west of the city, and begin the swift plunge across the province in a haze of spring sunshine that soon turns to light rain, and then, briefly, to fog.

An ermine weasel comes out on the black asphalt, looking ridiculously obvious in his coat of pure winter white. He stops, debating for a moment whether to dispute the right of passage with my car, and then dematerializes into a near-by ditch. Two tons of black machinery hurtling along with a potential of half a million foot pounds per second is enough to awe even an ermine weasel. Along the banks of the highroad the alder trees are in bud, giving off a bitter, resinous scent that stirs race memories of hunting in the boreal forests, and the leaves of the wild red currants have already unfolded like pale green stars.

The road is in beautiful condition. At present it is the best road of its length in the Atlantic provinces. There are other stretches of perhaps a hundred or a hundred and fifty miles that compare favourably with the Newfoundland road, but nowhere else east of Quebec is there a road of more than five hundred miles on which you can travel at an even 60 m.p.h. without once slowing for a turn, an intersection, or a blind hill. It is a two-lane road with extra lanes on grades and exits, and there are plans for increasing the more heavily travelled sections to four lanes as the traffic flow increases.

To Newfoundlanders, who grew up driving cars over dirt trails, this road seems almost miraculous, and driving on it is much like flying a small plane a generation ago. The geography unfolds under your wheels. An hour and fifty-five minutes after leaving St. John's I am passing Clarenville, a railway and ship-yard town on a beautiful fjord in the inner reaches of Trinity Bay. I can see chains of little fishing settlements dotting the blue land along the shores on either side, and the winding waterway that leads outward to the incredibly beautiful seascapes of St. Jones Within and Little Hearts Ease. A mere spit across the channel is Random Island, a squarish chunk of wooded ground twenty miles long, carved out of the coast by the narrow, river-like channels of Smith Sound and Random Sound, with more than fifty miles of marvellous boating waters all around it, and a chain of tiny settlements along its shore.

Half an hour later I have doubled the end of Bonavista Bay, **and Clode Sound** is stretching away behind me, the little white settlement of Charlottetown snuggled in a fold of the land on my right. I remember well when it took all day to reach Charlotte-town from St. John's by surface travel. Now it takes just a little over two hours. The landlocked waters of Sweet Bay and Alexander Bay, with their sheer cliffs and conical islands, lie just ahead, while Gander Lake and its international airport are just over the next range of hills.

I stop for an hour in Gander and have lunch at a restaurant where there is excellent, though rather expensive, Chinese food. Neither here nor almost anywhere else in Newfoundland is it possible to buy a restaurant meal of really fresh, locally produced seafood, prepared with imagination and flair.

From Gander I drive for an hour through dense pulpwood forests and along the shores of the Exploits River to the inland paper town of Grand Falls with its tree-shaded streets and omnipresent mill churning out newsprint by the square mile. There I make a short visit with a friend who shares my passion for bird-watching, before starting the long inland roll toward the west coast.

As I pass Springdale, where Indian River meets the sea, the overcast begins to break up, and a few minutes later I am coasting down the long, straight grade into the valley of Birchy Lake in a marvellous spring haze that makes the ranges of mountains on either side drift off into an infinite series of blues – a poetic equation with black and white as its limits, with the curve of the blue between, and the white light shining, the aleph-null of a transfinite reality.

Except in Labrador, where they soar more than 5,000 feet straight out of the sea, all our Newfoundland mountains are less than 3,000 feet high. But they are real mountains for all that, rugged, steep, faced with great slabs of rock, sometimes nearly unclimbable. The best of them are northern extensions of the Appalachian chain, but they are bolder, more rugged, more primitive than their civilized relatives to the south.

Golden shafts of sunshine fall through broken cloud in pools upon the still lakes, making long roadways through the hazy atmosphere. As the old people would say, 'The sun is drawing water', and they might go on to predict rain for the morrow – a not unlikely prophecy, either, when the clouds pile up like that, and the air is blue with haze. The spruces march up the clefts and sheltered valleys of the hills toward the skyline, turning from green to black, and then to purple as they go.

Soon I am gliding over a smooth saddle of hill and dropping down into the valley of the Upper Humber, one of the world's great salmon rivers, now dappled with cobalt and silver. Sandy Lake, a part of the ninety-mile Grand Lake chain, stretches off toward a far horizon on my left. The last clouds drift away, and I drive through the town of Deer Lake in a blaze of afternoon sunshine.

In the suburb known as The Water Chute (who remembers, now, the days when the trains used to stop there to take on water, and the half-wild, half-Indian children would come down through the fields to watch, and to wave shyly to travellers as the trains pulled away once more?) there are black-haired boys in shirtsleeves playing football – not true Indians, these, but descendants of Algonkians and Acadian French, newcomers to Newfoundland whose ancestors settled here after the expulsion of the Acadians from Nova Scotia in 1755. Just beyond the football game, three dogs are having an argument with a flock of crows in a field, while a pair of black ducks heads eastward across the sky.

Deer Lake is a town of loggers, and a power producer for the city of Corner Brook, but the lake, which takes its name from the migrating caribou herds that passed here each spring and autumn, is a broad expansion of the Humber River, hemmed in by mountains. As I pass Pasadena, a farm settlement near its western outlet, the banks at the end of the lake are still draped in mist gilded by the afternoon sun. Sizes and distances are distorted so that the modest Blomidon Mountains that surround Corner Brook emerge like a breath-taking view of the Rockies from a sea of cloud. Then the black ditch of the Lower Humber goes snaking between its steep banks, the white face of Marble Mountain on its left, the stark, reddish face of Indian Head on its right, the river everywhere soaking up the spring run-off and delivering it into the maw of the sea. The evening comes gently over Corner Brook, and the dusk has a touch of warmth as I crest the mountains above it and see this west-coast city, with its gleaming Bay of Islands, gathering soft gloom among its encircling hills.

The road slopes gently upward toward its highest point (marked with a large sign, as though you had here achieved the

Matterhorn, or, at the very least, the Great Divide), then grades away as gently toward Port-aux-Basques, the snow-creviced mountains of the Long Range on the left and the lush valley of the Codroy, full of sheep and river-bottom farms, on the right.

Dark is settling over the land as I drive down between the volcanic cones (millions of years dead) at the end of the Long Range, past the gleaming surf beaches of Cape Ray, and wind my way into Port-aux-Basques, with its twin harbours and its tarred fishing boats, and its multi-million-dollar terminal linking Newfoundland with mainland Canada, sixty-five miles away.

Though this sort of drive has its own kind of charm, it is, of course, not the way to see a province. But it is perhaps the commonest drive taken in Newfoundland, both by natives on their way to the mainland, and by visitors who wish to begin their tours at St. John's.

The great majority of tourists entering Newfoundland today come by car on the ferry from North Sydney in Nova Scotia. The trip takes six hours, and may be made by day or by night (with sleeping cabins). The two ferries on the run are large, comfortable, and well supplied with food and drink. It is sometimes possible, even in July and August, to get space on them by waiting in line, but reservations are usually required.

There are about 6,000 miles of highroad in Newfoundland, including private roads built by the paper companies for logging. These logging roads, in poor but passable condition, lead to some of the best hunting and trout-fishing areas in the Atlantic region – especially to the haunts of caribou, moose, and black bears, and to lakes full of eastern brook trout. Though for the best trout you have to get well off the travelled routes, no special effort is needed, paradoxically, to reach the lordliest of all fresh-water game fish – the Atlantic salmon. Many of the world's best salmon rivers are right beside the main highways.

Approximately 1,100 miles of roads outside the cities were paved by the end of 1968, and paving was continuing on various secondary highways. But there were still long stretches of road without pavement, including the 300 miles from Deer Lake by way of the Great Northern Peninsula to Labrador. This road is being extended another 550 miles from Forteau, on the mainland side of the straits, right across the face of Labrador to Goose Bay and Happy Valley, on to the giant power development at Churchill Falls, and finally to Labrador City and Wabush on the

Quebec border. The drive from St. John's to Labrador City will be about 1,200 miles, including a fifteen-mile ferry ride across the Strait of Belle Isle, but the ferry will eventually be replaced by a tunnel, if the Newfoundland government gets its way, and the road itself may well represent the beginning of a new Trans-Canada route in the north.

Many of Newfoundland's unpaved roads lead to landscapes and seascapes of almost awesome beauty – not to mention fascinating and remote villages, some of them changed but little since the days of the pirate Peter Easton, carrying on the in-shore fishery by substantially the same methods that were used by the fishermen from England, Ireland, and France who settled here in the days of the Tudors, Stuarts, and Bourbons. These roads lead out of the twentieth century into the pioneer period of our ancestors, to the days of ox-carts and water-wheels and cross-handed dories.

It would be a pity if any visitor with even a few days to spare were to confine himself to the Trans-Canada Highway and other paved routes, for at the ends of some of the dirt roads he will find the Newfoundland that existed before Confederation. These roads exact much patience from the driver. Except on paved stretches, speed limits are usually 40 m.p.h., and though you can safely exceed this limit in some places, on many routes it isn't even possible to maintain an average speed of forty without danger to springs, shocks, and ball-joints. You must have a spare tire in good shape and know how to mount it. It's also a good idea to know how to put a temporary plug into a tubeless tire, to carry a kit for this purpose, and to keep a full tank of gasoline, as it may occasionally be more than fifty miles between service stations, or even farther on the main route when you pass up the exits.

But apart from the need for a leisurely attitude, and very ordinary foresight, driving in Newfoundland presents no special problems. There is no need to pack picnic lunches. The restaurants and lunch counters are not the world's best, but there are enough of them, except on the most remote routes. They sometimes do annoying things like closing down at midday for a couple of hours, or not opening at all on Sunday, but they are gradually getting over these eccentricities. Along the Trans-Canada route there are plenty of hotels and motels (open seven days a week) with clean, plain dining rooms serving clean, unimaginative American food, badly prepared by people who can't cook. In this respect you'd hardly know that you were not driving through mainland Canada or New England. There is no need to bring special clothing to Newfoundland, other than the clothing required in any temperate maritime region, or, if you are camping, to bring special foods. The supermarket chain stores are here, too, with the same foods you can buy in all ten provinces and fifty states. The climate is not severe. Except in Port-aux-Basques, which maintains its own private fog bank, the summers are sunny, with no more fog or rain than in most other seaside regions. One of the commonest summer problems is drought, and on the side roads you are far more likely to be worried by dust than by mud.

4. Acadians, Gaels, and Deerslayers

Six miles from Port-aux-Basques and less than a mile off the Trans-Canada Highway, the John T. Cheeseman Provincial Park (named for a former minister of fisheries) lies in a sheltered valley in the midst of one of the wildest bits of countryside in Newfoundland. At Cape Ray, and the sands of Cape Ray Cove, the park also enjoys one of the wildest bits of coastline to be found anywhere.

It is popular with the people of Port-aux-Basques, as well as with campers from outside the province, for the sun often shines there in a cloudless sky while rain is falling in the near-by town or it is shivering under its private blanket of mist. In the six miles you have crossed into a new climatic zone.

The Cape Ray barrens, resembling the Barren Lands of the Canadian Arctic, surround the campground, in its small wooded valley, like Fate hemming in the characters of a Greek tragedy. The whole is dominated by the brooding mass of Table Mountain, the southern anchor of the Long Range.

On hot summer days there may be hundreds of people on the Cape Ray sands, but their sweep is so enormous that they still seem almost empty. Swimming on the ocean side of the beach is not recommended except for members of polar bear clubs, however, since a tail of the Labrador Current cuts around the cape and keeps the water temperature down to around 40° F. But on the landward side, separated from the sea by the sand beach, are two large lakes, or barachois as Newfoundlanders call them – bits of the sea cut off by sand-bars forming large natural pools warmed by the summer sun. The park also has its own little salmon river

— really just a brook — out of which more than a hundred salmon are taken by anglers in some seasons.

The village of Cape Ray lies two miles from the park. Back in the days when I was an unregenerate politician it was a fascinating place with some of the qualities of Dogpatch, where, when you cracked open a bottle of campaign rum, even the children came forward for a drink.

The shoreline is the main attraction. A two-mile road runs from the park through the village and on to the lighthouse, skirting rock cliffs and sand coves where mountainous surf comes thundering in from the Gulf of St. Lawrence to crash against beach or rocks in spectacular displays of spume and spray that grow fiercer as you approach the cape.

Here, if anywhere, the visitor can get a taste of the awesome power of the sea. After a storm in the gulf (one of the world's windiest spots) fifteen-foot or even twenty-foot waves will come racing toward shore, growing higher as they reach the shallows, and turning toward the cliffs as the drag of the bottom slows their shoreward ends. They crash upon the rocks with apocalyptic thunder and send spears of spray screaming through the air like bullets.

Surf-watchers need to be cautious, however. These waves expend enormous energy, measured not in pounds, but in tons per square foot. Each yard of wave-front carries more weight than a bull elephant, and travels faster than one in full charge. It can shift breakwaters and demolish sea walls, tear down cliffs and undermine highways a quarter of a mile, perhaps more, from normal high water. I have seen a solid reinforced-concrete block as large as a dwelling house split completely in two by such waves. If one of them breaks over you, it will do little good to cling to the rocks. You will be killed by the impact.

From the park, a two-mile road runs to the highway just opposite Table Mountain, and a good hiking trail leads to the top, where it divides, one branch going to the cliff face, the other leading into the fastnesses of the Long Range.

I strongly advise a hike up Table Mountain, which requires no rock climbing or special equipment, not even the 'strong pair of boots' always demanded by outdoor writers. You can do just as well in sneakers, or even thong sandals. The face of the mountain, which you approach from the rear, is a 1,700-foot drop to the valley below. In sheltered clefts unreached by the sun you may find snow-fields measuring thousands of square yards even in July or August. The Long Range has a sub-arctic microclimate with such wonders as gyrfalcons (the only place the famous bird is found in summer south of Labrador), but this can be dangerous country for the inexperienced, and bird-watchers or others who go much beyond Table Mountain into the wilder parts of the Long Range should have either a local guide or special equipment for wilderness travel. The particular nuisance of the table-land is scrub spruce growing about three feet high, too thick to walk through and too thin to walk over, and forcing very long detours.

On Table Mountain you are likely to meet anything from an eagle to a caribou. Rough-legged hawks nest there, and in the forest, lake, and marsh zones between the valley and the mountain-top you can find almost every bird that is known to the Newfoundland interior.

There is another easy access to the Long Range Mountains from Doyles, eighteen miles farther north. There you have to cross the Little Codroy River to reach the trail, which is a very good one, but there is a ford that can be waded when water conditions are normal, or, if you have a guide, he will supply a boat.

Cheeseman Park offers limited accommodation for tents and trailers, but there is a much better campground at the larger Barachois Park, an hour and a half away by car, and also at the foot of the Long Range.

Just north of Cape Ray is Red Rocks, Newfoundland's windiest spot, where gales of hurricane force come funnelling out of the Long Range to whip down through a dry gulch to the sea. Here Canadian National keeps a human wind-watcher to warn trains by phone whenever gusts exceed a hundred miles an hour, so their cars will not be blown off the tracks, as they have been, once or twice, in the past.

But just over the ridge from Red Rocks, twenty miles from Cape Ray, lies the peaceful Codroy Valley, presenting the highest possible contrast to the violence of the Cape Ray barrens. You can enter the valley through Tompkins, taking a long detour by way of farm roads that lead you through St. Andrews, Searston, and Upper Ferry, or more directly through Doyles, three miles farther on.

The Codroy Valley, sheltered from the east by the Long Range and from the west by the Anguille Mountains, is a picture of sylvan quietude, like something out of rural England. A broad river, the Grand Codroy, meanders across the flood plain, giving each farm its own little bit of waterfront, and providing hundreds of pools for salmon fishermen. There are boats, guides, and accommodation in lodges or cabins at all settlements hereabouts, and fishing is good all the way from the tidal pools to the fast waters of the river's upper branches. The lower Codroy, with its islands, intervals, and wide channels, is also excellent for boating, camping, swimming, and, in autumn, for hunting both big and small game.

The valley was settled first by Micmac Indians from Nova Scotia, then by French colonials escaping from persecuted Acadia. A few English families drifted in during the early nineteenth century. Finally came a colony of Gaelic-speaking Scots to begin sheep-farming and found a textile industry. This curious and fruitful mixture gives the people of the valley a distinct character, even today. They are gentle people, in a sense that coastal Newfoundlanders, for all their inbred courtesy and hospitality, are not.

An account of the Acadian migration to Newfoundland was given to me by an aged man named Placide White back in the 1950s. He was a member of the widespread family named LeBlanc, which once owned large tracts of land in Acadia, near Annapolis and the Basin of Minas. Some time in the last century, when being French was no longer respectable, they changed their names from LeBlanc to White.

Born in the Codroy Valley almost a hundred years ago, Mr. White preserved a family tradition dating back to the 1700s. His people came to Newfoundland, he said, in sailing ships and shallops – even in open fishing boats with oars and makeshift sails. They travelled by way of the Northumberland Strait, Cape Breton, and the Magdalen Islands, then known as the Isles of Ramea. They knew the routes well, for the French had been fishing at the Magdalens at least as early as 1596, and the Acadians had made annual voyages to Newfoundland for sealing and whaling for generations past.

They travelled four hundred miles and farther before making a landfall, settling 'wherever a river or a creek flowed into the sea and you could beach a boat'. One of their main landfalls was the estuary of the Grand Codroy, then much deeper and safer for shipping than it is today after two centuries of silting from the farmland. Ocean vessels could then sail up-river and anchor as far inland as Doyles.

'When I was a boy growing up beside this river,' the old man said, as we gazed out over the wide, meandering channels of the Codroy, 'we were almost completely cut off from the world, but we lived very comfortably. It was a simple life, of course. We wove everything that we wore out of homespun from our own sheep, except for skin boots that we made ourselves, for the winter. There was plenty of good food: fresh salmon and smoked salmon and game, and we raised so many vegetables that we could trade or sell a lot of them to the ships that came to the gulf to fish in the summer.

'We were a mixed-up lot, too. As you walked to church on Sunday morning you would hear people on the road speaking four languages: French, English, Micmac, and Gaelic, with French the commonest of all. But we got along well enough together. I don't remember a single feud or serious quarrel between people of different races in my whole lifetime.'

These languages have died out now. Gaelic is no longer spoken at all, French by only a few families on the most isolated part of Newfoundland's west coast, and Micmac by even fewer, in a cranny of Bay d'Espoir far off to the east. A hundred years earlier a fifth language would have been added to the spoken tongues of western Newfoundland – the old Norman dialect of the Channel Islands. Mr. White spoke French only as a second language.

'When I was a barefoot gamin about as high as a fence post, we all spoke French in our homes,' another old man, Charlie Blanchard of near-by Shallop Cove, told me, 'but we had to speak English at school, and later on at work, and French is almost forgotten today.'

Mr. White, a hunter and woodsman as well as a farmer, took part in the great caribou drive of the last century – the only attempt that I know of to round up caribou and treat them like Lapland reindeer. It began when a European company hired a crew of Newfoundlanders to go to the southern end of Grand Lake at the time of the autumnal caribou migration, to round up a herd of the animals for export. The plan was to drive them into a crude corral, as the Algonkian Indians used to do when they wished to slaughter a herd of white-tailed deer, then to tame them, as far as possible, and finally drive them to the coast. The camp was built on the central plateau just east of the Long Range Mountains within sight of the lake, and the caribou came past by thousands.

'You should see them – oh! my dear man! stretching off, you know, over the barren ground, as far as you could see, covering a whole hill at a time, thousands of animals on the move. And we cut out small sections of them, you know, like cowboys cutting out cattle from a herd. We rode horses wherever the ground was open enough. We had built a great enclosure of logs with an opening like a funnel in one side, and we'd drive the caribou in.

'It didn't work too well, though. They used to kill themselves from panic – break their legs, even their necks. And we couldn't get enough feed for them. But finally we got the survivors quieted down and drove them out, in small herds, to the coast. We lost some of them on the way, and we lost others trying to load them on a ship, but the ones that survived were stowed, at last, in the hold of a vessel, and taken to Europe to stock game parks, you know....'

The Grand Codroy is spanned at Upper Ferry by a narrow concrete bridge nearly a quarter of a mile long, built entirely by hand labour before the arrival of the first automobile. Fortunately, it proved to be wide enough to carry a single lane of motor traffic, and it is still the sole link with the towns of O'Regans, Millville, Codroy, and Cape Anguille on the right bank.

These towns are really farm settlements, centre of the carding, spinning, and weaving industry that was once important but is now in a state of decay. All but one of the carding mills at Millville had closed down the last time I visited it. The great looms of the weavers that had once produced Harris-type tweed from the local sheep were all silent. Most of the wool was being shipped away in a raw state for manufacture.

But it is to the credit of a handicraft organization known as the Jubilee Guilds that they moved into the Codroy Valley and re-established weaving at least as a part-time occupation of housewives. The women of the valley no longer weave homespun to make woollen trousers for their men and boys, but they produce, from linen, woollen, and even metallic yarns, finely woven cloths that are still in great demand by those who can afford the products of the artisan rather than the factory.

South Branch, at the upper end of the Codroy Valley, is unique in Newfoundland – the only town that owes its existence solely to a junction of rivers. Here the North Branch and South Branch meet, to form the Grand Codroy. Above and below the settlement the rivers are navigable only by canoes or special river boats that look like the offspring of a marriage between a canoe and a dory, but they took the place of roads through the wilderness in the days before the first highway was built.

This river town was founded not by a mining or a paper company, but by hunters, trappers, and farmers looking for a place to live off the land. They found at South Branch a spot exceptionally well endowed, where the products of river, forest, and soil have served them well for generations. Though farming is still important for the local supply of meat, milk, and vegetables, the chain-saw has replaced the plough as the chief tool of primary production, and tractors that still haul farm machinery double as work horses in the pulp forests.

The farms strung along both banks of the river are connected not by a bridge or ferry or anything else typical of the twentieth century, but by a knee-deep ford straight out of a folktale. It is approached on both sides by a sandy road that connects with the main local road that connects, in turn, with the Trans-Canada Highway. Knights on chargers might be expected to come plunging across this strip of rippling water, using one of the islands as a stepping stone, for the ford is set off by fields of supernatural green, springing from rich, river-bottom soil, by broad-leafed trees standing in rows, tamed and dignified by centuries of partnership with man, while the wild forest (that might, perhaps, harbour monsters) has been pushed far back to the foothills of the encircling mountains.

This is fairy-story country. But instead of princes on black steeds, or even ploughboys on the farm horses that waded this ford for generations, trucks come, up to their axles in water, and tractors churning foam with outsize wheels. Men wade across in rubber boots and boys in bare feet, but ladies and girls usually insist on transportation. You see them on Sunday morning, returning from church like a flock of gaily coloured birds, piling into a stake-bodied truck for the crossing.

South Branch literally takes its strength from the surrounding hills. Aeons of erosion by flowing rivers, by frost and ice and wind, have stripped from the mountains billions of tons of mineralized soil and spread them over the valley in an uneven layer. Roaring cataracts still plunge out of the Long Range, some falling nearly a thousand feet in a single drop. Fed by lakes and streams on the plateau, and by melting snows from the mountains, these streams continue the age-long process of tearing down the high rocks and feeding them, as silt, to the valley. There they become gravel bars, spawning-beds for thousands of Atlantic salmon that climb up the steps of the Little Codroy and Grand Codroy rivers each spring and summer, making the settlement of South Branch a centre for the gentle art of fly-fishing. During spring floods the gravel bars wash away, to lodge in the quiet bends of the river, where they finally dry out to become farmland.

The courses of the rivers are constantly changing and reshaping the valley floor. Men here have seen new islands appear and grow into cropland during their lifetimes, and old fields vanish into river channels. On some farms you can still see the line of old river banks, two or even three terraces, one above the other, fifty to a hundred yards from the floodmarks of today.

The first settlers of South Branch, frontiersmen of two centuries ago, trapped the forests and foothills of the Long Range, especially for foxes, in the days when the silver fox was ranked with pink pearls as one of the most precious products of the earth. Some took the fast money and moved on. Some stayed and squandered it. A few put it into the land. The fur market declined, then collapsed. The great depression came, with universal privation, and people in the fishing settlements of the coast literally starved to death. But here the little farms remained, a bulwark against hunger. Today the great-grandchildren of the trappers have returned to the forests as loggers, or are working for wages, riding the cash boom once more, as their ancestors did in the days of the fur trade, following the diesel engines as the landscape is changed by civilization, or the forests are fed into the bottomless throats of the pulp machines in Corner Brook. But they keep one eye on the land. It will still be there, waiting to feed them once more, if the cash should ever run dry as it did in the days of their fathers.

5. Land of the Jakitars

You can still get a fight by saying the word 'Jakitar' almost any-where on the west coast of Newfoundland. It was coined as a term of contempt – no one seems to know exactly how – to describe people of mixed French-Indian ancestry. Most of them, by now, also have progenitors who were English, Scots, Irish, and perhaps even Eskimo. But they are still a distinctive race or class of people – those who lived on the west coast before it was colon-ized by east-coast Newfoundlanders in the nineteenth and twen-tieth centuries.

The Jakitars are fascinating people, resourceful woodsmen and hunters, but able men off-shore in boats, too. They have some of the qualities of American hillbillies, including a fondness for home-made liquor, a proclivity for taking fish and game by any convenient method, legal or otherwise, in or out of season, a ten-dency toward sexual freedom (and sexual hospitality even at tender ages), and a healthy distrust of the law.

It is certainly true that they shoot or knife each other on rare occasions, and that their folk dances sometimes lead to minor bloodshed, but with visitors they are reserved and courteous, and you can safely attend one of their 'times' without the least danger of getting your head cracked, unless you choose, like a good Irish-man, to join the fight. I have always found them charming and warm-hearted people. Once they learn that you aren't a game warden, a detective, or a clergyman in disguise they will share their last drink of moonshine with you. Many of their children are almost incredibly beautiful.

Though the Jakitars are found everywhere along the west coast, their real home territory is St. George's Bay and the Port-au-Port Peninsula. Centre of the St. George's Bay region is the town of

Stephenville, 107 miles from Port-aux-Basques, and twenty-two miles from the Trans-Canada Highway. It is a modern town, built during the Second World War to serve the adjoining American air-force base of Harmon Field. It was preceded by a tiny Acadian village, where a very pure form of old Norman French was once spoken, but the village was submerged completely in a boom-town that took on some of the characteristics and much of the appearance of a cattle town in a Western movie.

The Americans came and went and left their mark in the form of fish-and-chip fryers, poolrooms, southern-fried chicken, and a whole generation of blond children where almost everyone had been black-haired before. There is, incidentally, at least one exception to the fish and chips. At a little two-by-four lunch counter on the main road, called 'The Chickenburger', they will serve you, instead of battered codfish, deep-fried clams or scallops with your chips at what I am sure are the lowest prices in North America.

When the base closed, Stephenville suffered a population crash, but it stabilized at around 6,000, and industry began moving in to take advantage of the ready-made accommodation that the Strategic Air Command had left behind. The town has comfortable accommodation in hotels and motels, a large airport, restaurants, bars, movies – things of that kind – and is enjoying face-lifting schemes by provincial and municipal governments; it may even soon become Newfoundland's second university town, but in spite of all that it is not especially interesting in itself. The interest lies in the region of which it is the commercial centre.

Seven miles west of Stephenville you come to the Port-au-Port narrows, the point at which the peninsula escapes by only the width of a road from being an island. Here the pavement ends, for the time being, and gravel roads run off in all directions. One runs north to Point-au-Mal (which richly deserves its name), on to Fox Island River, where there used to be splendid salmon runs until the Americans fished and dynamited it to death, then up into the Lewis Hills to the site of an ill-starred asbestos mine into which the Newfoundland government, led down the garden path by tricky promoters, poured a quarter of a million dollars during the 1950s without getting out enough asbestos to shingle a fish shed. This drive is not recommended.

On the peninsula the road promptly branches, the right-hand

branch going to the limestone quarries at Aguathuna, and on to the tiny fishing village of Boswarlos; the left-hand branch running out to Cape St. George. The Aguathuna workings, now abandoned, are of interest only to rock hounds. Five hundred and fifty men once worked in the pits and crushers, and played around with nitro-glycerine in thirty-ton lots, but they have now moved off to places as distant as the open-pit iron mines of Labrador, or as near as the gypsum quarries on the other side of St. George's Bay.

At Boswarlos, Piccadilly, and many other little villages on the Port-au-Port Peninsula, you can buy excellent lobsters, alive or cooked, at very reasonable prices. This, indeed, was the birthplace of the North American lobster industry early in the nineteenth century, and there are men still living who can remember when lobsters sold here for less than a cent each. At Piccadilly and West Bay you can buy not only lobsters, but strings of smelts or buckets of huge clams at ridiculously low prices from barefoot kids at the roadside. They spear the smelts in the brooks, dig the clams from tidal flats, and, if you happen to be there at the right time of the tide, they will take you out to the flats to dig clams yourself, if you have a mind. This particular kind of clam is tough, and must be minced for chowder, but the smelts are sweet and tender, and make excellent meals, especially if cooked outdoors at a beach party or campfire. You can also buy fresh salmon from the nets on either side of the peninsula.

If you continue through Piccadilly and West Bay until you come to Lourdes (fourteen miles from the junction) and then turn left, you will find yourself in the only truly French-speaking part of Newfoundland. In the other direction, off to the right, runs Long Point, a real geological oddity, fifteen miles long, and so low and narrow that you can throw a stone across it in most places. Beyond its tip it extends even farther, under water, as a long, narrow reef.

It is another fourteen miles to Mainland, the end of the road (which somehow fails to double the cape and join the other road on the south shore) and all along the route you will see houses of a kind not found anywhere else in Newfoundland. They have a strange, European look about them. They have peculiar styles of decoration. They are, in fact, rural French. All the people on this shore speak English as a second language, but many of them prefer still to speak the kind of French that they brought from

Europe with them in the seventeenth and eighteenth centuries. It is, so the experts say, one of the oldest, purest, and most beautiful forms of French that can be heard anywhere today. In another generation it will be dead.

On the south side of the Port-au-Port Peninsula another road runs for twenty miles from the Piccadilly junction past Jerry's Nose and Sheaves Cove to Petit Jardin and Cape St. George. Here the people mix farming with in-shore fishing, and the fields come down to the cliff tops, pasturing horses and cows. It is handsome, rolling country, rather like the Dover Shore, or parts of the Gaspé Peninsula. And it is one of the few parts of Newfoundland where the people continue to live in true rural simplicity. Here you may still see a woman milking her cow in a field, a small child driving geese, or a man splitting fish right on the beach as it comes from a boat. Do not hesitate to stop and talk with strangers – about their work, about the weather, about your own interests, or almost anything under the sun. No need to introduce yourself, or go through any other awkward formalities. Everyone here accepts a casual friendliness without preliminaries.

Just across the water from these quiet villages, a seven-mile sand spit encloses Flat Bay, Shallop Cove, and St. George's. The bar itself ends at a candy-striped lighthouse and the village of Sandy Point, once a pirate refuge, later the commercial capital of western Newfoundland, but now sinking into the last sleep of old age.

Here seagulls mew plaintively around the eaves of old houses that have long since fallen into decay. The streets are completely overgrown by grass. You will meet some sheep, but few people, except perhaps a fisherman or two spreading nets to dry on the sea-level tidal flats.

Sandy Point was once the most important town between Cape Breton and Labrador, a centre of trade that stretched northward into the sub-Arctic, the home of fish merchants and herring packers, boasting five public bar-rooms designed to ensnare all the fishermen of St. George's and Port-au-Port bays who might be tempted to spill a little red paint while 'in town' for supplies.

To west-coast fishermen of the last century 'the town' was Sandy Point. It was an old town, even then, the bones of its founders having been laid to rest in its sand dunes long before the end of the eighteenth century. It was a naval station during the disputed days of the French Shore fishery, with French and

English warships swinging there at anchor every summer. It was also a centre for the schooner fishery in Labrador.

Relics of past greatness are seen everywhere on Sandy Point – twenty-room houses with the sky shining through their roofs, a fine church with stained-glass windows backing an altar rich with vermilion and cloth of gold, a large school where the children sometimes were marooned by high tides, big fishing boats, long abandoned, now almost covered by drifting sand.

The town maintained a precarious perch for two centuries on a strip of beach held together by nothing more than the roots of dune grass. You can walk all over it without ever being more than ten feet above high water. Its great days were those of the west-coast herring fishery, when men pursued the herring spring and fall in St. George's Bay itself, and sailed out in summer to the Quebec North Shore, or beyond the Strait of Belle Isle to the bleak outer islands of Labrador, seeking the remarkably large, extra-fat herring of the Labrador summer run: fish that have since vanished completely, though an American firm with a branch at Stephenville is now trying to find them again to convert them into fishmeal for animal feeds, and perhaps, later, for high-protein human food for underdeveloped countries.

The Sandy Pointers built their own boats from pit-sawn lumber, knit their own nets, made their own herring barrels in home cooperages, splitting logs for staves and carving them by hand with draw-knives. A man, with the help of his children, could sometimes make a hundred barrels this way in a winter.

Down on the point near the lighthouse there is an old graveyard whose stones are so eroded by time and salt spray that no inscriptions can be read. Most of them lie broken, some in small fragments. Here lie the men and women and children of the century before last, their names now lost for ever.

Nearer the church is a later graveyard, whose stones date from 1860, telling of more than a century of struggle by a people to whom death was a daily companion. Here lie the Hunts, the Banfields, the Sawyers, the Parsonses; others with names from the Channel Islands: Renoufs, Messervys, Leroux. You had to belong to the ruling class to rate such stones. The graves of the Jakitars – Benoits, Beaupatries, Blanchards, LeJeunes – are not so marked.

Here are the six children of John and Elizabeth Renouf: two died as young men, two as boys in their teens, two as little girls of three and seven. It was the same with other families. The old churchyard tells of the other side of the good life of the pioneers. It was no easy road they walked, even those who looked down their noses at the Jakitars.

Sandy Point was doomed from the day the railway reached St. George's in 1896 and its people began drifting away. One by one its general stores closed, its merchants moving off to mainland points. Slowly its wharves fell into disrepair and were covered by the sand. It became a sheep pasture, and a picnic ground for weekend excursions by people from the new rail town across the water. Towns die hard when they have roots hundreds of years deep, and more than thirty families still clung to this sand bank right into the 1960s, but all its young men had gone away to work. Then came the highroad, and it, too, passed by.

Last of all came the sea. The ancient, all-powerful ocean that had given Sandy Point its life began, in the second half of this century, to reclaim it, bit by bit. At first during storm tides, then more and more often during normal weather, the high water crept across the bar, washed out channels, gradually cut the point in two, and made the outer section, where the town once stood, into an island.

The channels are widening, the sand washing forward into Flat Bay. New gaps are opening. Gradually, it seems, this whole flat peninsula of sand will vanish, and the sea will then begin eating away at the inner shore, until sand and soil are worn back to the hills of limestone, granite, and gypsum that face St. George's Bay with the solid look of eternity.

Flat Bay, which is shallow, enclosed, and protected from the sea by Sandy Point, has many excellent swimming beaches. Just east of St. George's there is a fine beach at Black Bank, somewhat defiled with litter. Just west of Shallop Cove another beach, about three miles long, runs to the mouth of Flat Bay Brook. Here midsummer water temperatures rise into the fifties and occasionally into the sixties. The beach is perfectly clean, and, except for a few local children, almost wholly deserted.

Offshore there are low, sandy islands, the home of terns and plovers, horned larks and water pipits. The islands are overgrown with wild grass and with pink morning glories that bloom there in a riot of colour unseen except by the chance fisherman who passes by on his way to a salmon berth up or down the coast.

St. George's, a staid old town that was until recently the seat of a bishop, has been troubled from time to time by the encroachments of industry, especially mining. Steel Mountain, just back of the town, is almost solid magnetite. Flat Bay, a western suburb, has cliffs of white gypsum that are being blasted down, ground into rubble, some of it loaded on trains for the plaster mill at Corner Brook, and the rest sent in buckets on an endless chain right through the centre of the town to a ship-loading pier. St. George's is surrounded by a cluster of aboriginal villages: St. Teresa, Shallop Cove, Barachois Brook, and Mattis Point – the latter name, believe it or not, a corruption from St. Jean Baptiste.

Nine salmon rivers flow into St. George's Bay, all of them carrying major runs of fish at one time or another throughout the summer, and there is usually good fishing, somewhere or other within an hour's drive of St. George's, from the day the season opens in June until it closes in mid September.

I once camped for seven days near the mouth of one of those little rivers, and counted more than a thousand salmon taken by anglers out of a quarter-mile stretch of water between the road and the sea. Most of the fish were grilse – young salmon on their first run into fresh water. Unlike the inferior creatures of the Pacific coast, the Atlantic salmon do not die after spawning, but return to salt water, to make second and third runs into the rivers, growing heavier each year, until they reach forty pounds or more.

One of St. George's Bay's nine rivers – Little Barachois – flows through Barachois Pond Provincial Park, which abuts the Trans-Canada Highway and overlooks the bay. It is a fair-sized park with more than ten square miles of forest, lake, mountain, and stream inside its borders, and with one of the best camp and trailer sites in the province.

There is licensed salmon-fishing in the river, and guides with boats to take anglers to the pools where the river flows out of the mountains. There is also trout-fishing, for which no licence is required, a supervised sand beach for swimming, and a trail to the top of a rugged hill overlooking the lake.

The park has many wild birds and animals, including moose and caribou. Pigeon hawks nest at the campsite, and there are waterfowl on the lake. A lynx is sometimes seen at evening on the beach beside the camp-ground. The setting, in the foothills of the Long Range, is exceptionally beautiful, and every campsite has immediate access to the lake. Barachois Park is an hour and a half by car from Port-aux-Basques and less than an hour from the city of Corner Brook.

6. City on the Humber

Corner Brook, a modern city of 30,000 based upon one of the world's largest paper mills, was a tiny logging town of less than thirty families half a century ago. The whole Bay of Islands region, of which it is now the centre, then held less than 3,000 people scattered in a dozen villages around its thickly wooded shores, subsisting by combining the arts of forestry, hunting, farming, and fishing.

The people of Corner Brook insist that their city is the most beautiful in eastern Canada, and though this claim may not be justified by close inspection of its east and west wings, which sprouted unbidden and unplanned even before streets were laid out, the city certainly has the most beautiful setting in the Atlantic provinces. It lies in a lovely valley and climbs the slopes of its encircling hills beside a splendid fjord where a great river comes down to meet the sea. As you approach from the south along the Trans-Canada Highway the first view of Corner Brook is a sight to make even a stranger catch his breath.

The city also enjoys a fine climate. Protected on all sides by the Blomidon and Long Range mountains, and thirty miles from the open waters of the Gulf of St. Lawrence, it has inland weather in a maritime setting, warmer summers and colder winters than most Newfoundland cities and towns, less fog and fewer windstorms than St. John's, Gander, or Grand Falls.

It is essentially a mill town, manufacturing not only paper, but cement, plaster, plasterboard, and a variety of pre-stressed concrete and other building materials. It has always been a pleasant place to live, and the manufacturing companies have recently taken steps to improve it by reducing air pollution, which was becoming a nuisance, though hardly a major problem.

The city has excellent recreation facilities, and is a major centre for winter as well as summer sports. The Marble Mountain ski resort, equipped with modern tows and lifts, and with a full range of slopes, has, throughout the months of January, February, and March, one of the most consistently good snow surfaces in eastern Canada, and attracts skiers from all parts of the country. Moreover, you do not have to mount an expedition to reach it. It is right on the Trans-Canada Highway, five minutes' drive from Corner Brook.

There is a well-equipped sports field and a modern stadium, both built by public subscription, and – unlike most such institutions in Canada – actually making money. There are two public parks, one inside the city devoted mainly to swimming, and a larger one, twelve miles up-river, with swimming, boating, two children's playgrounds, a canteen, a dancing pavilion, a wildlife exhibit, a spacious lakefront sand beach, space for more than a hundred tents and trailers, and, just outside the park's borders, a float-plane base and three fishing rivers.

The Blomidon Golf Club has a number of unique features. It is on a hill-top with an absolutely stunning view of the city and bay. Devotees say that its greatest hazard is the scenery, which practically murders your concentration. There are other distractions, too: wild animals occasionally wander out on the greens and fairways; moose, lynx, and varying hares are sometimes seen by those who rise for a round of golf while the dew is still on the sward. But the Blomidon Golf Club's unique feature is its position – right *inside* the city, within easy walking distance of the two major shopping centres and all the major hotels and motels except those to the east in the Humber Valley. It is a democratic club with open membership and welcomes visitors.

Humber Arm has a growing corps of yachtsmen, though this recreation, strangely enough, took a long time to develop. Not for any lack of natural advantages, however. Bay of Islands is beautiful boating water, well protected from the ocean, and with four fjords running into the mountains. Though it has six large islands and dozens of smaller ones, it is fairly free of serious hazards to small boat navigation, and an hour's run by motor launch from the mouth of the bay takes you into spectacular Bonne Bay and the awesome grandeur of Gros Morne National Park.

Small boats also have access to the Lower Humber River for cruising and fishing, but are almost always barred from entrance to Deer Lake, out of which it flows, by a log boom that plugs its lower end like a cork in a bottle except on the very rare occasions when all the logs are released to float down-river to the mill.

The biggest salmon taken by fly fishermen come consistently, year after year, from the Lower Humber. But these monsters, which are never plentiful, and exact great patience from the angler, often require several hours to land, if they can be landed at all.

For a new industrial city, Corner Brook is surprisingly well-rooted in the pre-industrial population of Bay of Islands. When I visited the mill last year, I found that many of its employees, and many others recently retired, had actually grown up in Bay of Islands before the first paper machine arrived.

'Christopher Fisher built the first sawmill here in 1885,' one old man told me, 'and it was still turning out lumber when I was a boy. We lived just across the arm from Corner Brook, and hardly thought about the outside world at all. It was a rough and happy sort of life – fishing, hunting, trapping, a little farming. We were always out in boats, down the bay, up the arm, bringing hay from Summerside for the horses that worked at the mill. There were cart roads all along this side of the arm, for six or seven miles, built partly out of sawdust from the mill.

'You might almost say we ran wild in the summer, though we had some work to do, too, but it was a free and glorious life for a boy. . . . I can still remember having to put on boots after running about barefoot for three months – God, how we hated it! And we went swimming, of course – not in the river, it was almost always too cold, but in the brooks and ponds.

'I was up at Howley one day in the 1940s – a small logging town, you know, about fifty miles from here, where Sandy Lake and Grand Lake join, and I went down on the wharf, on the Sandy Lake side, you know, and it seemed like half the kids in town were there, chasing up and down the wharf in their bare pelts and diving into the lake, and it made me think of the old days here. We were brought up kind of rough and strict, but life was great fun for all that.'

'We used to go out to the islands on week-end picnics,' one lady recalled, 'and we took turns going to Labrador in the summer – on the schooners that used to sail north to fish and trade. Later you could take holidays on the paper boats – $40 for a round trip to New York, $60 for one to New Orleans. Some of us became great travellers.'

'We lived at Meadows Point across the arm,' another man told me, 'and we ate mostly fish and potatoes and rabbits, all of which we got for ourselves. We were never hungry. We wore home-knit caps and sweaters, and some people even had home-knit underwear. We used to make our own boots for the winter, or buy sealskin boots from Labrador and then tap them with sole leather that we bought at the general store in Curling. But some people tanned their own leather, from cowhide, too.

'I sailed to Labrador when I was fifteen and spent six summers fishing there, but I went to work on construction when they began building the paper mill in 1923, and I have been here ever since.

'The winters used to be much colder than they are now.* We used to haul logs for the mill with ox teams, and I remember one winter when my ox actually froze his nose. I used to see my father get up and break the ice in the water bucket in the morning, and put bread in the oven to thaw it.'

All this was before the Hungry Thirties. When the depression hit the paper industry, and the workers had no farms or fishing gear to which they could return, people began, for the first time in Bay of Islands, to feel the pinch of hunger.

The mill was cut back to four days a week, then to three, then to two. Shifts were shortened from eight hours to six. Wages were cut. Men were laid off. Those who had formerly walked straight and proud went from door to door, begging. Children went half-naked and died of malnutrition. The government dole, given only to the totally destitute, amounted to six cents per person per day. At least one fisherman, who had begged at the relief office in vain for an advance against his next month's dole, went back to his fishing boat and cut his throat rather than go home to his starving children. Corner Brook was just beginning to revive when the Second World War began. It has now enjoyed continuous prosperity for thirty years, and to most of the young adults of today the stark horrors of their fathers' time sound like fables out of the dark ages.

The Bowater organization bought the Corner Brook mill in 1938 – the first overseas property acquired by this British indus-

* This is a fact, not an old man's fancy. Climate records bear it out.

trial giant. By 1940 they were turning out an average of 881 tons of newsprint daily. By 1966 this had increased to 1,121 tons, and, in addition, sulphite pulp was being exported for manufacture into paper in Europe. The Corner Brook mill was the foundation stone of an industrial empire that now has branches in thirteen countries, fixed assets of over half a billion dollars, 31,000 employees, and 68,000 shareholders.

One man who has worked for all the logging and paper companies in turn at Corner Brook, starting with the old Fisher sawmill, says, 'Sure life was good here in the old days. We'd go up-river and get our three caribou for each family, grow our own potatoes, and catch all the salmon we wanted. But life now is better. You can't have comfortable, modern homes, paved streets, and motor cars, without modern industry. We have all those things, plus the guarantee of a high standard of living and a comfortable retirement. You may have to go a little further for your fish and your deer, but it's well worth it.'

Westward from Corner Brook's oldest section (the fishing town of Curling that the city absorbed in 1955) a cliff-hanging road runs for forty miles along the base of the Blomidon Mountains and the Lewis Hills, skirting the south shore of Humber Arm and Bay of Islands – an exciting and exceptionally scenic drive for the motorist who isn't in a hurry. Past Halfway Point and Benoit's Cove, with its little white church and French Stations of the Cross, the road runs to Frenchman's Cove, where the arm opens into the outer bay.

At this all-fishing community you can go cod-jigging for sport. It is a kind of fishing that requires no skill, no bait or lures, and no equipment other than what comes with the boat, but guarantees that you'll catch something weighing ten pounds or better. If you can drop a lure overboard on a line, and retrieve it in short jerks, you can jig a cod. They can hardly be classed as game fish, but many people who have never landed anything bigger than a bluegill or an eight-inch trout get an enormous thrill out of boating a fish three or four feet long, even if it doesn't put up much of a fight.

The cost of this form of recreation varies, but is negotiable. It shouldn't be more than a reasonable hourly fee for a kid with a boat. But if you prefer you can make more luxurious, touristy expeditions for cod in regular, organized, trap-boat tours on the east coast. Either way, you have the satisfaction of knowing that you are taking part in an activity that has been going on along the coast of Newfoundland for approximately five hundred years.

Beyond Frenchman's Cove is York Harbour, and, beyond that, Lark Harbour, a typical headland and fishing community clinging to bare rocks and smelling of cod guts. From any of these three places (but Frenchman's Cove by preference) you can take a boat to the off-shore communities of Woods Island and Innismara.

On the other side of the arm a road runs from Humbermouth (like Curling, once an independent village now absorbed by the city) across the Humber River, and then through the mountains, roller-coaster-like, to Cox's Cove, separated from Humber Arm by a range of hills, and the only community in the neighbouring fjord of Middle Arm. Goose Arm, further inland, and North Arm, beyond the next headland, are wholly uninhabited.

The road to Cox's Cove drops down at an almost frightening angle from its overhanging hills. It is a completely hemmed-in community where everything is crowded against the picturesque waterfront, and the people maintain a stoutly independent outlook against the urbanizing influences of the near-by city.

Here I was fortunate enough to meet the oldest resident of the west coast, and one of the longest-lived of a long-lived race of Newfoundlanders – Pierre Beaupatrie, who claimed to be 112 when he died, and was certainly within a very few years of that mark. When I met him, and we sat down to kill a bottle of Demerara rum together, he was married to his third wife, living half-way up a hill that would have killed many a younger man to climb, and was making daily rounds of the village on foot, splitting a beer with his neighbours. He was still a strong drinker, a full century after he had taken his first mug of grog.

He was the only man I ever met who, besides three wives, had also had three surnames. His English-speaking neighbours had corrupted his name in two directions – to 'Peter Patrick' and 'Peter Barefoot', and it was many years since he had been commonly called by his real name of Pierre Beaupatrie.

He recalled incidents of his first landing on the coast in 1868, and gave a detailed description of the parts that he visited with the French fishing fleet up to 1879, when he settled in Bay of Islands.

In those days there was a vigorous three-way trade between the French island of St. Pierre just south of Newfoundland (from which M. Beaupatrie originally came), the province of Quebec, and the French Shore of western Newfoundland. The trade included the Cape Breton shore of Nova Scotia as an incidental point, and flourished on such commodities as fish, agricultural products, tobacco, and rum, as well as manufactured goods that flowed into St. Pierre duty-free from Europe. The French islands were never able to produce half enough fish to supply their own export trade, or any hay or vegetables for their own use, so they formed an excellent half-way house for trade. Some of this trade was certainly illegal, but the whole area was outside the ambit of the law for all practical purposes. The Newfoundland government had not even 'discovered' the west coast until 1874, when the first census showed 8,651 people living there, more than half of them of French or Jersey descent, apparently having appeared there out of thin air. During the first four centuries of English rule in Newfoundland, the colony consisted of a varying strip of the eastern shore, sometimes only a part of the Avalon Peninsula, but never included the west or south-west coasts. Aside from this old 'English Shore', Newfoundland was *terra incognita*, given over to the French and the Indians.

If you want a special adventure in trout-fishing, you may be able to persuade someone at Cox's Cove to take you up Goose Arm in a boat (the trip is well worth the time anyway, even apart from the fishing) and show you the places where the sea trout run in and out of the rivers. With any luck you may strike a run of really exciting fish in this uninhabited and unspoiled corner of the Bay of Islands, where the waters of the Blomidon Mountains empty into the Gulf of St. Lawrence.

Corner Brook is, of course, replete with accommodation for tourists. The oldest hotel, Glynmill Inn, is still to be recommended for those who like quiet, comfortable surroundings, a shady garden, and a well-kept ornamental lake. It has reasonably good food and bar service, and a dignified, Old-English style of architecture. And if you can't stand the gaudy murals on the walls of the main dining-room (they are a late vulgar addition to this fine old house and tend to put me off my feed) then maybe you can wear dark glasses at dinner.

Westport Inn is a 'hotter' spot, with a well-patronized bar, and dancing. The Holiday Inn is much the same as so many other Holiday Inns from coast to coast except that the portion of the chain in Newfoundland was built and is owned by the Newfoundland government as a gesture toward the tourist trade and socialism. There are reasonably good motels on both sides of the city, and in Humber Valley, between Corner Brook and Deer Lake, there are also cottages, lodges, restaurants, and night spots devoted mainly to the pleasures of bed and bottle.

The city has two television channels, three radio stations, and a daily newspaper, the *Western Star* – a small but well-produced journal that has won a number of awards in national competitions for its presentation of features and news.

7. The Road to Labrador

At Deer Lake, half an hour's drive by the Trans-Canada from Corner Brook, you may continue eastward toward St. John's or take the road to the north, by way of the Great Northern Peninsula to St. Anthony and Labrador.

The road to St. Anthony is gravel-surfaced, three hundred miles long, and not always in the best repair. But at least a small part of it – that serving Gros Morne National Park – is due for paving soon.

The first forty or fifty miles, a spectacular drive through mountains, also happens to have an excellent surface, often as smooth as pavement. At Wiltondale, a tiny logging settlement fifteen miles from Deer Lake, the road forks, the right branch going into the park, the left to the south side of Bonne Bay and on to Trout River, a total distance of thirty-five miles.

This short drive is well worth the trouble, for the mountains are really beautiful, and Bonne Bay has a reputation for the loveliest marine scenery in Newfoundland. Besides, Trout River is worth a visit for several reasons.

The branch to Trout River climbs over a tableland that is undoubtedly the most desolate spot visited by any road on the island. It looks less like anything earthly than like the surface of the moon. Bare boulders lie everywhere, many of them pitted and brown, others of an unnatural, sulphurous hue. Stark mountains rise against the sky, with sharp and precipitous escarpments.

The settlement at the end of the road is a fishing and lobstering village of no special interest, but the short river that gives it its name, and the lake out of which it flows, carry excellent runs of salmon and trout.

Just beyond the Trout River branch lies the settlement of

Woody Point, notable for its air of settled gentility and for the profusion of Lombardy poplars with which its gardens are filled, giving it a European, almost Italian look, as you approach along the shore.

Woody Point is connected to Norris Point, just across the Bonne Bay Narrows, by motor ferries that run continuously. The fifteen-minute trip with its changing views of the bay is certainly a most interesting short boat ride. If you are driving to St. Anthony or Labrador it is well worth considering going by way of Woody Point and the ferry, and returning by way of Gros Morne National Park.

The road to Labrador really begins at Bonne Bay, and the choice is either by way of Woody Point and the ferry or by way of the branch that leaves at Wiltondale and runs through the mountains of the park – a new one, now under development. It will be two or three years before this park has many attractions other than scenery to offer visitors. But the scenery is something to see. There is nothing in Canada east of the Rockies or south of Labrador to compare with it. The route through the park is a few miles shorter than the route through Woody Point.

From Rocky Harbour, where the road through the park comes out on the coast near the mouth of Bonne Bay, you skirt the shore on beach and cliff-top for the next 192 miles, rarely more than a stone's throw from the sea. The ocean is always in your ears. Sea birds circle overhead. There are numerous wonderful spots for beachcombing, for this is a lee shore, where both winds and tides set toward the land, and the sandbanks up to the line of the storm tides are sprinkled with gifts from the sea.

Some of the route along this shore is actually over old beach terraces that lay at sea level geological ages ago but were lifted by the forces of nature high above the waves to form a convenient flat roadbed for highway-builders of the twentieth century. Skeletons of great whales were among the things dug out of the gravel-pits when the road-building machinery moved in.

Some stretches of this road are monotonous, but there are some scenic areas, as well as interests of other kinds, and there are many really exceptional salmon rivers – probably the world's best south of Labrador.

About twenty miles from Bonne Bay the road bridges the entrance to St. Pauls Inlet, a totally landlocked bay ending in a spectacular rock-girt fjord, where cliffs more than 2,000 feet high drop into the water. A trip of half an hour by small boat will take you to the head of St. Pauls Inlet, and to one of the true scenic wonders of eastern North America. There is excellent fishing here, too, especially for sea trout.

St. Pauls is a possible Norse site. Farley Mowat, after an exhaustive study of the Icelandic and Greenlandic sagas, personal visits to the area, and the most detailed reconstruction of the Viking voyages ever undertaken, is convinced that St. Pauls was one of the ports mentioned in the early accounts of voyages by the Icelanders. Specifically, he says it is the *hop* described in the account of the Thorfinn Karlsefni colony, which set out to find Leif's Vinland in A.D. 1005. The colonists never succeeded, but did spend three years somewhere in North America, probably in this region. To the Norse, a *hop* was the kind of harbour that Newfoundlanders call a barachois. St. Pauls is not only a harbour of this type, but fits exactly all the other descriptions given in the saga. Mr. Mowat also claims to have discovered evidence, on the site, of probable Norse occupation. The question has not yet been investigated by archaeologists.

Just north of St. Pauls are the remarkable beaches and sand dunes of Cow Head, one of the landmarks for sailors along this shore, and one of the few places on the north-west coast where sea bathing is a practical possibility. North of these is Parson's Pond – settlement, lake, and salmon river, and also the site of the only oil-well ever developed in Newfoundland. It produced little, and was soon abandoned, though there is a lot of oil in the area, lying in faulted strata, and forming pools too small to be worked profitably.

Twenty-six miles from St. Pauls is Portland Creek, one of the great salmon rivers, and the centre of the whole salmon-fishing area of the north-west coast. There are several motels and groups of cabins here and at Daniel's Harbour, catering to tourists and anglers, and I can recommend the Benfield Motel at Daniel's Harbour without reservation. Trevor Bennett, owner and manager, is most helpful and obliging. He operates a restaurant, bar, and small general store as well as the motel. His rates are low and his menu is limited, but he serves the best food on the north-west coast. His platter-sized halibut steaks (the choicest of all fish) are the best you can get anywhere in Newfoundland. Sometimes, too, you can buy hooked mats in the store. A hooked mat is a sort of tapestry made by Newfoundland women who got the art from their mothers who had it handed down to them from the first European settlers. They were originally used on floors instead of carpets, but now are usually hung on walls as art objects.

Mr. Bennett also keeps a group of cabins facing a small lake separated from the road by a strip of forest. The lake has trout and a bathing beach. But among the cabins is one that he never rents to tourists. It belonged to the famous sportsman, author, and photographer Lee Wulff. The cabin, with its equipment, is kept exactly as Mr. Wulff left it, a sort of private museum. Wulff made a number of his movies in this region, and spread the fame of its salmon rivers among wealthy sportsmen all over North America. Portland Creek, and River of Ponds, twenty-five miles farther along the road, were two of his favourite haunts.

River of Ponds is now the site of a provincial park with camping, boating, and swimming facilities. The park has a long sweep of sand along the shore of a lake, and many of the campsites have what amounts to private beaches for swimming and boating, as well as the public beach adjoining the picnic area. A highly productive salmon river flows into the lake's upper end, a few minutes by boat or canoe from the campsite. There is also down-river fishing in a number of fine pools between the outlet from the lake and the point where the river falls into the sea. There are cabins for rent, and a small store where you can buy supplies and fishing equipment. The cabins are in great demand during the July salmon runs, and anglers who wish to use them at that season should make advance reservations.

North of River of Ponds the road makes a wide circuit around Hawke's Bay, a logging centre and site of another excellent salmon river, then swings past Port Saunders to Port-au-Choix, where archaeologists discovered the largest and most important Dorset campsite so far known, and where, more recently, they unearthed hundreds of skeletons and truckloads of artefacts belonging to the Red Paint Culture.

Port-au-Choix lies on a big, flat peninsula – all but an island – with harbours on both sides. In prehistoric times it was the jumping-off place for journeys between Newfoundland and Labrador, for hunting expeditions into the mountains to the south, and for sealing expeditions into the Gulf of St. Lawrence.

Unlike most such campsites, Port-au-Choix was occupied for a very long time by a single culture. There are many cases (at Jericho for example, and at Troy) where a village or town was occupied by a long succession of different peoples. But Port-au-Choix was occupied continuously by the Dorset people for at least 2,000 years, probably longer. There are few opportunities for scientists to study the evolution of a single culture on one site over so long a period.

In addition to the Dorset and Red Paint cultures, remains of Beothuck Indians have been found on or near the Port-au-Choix Peninsula. Beothuck and Dorset were in Newfoundland at the same time, but what contacts there may have been between the two peoples is not known. Fantastic numbers of stone tools have been found at the Port-au-Choix site – sometimes thousands of points, or broken parts of points and blades, in a single plot of a few square yards.

Dr. Elmar Harp of Dartmouth College spent five years digging into the Dorset village. He found, under the turf, layers of seal bones almost a foot thick in places, as well as beautifully fashioned tools and other native work. It seems that the Dorset people depended very largely on seals, and that any forest hunting that they did was conducted from bases farther inland or farther south.

The Dorsets were neither Eskimo nor Indian in the modern sense, but a prehistoric people of Asian origin who more or less antedated both, developed their culture in North America, and occupied most of the Arctic and eastern Canada down to A.D. 1100 or later.

They were physically powerful, decidedly bigger than today's Eskimos, and modern Eskimo folk legends relating to them describe them as giants. The legends are exaggerated, of course, but they may well have averaged more than six feet, about a foot taller than the Eskimos of that time.

The Dorset stone culture was one of the most beautiful and skilful in the ancient world. The tools were so small that they are sometimes called 'microliths'. They were made from quartz and flint, with edges that were almost as sharp and efficient as steel. The Dorsets did not need to make massive, heavy stone weapons. They could produce deadly little arrowheads no bigger than a thumb-nail, and razor-sharp knives and scrapers only three or four inches long. They produced stone and bone sculpture of as high a standard as the soapstone carvings of today's Eskimos, and made lamps and pots from carved stone as well.

Apparently about 700 or 800 years ago they were caught in a

gigantic squeeze between warlike Indians (the Algonkian peoples of eastern Canada) who began moving in from the south and the west, and Thule Eskimos, moving in from the north and the east. Sedentary and unwarlike, and unable to adapt themselves to new hunting methods after thousands of years of seal hunting, the Dorsets quickly vanished. Some of them may have survived in isolated tribes right down to the time white men began coloni-zing North America, but as a widespread culture they were doomed shortly after the time of the Viking voyages.

Thirty-eight miles north of Port-au-Choix there is a road junc-tion giving access to Roddickton, Main Brook, and Englee, 47, 53, and 58 miles away on the other side of the Great Northern Peninsula.

There are people – most of them social workers for the Gren-fell Mission – who profess to enjoy visiting Roddickton. Person-ally I find it very depressing.

I met one man there who remembers it when it was inhabited by only two families, and by thousands of ducks and geese, when its hills were covered by sea-dipping forests and its valleys laced by trout and salmon streams, giving an affluent living to the few pioneer inhabitants.

Today it is a squalid mill town with a much-too-large popula-tion living in balance between life and death, where men soured by discontent and a vague realization of their status in a vicious industrial system perform indifferently tasks of numbing monot-ony, or sit in the sun doing nothing but feel mad at the world.

The Roddickton churches are a revealing thing to see. The Salvation Army (which in Newfoundland is a religious denomina-tion rather than a welfare organization) flourishes, along with a very shabby version of the United Church of Canada. There is a meeting hall for the Pentecostal Assemblies, where people gather to 'speak in tongues' and give other manifestations of possession by the Holy Ghost. But above them all, in Byzantine splendour, stands the Apostolic Church of the Full Gospel, domed like St. Sophia's, except that the domes are green-painted wood, and fronted with a billboard painted in black letters six feet high. Perhaps these various brands of emotional fundamentalism give people some relief from the misery of their surroundings.

There is a widespread belief that religion occupies an impor-tant place in Newfoundland outport life – that Newfoundlanders are essentially devout people who, in their closeness to nature and to the bare bones of life, also feel close to God. But sociologists working out of Memorial University in St. John's discount all this. According to their findings, religion occupies a very superficial place in the outports: at most it is a sort of club activity, something to 'belong to' and something to do on Sundays, when a deep-rooted superstition forbids practically all forms of work and many kinds of play as well.

The harbour front at Roddickton is quagmired with sawdust. The streets wind crookedly between the little houses, their mud smelling of inadequate sanitation. A sign in the restaurant proclaims: 'Full Coarse Meals'.

In the midst of this squalor I met groups of lovely children. Some were rather dirty, it is true, but many even of the dirty ones were beautiful. There were little blonde girls whose eyes danced with pleasure in the simple joys of life and summer, sturdy brown boys as lithe as young panthers doing daring high dives from the end of the pier. The surrounding ugliness had not yet touched the children. They were like flowers on an offal heap.

Though the Newfoundland birth-rate is dropping in recent years, it is still the highest in Canada. Everywhere there are troops of children. The schools are bursting at the seams, and some have even adopted a shift system to try to meet the demand for space. The outport children are among the most natural, friendly, and unspoiled in the world. Though they may be shy with strangers at first, they quickly get over this, for to any outporter a stranger is just a neighbour from a little farther away than the ones he meets every day.

The children of Roddickton (and other depressed 'growth centres') are no different from the others: just as full of high spirits, confidence, hope. . . . Perhaps most of them will escape, as teen-agers, to happier places. It would be a shame, indeed, for them to grow up into the scolding women and bitter men whom you meet in Roddickton today.

Far better for life to be harsh and beautiful (as it was for the pioneer families) than for it to be soft and ugly and sour, as it is here. Nobody any longer dies of appendicitis without help in the woods of Canada Bay. But too many live without hope and die in a trap, spending life without risk, challenge, adventure, or expectation of high reward.

Here, if anywhere, I am convinced that life cannot be valued in quantity. Roddickton is not better because its twenty people have increased to 2,000 (many of them now scattered, seeking the means of life). A country's progress is not measured by the increase of its areas of squalor. Not Roddickton alone, by any means; dozens of similar Newfoundland communities have sprawled out over square miles of countryside, their populations doubling every ten years or so, sinking progressively into deeper and more hopeless futility, fed by government welfare, or half living by performing useless tasks for which they are half-paid, and filled full of rapacious desires for mere things which, once acquired, become an added burden.

Perhaps, somewhere far off, there is an industrial 'Kingdom coming', as they sing in the strange wooden temple above the muddy street. There, perhaps, the economic lion and lamb will lie down together. Meanwhile, the sort of primitive industry that has come to rural Newfoundland seems only to corrupt and brutalize and to turn the green earth into a vast pigsty, where the majority of children, being adequately fed and visited by nurses, no longer die in infancy, but grow up, instead, to die in spirit, or to become expatriates for whom their land will shortly dwindle to a remote, nostalgic, and sentimental dream.

Twelve miles past the Roddickton junction (160 miles from Bonne Bay) is St. Barbe, the Newfoundland terminal of the Labrador ferry. The ferry runs from a pond-like nook in St. Barbe Bay, making two round trips daily to Blanc Sablon, twenty-two miles away on the Labrador side of the Strait of Belle Isle.

Schedules on this ferry may change with traffic demands, but at present it runs for six months a year, May to October, leaving St. Barbe at 7 a.m. and 3 p.m., and Blanc Sablon at 10 a.m. and 6 p.m. The voyage takes about two hours each way, but this can vary considerably depending on how the tide is running at the time. The Norse, with good reason, called the Strait of Belle Isle 'Straumfjord', for the tide there does, indeed, run like a river.

Though Blanc Sablon is in the Province of Quebec, for most practical purposes it is part of Newfoundland Labrador. The border runs north from Blanc Sablon Brook, and the little fishing settlement is one of the chain of English-speaking settlements that skirt the shoreline northward past Belle Isle. Its ties are with Newfoundland, and its only road connection was built by the Newfoundland government.

From Blanc Sablon the road runs mostly along the shore for forty miles to Red Bay, and there it ends. If you cross the Strait at 7 a.m. you can pay a brief visit by car to all the Labrador settlements and be back for the return crossing at 6 p.m.

If you happen not to be interested in fishing, that is. Any angler will certainly want to try the Labrador salmon and trout streams, particularly Forteau Brook, ten miles from Blanc Sablon. I have never fished this small river myself, but people who have done so assure me that it is the answer to any angler's prayers – populous with salmon, and consisting of a long series of pools, all of which can be fished comfortably from the bank without a boat.

Over a ten-year period, anglers on this river have averaged better than one salmon a day each. There is a good range in size, and more than two hundred fish running from ten to twenty-five pounds have been landed there.

There is cabin accommodation for anglers on Forteau and Pinware rivers. And though the rates include guiding fees, they are still far too high – $50 a day and up. If you think fishing is worth this kind of money, they can, at least, guarantee that you'll actually catch salmon. The fishing at Pinware is reported to be even better than at Forteau, but the river is a much more difficult one to fish.

It is also possible to fly by bush plane to any part of Labrador for trout- and salmon-fishing, some airlines even maintaining regular schedules for this purpose. In addition to salmon and brook trout, there are lake trout, pike and arctic char, all plentiful and all in trophy sizes. The trips are expensive, but they assure the fisherman of the finest fresh-water sport fishing that it is possible to get anywhere in North America.

8. The Land of Grenfell

St. Anthony, headquarters of the Grenfell Mission and self-styled Gateway to the North, is eighty-five miles by road from St. Barbe Bay. With a population between 2,000 and 3,000, it is the 'city' of Newfoundland's northern tip, and roads from it run out in five directions to clusters of fishing settlements within a radius of twenty miles. These villages have such names as Griquet and Quirpon (Car-*poon*), St. Lunaire and Little Brehat (Bra-*hah*). All of them are relics of a French fishery dating back to the early days of the sixteenth century.

On this shore, more than three centuries ago, we had the only massacre of white men by Indians in Newfoundland. How the trouble between the French fishermen and the natives first arose we do not know, but in 1609 the fishermen applied to the government of France for permission to outfit two armed vessels each year to 'make war upon the savages of Newfoundland'. They continued to outfit ships of war for this purpose for at least the next quarter of a century.

An account of only one battle has been preserved, and in that one the 'savages' had it all their own way. In 1640 a raiding-party of eighty natives descended upon St. Julien's Harbour (just across Hare Bay from St. Anthony) and killed seven men whom they found there working at their fish. They then crossed a hill into the adjoining harbour, now called Grandois, and killed nine more.

Sixteen of the natives then dressed in the dead Frenchmen's clothes, and next day appeared at Croque, where they killed twenty-one more fishermen, a total of thirty-seven, apparently without losing a single man themselves.

One of the puzzles about this ancient skirmish is the identity of the 'savages' involved. They could have been Eskimos or Algonkians. If they were Beothuck Indians, then this is the only known case of Beothucks engaging in organized warfare. It is also uncertain that the Beothucks ever penetrated as far north as Hare Bay in historic times.

There are many Dorset sites other than Port-au-Choix on the Great Northern Peninsula. One of them is at L'Anse-aux-Meadows, at a place that the local people always called 'The Old Indian Camp', but that turned out, on investigation, to have been occupied by a succession of cultures, including Norse colonists from Iceland or Greenland around the year A.D. 1000.

L'Anse-aux-Meadows (the name is a corruption of the French L'Anse-aux-Meduses, the Bay of Jelly Fish) lies in a flat, shallow depression seventeen miles north of St. Anthony on the extreme northern tip of Newfoundland. There is no harbour, but a tiny stream flows into the sea, providing fresh water; there is a small area of wild sheep pasture, and it is possible to beach a shallow-draught boat there.

A succession of peoples were attracted to L'Anse-aux-Meadows in ancient times because of its location in the Strait of Belle Isle, with access to both sides of the peninsula, and to the great herds of whales and seals that passed there every year on migration, going both to the west, into the Gulf of St. Lawrence, and to the east, into White Bay, Notre Dame Bay, and along the east coast of Newfoundland to the Grand Banks.

As long ago as 1914, the Newfoundland historian W. A. Munn argued on the evidence of the Viking sagas that there must have been a Norse settlement in this general region, and urged archaeologists to investigate, but nobody did anything about it until the Danish archaeologist Jorgen Meldgaard landed there in 1960, having read and been convinced by Munn's book. He found nothing, but his work was followed up a year later by the Norwegian Helge Ingstad, who used the same local guides that Meldgaard had employed the year before. The guides took Ingstad to 'The Old Indian Camp' which, somehow, Meldgaard had missed, and it proved to include the first authenticated Norse settlement ever found in North America.

Unfortunately the determination of its discoverers to prove that L'Anse-aux-Meadows was the landfall of Leif the Lucky caused many other interesting finds there to be ignored. There is little reasonable doubt that it was, indeed, a small Norse farm complex, and carbon dating of approximately A.D. 1000 confirms that it was probably a stopping place for one of the saga voyages. It could not have been the 'Vinland' of Leif Ericsson for a number of reasons, strongest of which is that it does not bear even the faintest resemblance to the landfall described for Leif in the sagas, but it was probably the wintering-place of the Karlsefni expedition, the first true colonizing attempt, made by Icelanders around the year A.D. 1005.

The Dorsets were there long before the Norse, and apparently long afterwards as well. Not only was a Dorset flint factory discovered on the site, but a Dorset stone lamp was dug out of the floor of the 'smithy' where iron was apparently smelted from bog ore, and no doubt worked into harpoons and other weapons for sealing and whaling. It was not, of course, the Dorsets who worked the iron, but the Norse, or other Europeans. Though most of the carbon dates are clustered around A.D. 1000, one piece of charcoal from the 'smithy' has a date approximately 350 years earlier, indicating that somebody was using it by the middle of the seventh century.

There is a road to L'Anse-aux-Meadows for those who wish to stand on the spot where Karlsefni and his Icelanders probably came ashore almost a thousand years ago. But there is very little for the visitor to see – just sheds covering shallow depressions in the turf, empty shore, bogland, a stretch of shallow bay dotted with islands, and, far off to the north and west, the looming coastline of Labrador.

The little settlements founded in the Strait of Belle Isle by the Basques and the French maintained a tiny fishing population down through the centuries, but St. Anthony itself was practically an empty harbour when a young English doctor arrived in 1892 with a bunch of religious tracts under one arm, a stethoscope under the other, and a determination to make this the capital of his private empire.

Sir Wilfred Grenfell was a strange and contradictory man, but he had such force of character that northern Newfoundland and much of Labrador is still deeply imprinted with his personality. Even today it is impossible to buy a drink in St. Anthony. The nearest licensed room is at the Loon Motel, seven miles out of town. And, if Sir Wilfred were alive, it is a safe bet that the demon rum would never have gotten even that close to the town which he named after his patron saint. St. Anthony lacks public restaurants and hotels, and there is little that could be described as entertainment. Until a few years ago the power supply was cut off each night at eleven o'clock.

It is a clean, well-built town, with an impressive collection of public buildings, most of them the property of the Grenfell Mission, for Sir Wilfred not only built a general hospital here, but started industrial shops, handicraft industries, a dry dock, dairy and pig farms, and founded schools and orphanages where children from all parts of his domain were brought up on strict Victorian principles in the fear of God and the fear of the rod. Some of them were taken by force or coercion out of what he regarded as appalling home conditions.

He had himself appointed a Justice of the Peace, so that he could hold court on his ship and punish wrongdoers. There is one case on record where he and his assistant tried a woman for neglecting her child, convicted her, and sentenced her to jail, then suspended the sentence on condition that she sign the child over to them. She agreed, and the child grew up as a Grenfell 'orphan'.

Grenfell was a visionary and a fanatic, a compassionate dictator, a shy, even timid, publicity hound who had no compunction about stretching or distorting the truth in what he regarded as a good cause. Though he never spent a winter in Labrador in his life, he loved to have himself photographed in the furs of a polar explorer, and encouraged the growth of legends about his adventures on the drift ice. He trumpeted his own name around the world and made himself into an almost mythological figure decades before his death in 1940. What the name of Schweitzer meant in the 1950s, the name Grenfell meant forty years earlier.

He was appalled by the misery that he found among the Newfoundland and Labrador 'livyers' in the 1890s – boys and girls with hardly a shred of clothing, even in winter, fishermen spitting blood as they hauled their nets, mothers gaunt with sickness nursing dying children while carrying others still unborn. He devoted his life to trying to change those conditions. He did not succeed. When I first visited Labrador in 1949, babies were still being fed on flour and water for lack of milk, and hundreds of the 'livyers' were housed in one-room shacks with nothing but the bare earth for floors.

Dr. Grenfell and his Mission saved many lives and improved living conditions for at least some of the people of the coast. He was determined not only to heal men's bodies, but to reshape the whole course of their lives, and the towns where he built his hospitals were, until quite recently, run by the Mission, with no nonsense from the natives.

Some of his schemes bore fruit. He even managed to create a real farming enterprise in central Labrador, where one of his stations raises enough crops to be almost self-supporting. Some of his schemes were bizarre, and came to nothing. Such was his plan to introduce Lapland reindeer, which he felt might be herded like cattle, pastured on the wild barrens of Newfoundland and Labrador, and used both as meat and as draft animals. The only result of this ill-advised venture was the introduction to North America of two new parasites (brought here by his reindeer herd) that infected the Newfoundland caribou and have plagued them ever since.

His town-building schemes began a new era. Where two or three families of hunters had lived before, sawmill towns sprang up. Where a few trappers had lived in sylvan solitude, docks and tankers and modern machinery and finally airplanes invaded the wilderness. Where necessary, the Mission undertook such public works as are usually left to town and provincial governments. They not only built hospitals, schools, and industrial institutions, but also built roads, public water-supplies, and installed diesel electric systems.

Though in the early days Mission schools taught only up to grade nine, hundreds of students went away for higher education. Many of them became doctors, nurses, engineers, business managers, social workers, teachers, and many of them returned to serve the Grenfell empire. Even some of the bush pilots who fly planes serving the northern hospitals are Grenfell-educated men.

Grenfell nurses are a special breed. They come from all over the world, volunteer for northern service, and often carry responsibilities that city nurses would never dare to face.

Edith Summers, an Australian who joined the Grenfell organization in Montreal, told me of her arrival on the coast. She drove north by car, but before reaching St. Anthony was diverted to the little nursing station at Flower's Cove, seventy miles short of her goal, where she found herself in sole charge of a 'hospital' serving hundreds of loggers and fishermen.

The morning of her arrival a burly lumberjack rolled up to the door.

'Be ye haulin' teeth today, ma'am?' he demanded.

Miss Summers was shocked. She had never heard of a nurse doing dental extractions. But the radio-telephone link with St. Anthony assured her that this was purely routine. She dug out a pair of forceps, flexed her muscles, and tackled her first molar.

A few weeks later she was joined by an assistant, but life continued to move from one crisis to the next.

'We never knew when the sky was going to fall on us,' she related. 'One evening when we were ready to quit after a hard day, a woods truck pulled up to the gate, and two men got out, carrying a third between them. He was unconscious from a scalp wound, and had lost so much blood that we couldn't find any pulse at all. But he was still breathing.'

They had neither plasma nor whole blood, so they laid the patient on a cot, closed the wound, filled him full of liquids in an effort to counter the loss of blood, and sent off a frantic call to St. Anthony for help. Just then a second patient arrived, with the tip of his finger amputated by an axe.

'I was just putting a dressing on this ugly wound,' Miss Summers recalled, 'when a young boy came hobbling in, all by himself.

' "What's the matter with you?" I asked, maybe a little impatiently.

' "I got a sore knee, ma'am," he replied.

' "Oh, for heaven's sake – a sore knee! Can't it wait till tomorrow?" And he was actually hobbling out again when it struck me that he might actually be worse off than he seemed. I called him back, felt him stiffen as I touched his leg, and then, as I rolled up his pants, I was horrified to find his knee-cap hanging loose by a flap of skin.'

So while her assistant hovered over the shock victim, trying to prevent him from slipping into final oblivion, and the man with the amputated finger went home, promising to return tomorrow, Nurse Summers gave the boy an anaesthetic and inserted fourteen sutures to close the wound. All three patients made a complete recovery.

'Much more interesting than city hospital work, where you can't even give a patient an aspirin tablet without a signed order from a doctor,' she assured me.

I was in St. Anthony when the first fatal motor accident occurred on the road to Bonne Bay, the year after it was opened. Besides one man killed, two carloads of men, women, and children were injured, five of them critically. Dr. Thomas, the present director of the Mission, left to fly to the scene, ninety miles away, but his plane was forced down on a small lake, with a broken piston. The Mission now faced a complicated emergency – its plane out of action, its chief surgeon marooned in the bush, and one nurse at Port Saunders, near the scene of the accident, fighting for the lives of five people who might die at any moment. They radioed emergency calls to Gander in central Newfoundland, and by early afternoon bush planes were arriving in relays with doctor and patients, all of whom were rushed to the emergency ward of the hospital, and all of whom survived.

One of St. Anthony's attractions to the visitor is the handicraft shop and workshop, where beautiful knitted, sewn, woven, and carved articles are offered for sale, all of them made from designs unique to Newfoundland and Labrador. Here, again, you can get hooked mats, some of them with Eskimo designs or arctic scenes. Among the articles sold are beautiful and highly practical parkas of Grenfell cloth, decorated with hand embroidery. The ivory carvings were once made from walrus tusks – an art that goes back to prehistoric times among the Eskimos. But walrus ivory is now so scarce that the mission imports elephant ivory from Africa as a substitute. There are also wood carvings, bead work, and embroidery, not only from St. Anthony, but from Mission stations in Labrador as well.

The town that Grenfell built has since declared its independence, has its own town council, runs all its own public works, and has even taken the school out of the Mission's hands. But the orphanage, the hospital, the farms, and industrial shops remain. And, even in death, the little English doctor continues to dominate his surroundings.

On a wooded hill overlooking the town, approached by a primitive woods trail that can be traversed only on foot, there is a modest grave plot and a modest memorial. Kings and other lesser men might need great tombs to honour their memory. Grenfell, whose achievement was real and not merely symbolic, needs nothing more than a tablet to mark his resting place. Here, overgrown with Labrador poppies, are the graves of Sir Wilfred Grenfell and his successor, Dr. Charles Curtis, and to this small shrine people from all parts of the world come to gain a sense of dedication. It is only among the people whom he served and ruled with such inflexible purpose that Grenfell is remembered with mixed emotions. Few other men have been so loved and so hated.

9. The World's Greatest Inland Game Fish

Newfoundland's national sport is angling. Practically every boy (and nowadays many a girl, too) begins catching trout as soon as he is big enough to hold a rod. In their teens, thousands of these young anglers graduate to salmon-fishing. A few go on to the millionaire's sport of deep-sea fishing for tuna, for 600-pound bluefins are caught by the hundred every summer off Newfoundland's coasts, and the annual world record tuna frequently comes from Conception Bay.

But salmon-fishing is still regarded by most anglers as the highest form of the art. The west coast of Newfoundland and the adjoining east coast of Labrador are the centres of this sport. There are other parts of Newfoundland with salmon rivers. The Gander, in central Newfoundland, is one of our most heavily-fished rivers. And there are some good salmon streams on the south coast. But on the west coast there are thirty-six rivers, not including tributaries, that I would class as major streams, with excellent runs of fish at one season or another between late June and early September. The best time for fishing the great majority of these rivers is from the middle of June to the middle of July, but a few rivers, with their own local population of salmon, do not reach their peak until August, and some inland pools, far from salt water, are at their best in September.

There are six rivers in southern Labrador that are at least as good as any in the world, but generally speaking they are rather difficult to reach and rather expensive to fish.

When I started salmon-fishing in the 1940s, the bag limit was eight salmon per day, and it was not uncommon for an angler to get his limit. This was later cut to six, and recently to four. The four-fish bag limit is really quite generous, however. Salmon average about six pounds each, and twenty-four pounds of fish is a reasonable catch for any day's angling. The limit, of course, is on the number of fish killed. There is no limit on the number that you may hook, play, and release.

I camped near a pool on the Upper Humber a couple of years ago and watched nineteen anglers, all fishing a single large pool, take four fish each between breakfast and lunch. An even larger number of fishermen were angling in the famous Big Falls pool, about five miles farther up-river, and taking several fish each every day.

It is not necessary, however, to share your sport with crowds of other anglers. I have often left the crowded pools near the roads and found a totally unoccupied pool only a mile or so up-river. There is a special thrill to playing one of these great fish in total solitude in a wilderness setting. The rivers are so plentiful, and the pools so numerous, that it is rarely necessary to share a pool with another angler if you prefer to fish alone.

All Newfoundland rivers are open to all anglers. None of them is leased or restricted, except for a very few spots that, for conservation reasons, are closed to all fishing. Once you buy a licence, you are entitled to fish any river or lake in the province. About 15,000 licences are issued each year, and the anglers who buy them report catching about 200,000 pounds of salmon. The catch is probably very much under-estimated, however, since the report depends mainly upon the returns sent in by river wardens, who never see more than a minority of the fish taken or the anglers fishing.

Licences cost $5 a day, $20 a fortnight, $30 a season for non-residents, $5 a season for residents. You can fish for trout without a guide, but non-residents require a guide for salmon-fishing. Guiding fees vary greatly, depending on the services provided. Some guides include cabins or camping equipment and food in their guiding fees. Others provide all-in trips including transportation at a daily fee. But guides without these extras charge about $15 or $20 a day. Two fishermen are allowed to share a guide.

All fishing for salmon must be by fly-rod only. In fact, the fly-rod is by far the most productive, as well as the sportiest, fishing tackle for summer fishing in Newfoundland. Bait, plugs, spinners, and the like are permitted on lakes and trout streams, and are quite effective in spring, but for summer fishing for trout as well as for salmon the fly-rod is the universal favourite. Most New-foundland anglers favour light tackle – rods of no more than five or six ounces, tapered lines, leaders with tippets of four, six, or at most eight pound test.

Small, lightly dressed flies are usually the most successful. Many a visiting angler has been appalled to see his guide take scissors or nail-clippers and strip away almost all the fancy feathers from his over-dressed, European-style (and very expensive) salmon flies. Hundreds of Newfoundland anglers tie their own flies, some of them right at the stream-side, and rarely use more than a bit of black moose hair, a strip of silver tinsel, maybe a tiny bit of white feather or a bare touch of red. You do not need a host of different patterns. The moose-hair wet fly, in various sizes and lengths of shank, or the Royal Coachman dry fly, will almost always take fish. Trout, too, and especially sea trout, rise hungrily to the moose hair.

Most of the rivers that carry salmon in their up-stream pools are also good sea-trout streams, especially at the estuary. Unlike salmon, trout carry a weight limit. You make the limit when your catch totals ten pounds with one fish taken out. This curious formula protects an angler who lands a single large trout from being forced to release it because he is already close to the day's weight limit.

The largest sea trout (a brown) ever taken in Newfoundland was landed by a woman, and weighed twenty-six pounds. The largest brook trout weighed twelve – approximately two pounds short of the world record.

Labrador has lake trout and pike, as well as the trout and salmon common on the island. The lake trout tend to run to huge sizes (I have seen a photograph of a sixty-pounder taken on a set line through the ice in the winter) and there is a limit of four per day. Pike – among the largest and hungriest of fresh-water fish – are regarded as food fish rather than game. There is a bag limit of twenty-four per day, a possession limit of forty-eight, in a season running from January 15 to September 15.

The summer visitor who plans to fish for salmon and trout needs one light fly-rod and a reel with plenty of capacity and ample backing behind his line, since salmon sometimes make very long runs. If he plans to do much lake fishing, he may bring a spinning rod as well.

Apart from big-game hunting and deep-sea fishing, salmon-fishing is the really élite sport in Newfoundland. It is not, however, excessively expensive, as, apart from travelling, a short salmon-fishing trip can be managed well within a budget of $200. It is, in consequence, a popular, democratic sport, with an increasing number of participants. How long the salmon runs will be able to stand the pressure no one can predict. At the moment there are still populous runs of excellent fish in dozens of rivers, especially in good years when water conditions are neither too high nor too low and there is a successful return from previous breeding seasons. Most of us feel, all the same, that great salmon angling is a phase that will not out-last the wilderness, and that with increasing civilization the sport is likely to die. Perhaps, in consequence, we try to make the most of it while it lasts.

10. Notre Dame Bay and the Road to the Isles

The last glacial epoch – which ended rather suddenly about 7,000 years ago – buried Newfoundland under an ice sheet a mile thick, tilted the island by sheer weight into a long, gradual northeast slope, then melted and left its tilt behind. Along the south coast stark cliffs were tipped upward out of the ocean. In the north, hills sank down to become islands, and the sea rushed in to drown the valleys.

As the ice retreated, leaving the land scarred and scoured, the depressed coastlines began to rise again, and they have been rising ever since, at rates varying from a few inches to a foot or more each century. But vast stretches of the north-east coast remain buried beneath the sea, creating a fanciful complex of islands, bays, runs, and tickles, more complicated and more picturesque than anywhere else on the Atlantic shore. It is literally true that experienced sailors, using good charts, could still lose their way in the intricate passages of Dildo Run.

Most of the drowned region is known as Notre Dame Bay, a large area incorporating many smaller bodies of water such as Green Bay, Gander Bay, Hall's Bay, and Bay of Exploits.

The Trans-Canada Highway makes a big bend past Notre Dame Bay, coming down to the shore at only two points: South Brook on Hall's Bay, and Norris Arm on Bay of Exploits. The rest of the region is served by over 700 miles of secondary highroads, and a number of causeways and ferries.

On the western side of Notre Dame Bay a highly mineralized bit of the Precambrian Shield known as the Burlington Peninsula forms one of Newfoundland's principal mining centres.

Here, when the world was young, its crust shifted repeatedly, allowing molten rock with many kinds of metallic ores to flow into the cracks as intrusive masses of all sizes, big and small. These pockets form today's ore-bodies.

Copper is mined at Little Bay, Tilt Cove, and Gull Pond. Asbestos is mined from a very large reserve of good ore at Baie Verte. At Rambler, near by, copper, zinc, gold, silver, and cadmium are mined. Hundreds of other deposits have been drilled, and some of them show excellent prospects for production. The whole peninsula is a rock-hound's delight, with numerous mineralized outcroppings that yield beautiful samples but have no commercial value. The area is worked and prospected by a group of companies controlled by Canadian mining magnate Jim Boylen.

The Baie Verte road and its various branches, beginning sixty miles east of Deer Lake, reaches most of the peninsula. Still unpaved, it carries such a heavy flow of traffic that its surface is often in bad shape, though it is passable at all seasons. Baie Verte is fifty miles from the Trans-Canada Highway, and the road continues another sixteen miles to the headland fishing village of Fleur-de-Lys. There are branch roads to such fishing villages as Ming's Bight, Pacquet, Harbour Round, and Shoe Cove, all of them typical northern fishing settlements, some of them in very picturesque surroundings.

Shoe Cove, the smallest, is just a cleft in the cliffs with a pocket-sized harbour that will admit nothing larger than a motor boat. Though there is room for half a dozen fishing skiffs, the sea heaves in with such force that they can ride on their moorings only a few weeks out of the year. At other times they must be hauled out of the water on skids, or moored in neighbouring harbours.

In the 1950s the Newfoundland government decided that the people ought to move out of Shoe Cove to some place where it would be easier to deliver their family allowance and unemployment insurance cheques, but the half-dozen fishing families that lived there dug in their heels, refused to move, and, to reinforce their decision, built themselves a new school. They are still there, and, since Shoe Cove happens to be a place with a productive cod bank right on its doorstep, they are making a good living, while many of those who moved from similar places spend most of their time on welfare.

The widespread belief that Newfoundland fishermen are desperately poor is no longer true. In 1967 herring fishermen of Harbour Breton shared $20,000 a man for a five-month season. And though this is still exceptional, it is not unusual for a fishing family in a good location to net $6,000 to $10,000 for its season's work. In places where the fishery is always poor, and frequently fails, fishing is still a mug's game, but in settlements near prolific fishing-grounds the people are prosperous if not affluent.

Nevertheless, the movement from the fishing settlements to the big towns and cities continues, with government help and approval, and even with strong government prodding when inducements fail. Three miles over the hill from Shoe Cove lies the Horrible Example. It is the town of La Scie, where federal and provincial governments combined under a single master plan to build a fishing metropolis in a place where a handful of seal-hunters had lived before. They created an artificial harbour, laid out a townsite, piped in water, built fish filleting and freezing plants, erected docking facilities, and invited fishermen from near and far to move there at public expense. Many of them did, and some of them lived to regret it, for, because of its geography, La Scie can never become a great fishing centre, and today its largest industry is government welfare.

Five miles off Cape St. John at the tip of the peninsula, and ten miles from La Scie, a bare dome of rock rises out of the ocean like an egg from an eggcup. This is Cape St. John Gull Island, where the brigantine *Queen* ran aground in a snowstorm on December 12, 1867, on her way from St. John's to the Tilt Cove mines. She carried captain, pilot, a crew of eight, and six passengers, including two young women, one of them the daughter of the mine manager. When the ship struck the island and lodged in a cleft of the rocks, all of the people got ashore.

Three of the crew then returned on board to try and remove supplies. But before anything could be landed a heavy sea lifted the ship off the rocks, she slid seaward, vanished into the blizzard, and was never seen again. The three men went with her. One of the passengers, a doctor, kept a diary for the sixteen days that followed, recording the death by exposure and starvation of the company. There was no food or shelter. They tried to signal to the land by lighting fires at night. The fires were seen, but the superstitious fishermen regarded them as 'spirit lights' and warned one another to stay away from the island. The doctor and the daughter of the mine manager were the only ones still living on December 27, the day of the last entry in the diary.

The entire tragedy occurred within sight of the homes of some of the people, for Gull Island is only twelve miles from Tilt Cove. Sealers, the following spring, found the bodies and took them there for burial.

Tilt Cove today is reached by a branch road that leaves the highway near La Scie. It is a town that came back from the dead – a former ghost town that sat over an abandoned mine for more than a generation, then suddenly, in 1955, became a boom town once more.

Mining began there in 1857, the first of four copper mines that were opened in Green Bay in the nineteenth century and made Newfoundland the world's sixth largest copper producer. Tilt Cove employed 1,200 men, and paid out five million dollars in dividends to shareholders in twenty-four years.

Then came the first close-down, followed by sporadic workings until 1914, when the mines closed 'for good'. It was not until the 1950s, after Canadian prospectors discovered gold and nickel as well as new bodies of copper ore, that the ghost town, then down to six families, woke up to the roar of diamond drills and heavy diesel engines. Once again 700 men worked there. A new town was built. Ore production reached 2,000 tons a day. And then, again, the mines closed, outclassed by richer ore-bodies a few miles away. But there are still extensive lodes of ore at Tilt Cove, and the town seems destined to lead a sporadic on-and-off existence depending on the world market price for copper.

Other roads on the west side of Notre Dame Bay lead to such picturesque spots as Rattling Brook, Wild Bight, and Pilley's Island.

The latter is both the name of a large island and its chief settlement – one of a group that includes Brighton, Triton, and Robert's Arm. The group of islands is linked by road and causeway, in one of the loveliest maritime settings on the Atlantic shore. Though the islands and villages can be reached by road, it is still best to visit some of them by motor boat, using the beautiful inside runs that look more like lake and river than inlets of the ocean, until you notice a shingle beach with strings of kelp and rockweed, or tidal pools between the islands, red and purple with starfish and false corals.

It is fifteen miles from South Brook, on the Trans-Canada, to Robert's Arm, another six to Pilley's Island. And that is an excellent spot to get a boat, for half a day or so, to visit Card's Harbour, Brighton, Triton, and Lushes Bight. There are also hundreds of small islands, all of them well-sheltered from the sea, many of them partly forested or covered with wild pasture. This is a place where you could buy a private island for less than the cost of a suburban building lot.

Farther east in Notre Dame Bay lies an even larger group: Chapel Island, New World Island, Twillingate, and their attendant flotilla of islands and islets. The highway to this beautiful region begins at Notre Dame Junction on the Trans-Canada, skirts a magnificent series of bays, and hops by bridge and causeway from island to island until it reaches the important fishing town of Twillingate, some seventy miles away.

As I drove over this new road recently, I could at first see little change in the quiet and remote settlements that I had last visited ten years before. Here where some of my ancestors had lived for generations, the peace that has always blessed the Newfoundland outports still brooded over white villages and jewel-like harbours set among blue and green hills. Open trap boats and little decked motor vessels swung to their moorings in the runs and tickles. A man and a boy waded in the shallows among the rockweed collecting bucketfuls of blue mussels. Long vistas of wooded islands stretched away on either hand. Wild roses and irises invaded the edges of the potato patches. A few cows of uncertain breeding wandered freely about the landscape, poking their noses through the white picket fences that protected small plots of flowers and vegetables beside the kitchen doors.

Not until next morning did the change strike me. As I walked along what used to be called the Front Path, now become in very truth a road, where fish stages and curing flakes used to stand on the right while stores filled with salt and tar-scented nets flanked the left, I realized that the flakes – once the very badge and signpost of the outports, and still to be seen in a hundred small places – had vanished. For here the fishermen no longer cured their fish, but sent it up the bay by truck to be processed in a plant, or sold it in bulk to collectors to be dried artificially in ovens instead of in the autumn sunshine as it was done when I was a boy.

While I pondered these changes, a transport truck with a Nova Scotia licence plate came lumbering around the corner, reminding me that the outside world had descended in force on these villages only the year before, when Premier Joey Smallwood, redeeming an election promise, had built the causeways to link New World Island's 5,000 inhabitants with his burgeoning system of roads that now connected 900 Newfoundland settlements to the rest of Canada.

I stopped to talk with a fisherman mending a net – an old man with a leather-brown face and wonderful, knotted hands that were like poetry among the meshes of his seine. Two boys in bib overalls came and stood to one side, deferentially, listening to our talk.

'The road, yes, 'tis a great blessin',' the old man was saying. 'Before it come through only the old ones was bidin' here – the likes o' me, and bits o' boys like they two yonder. All the fishin' crews was nigh old enough fer the pension, or green youngsters ye knew'd be gone come next year. Soon as they stopped gettin' the baby bonus they was off to St. John's or Corner Brook or one o' they places lookin' fer jobs. 'Twere different in the old days. Then everyone worked at the fish – even the women in aprons with bonnets to keep the sun off their faces – ye from the Mainland?'

I disclaimed this distinction, and asked about the regrowth of the fishery.

'Oh yes,' the old man said. 'There be a lot o' fellers goin' back to fishin' now. Since they heered tell o' the road comin' through people been stayin' here, mostly, instead o' movin' off as they was doin' before. Lot o' the young men goin' fishin' too. Some even come back, after movin' away.'

'And how about the sawmills?' I asked. 'Much lumber being cut?'

'Oh yes,' he assured me. 'They be doin' pretty well I 'low. Small's mill, up there alongside the causeway, cuts nigh on quarter of a million feet a year. They's talk they'd cut an' sell half a million, could they get the logs.'

'Are you planning to stay here yourself?'

'Maybe yes, maybe no. Twillingate got the lights, ye know, an' a fish plant. They be ahead o' we, that way. But they say the lights'll follow the road, sooner or later. There still be those as wants to move to Lewisporte or Twillingate. But meself an' the old woman, if we makes a move, 'twill be to live with our daughter in St. John's. The old woman, she be gettin' the pension now, an' I be due next year, so we'll be beholden to no one fer the rest of our lives.'

I thanked the net-mender and asked the boys to show me over the hill to The Arm, though in fact I knew the way well enough. They were shy at first, answering only 'Yes sir' and 'No sir' to my questions. Yes, they still set snares for rabbits in the woods in winter. No, they never went out with the men to the cod traps, except maybe for the ride. Yes, they had been across the new causeway in a car, and over the road to Lewisporte, which is now the 'city' of Notre Dame Bay. No, they had never been to St. John's or any other big town. Yes, they both wanted to go. They both wanted to drive trucks or bulldozers or maybe even airplanes.

As their shyness left them, they told me about their families. Children were no longer named Solomon and Eli and Joshua, as they were when I was growing up. Names now came out of the movies instead of the Old Testament. One boy was called Gary and the other Wayne. But the family names hadn't changed in two hundred years: Nippers and Kings, Coles and Smalls, Rowsells and Nobles, even a few Horwoods – most of them descended from English adventurers who had fought and exterminated the Indians on this coast back in the eighteenth century.

I had known the older boy's father. Where was he now?

'Working at Goose Bay, sir. He comes home at Christmas, sometimes, and for a couple weeks in the spring. We've a salmon net that we set out when he's here on holidays. He takes me with him to the nets in the mornings, and I set out some lobster pots, too.'

'How does he get his salmon berth, if he isn't home?'

'I draw for his berth, sir. The teacher lets me off from school, and I go to the store and draw for a berth with the men.' There was more than a touch of pride in his voice as he said it.

'Why don't we go and have a look at the general store?' I suggested.

They grinned eagerly. A trip to the store with a visitor to stand treats was something that the road hadn't changed. But the store itself was hardly recognizable. Instead of the owner, looming over the end of the counter and examining his ledgers like the Angel of the Apocalypse with the Book of Life (as I remembered him), were two teen-aged slips of girls with toothpaste smiles and gleaming hair-dos. Gone were the odorous recesses where, only yester-

day, sole leather, bacon sides, and harness straps used to hang.
The shelves were lit by neon tubes supplied by a generator hum-
ming busily in a small shed on the wharf. A glass-fronted frozen-
food dispenser. A juke box. As we went in, it was playing a sentimental ballad about a cowboy who had lost his love. 'Country
and western' has become the national music of the outports.

'Maybe you could fix us up with whatever it is kids like to buy,'
I suggested to the nearer of the toothpaste girls.

'Popsicles?' she asked, and perhaps I winced, for she went on,
'for the boys I mean, sir. We won't have ice-cream today until the
truck gets back from Lewisporte. But there are fudgsicles, dream-
sicles, frozen drumsticks . . .'

I wasn't listening. I was thinking of the huge molasses puncheon with its hand pump that used to stand in the corner, and
the six inches of delicious molasses sugar that you could get out
of the bottom of those puncheons when, after an eternity of sitting in the same spot, they were at last empty. I was thinking of
the buff-and-brown taffy and the striped peppermint knobs that
used to fill the departed glass jars. For this used to be a store just
like the big old one at Port-au-Port, where Abbott and Halibur-
ton still do half a million dollars' worth of business over the
cracker-barrel each year. I was examining the shelves. Cake mixes.
Canned marmalade. Bottled jam. Meat balls. Jelly-roll made in
Montreal.

The boys were sucking popsicles and looking at trinkets, including small American flags made in Japan, offered for sale at
the notions counter.

'Give them something to eat, too,' I suggested, 'chocolate bars
or bananas or something.'

'No fresh fruit, sir, I'm sorry,' the girl said. 'What sort of bars
would you like?'

After a while we walked out into the warm sunshine.

'Do you still pick berries on the hills back there?' I asked.

'Oh yes, sir, but they won't be ripe for a month, yet.'

'And do your mothers make them into jam and fruit pies?'

'Oh no, sir,' the older boy said. 'A truck collects them, you
know, and takes them to the plant, and we get fifty cents a gallon.
At least, that's what we got last year.'

Trucks, indeed, have become the very centre of the life of this
community. Trucks bring in food and clothing and other supplies from the mainland. Trucks collect their fish, right from the

boat or the splitting table. Trucks running all the way from Prince Edward Island, a thousand miles by road and causeway and ferry, pick up their lobsters. A dozen little stores have sprouted up where the trucks of wholesale jobbers have brought goods to set up ambitious men or women in small businesses of their own.

Out at the small harbour called Cottle's Island, on the western tip of New World Island, lives a man who flourished mightily by trade before the first truck arrived. Arthur King invested $40 in job goods twenty-five years ago, then began buying and selling lobsters and fish. Today he owns the biggest single premises on the island, has three branch stores and a service station, rents a modern building to the Bank of Nova Scotia, and runs a fleet of trucks and boats.

'The roads are making a great deal of difference to the fisheries and the lumber industry,' he says. 'Lumbering is almost as important as fishing here, you know. The mills are all small, and they sell locally in various parts of Notre Dame Bay. Shipping by road is a great help to them.

'Prosperity has increased, too. I bought a quarter of a million dollars' worth of fish last year, and I'm competing with a dozen other buyers. New churches and schools are going up all over the place – new homes, too, much better types of homes than people were building before. We have eighty-two miles of local road on the island, and hundreds of cars – junk, a lot of them, but they all run, somehow or other.'

King's lobsters were shipped in trucks, insulated and refrigerated, to Prince Edward Island, but his closest competitor, Notre Dame Bay Fisheries Limited, shipped their lobsters to near-by Gander Airport, then flew them to market in the United States.

'It's a matter of price,' he explained. 'Either way you can market them in good condition, and both are a great improvement over the collecting boats that we had to rely on before.' He had to break off our talk to see to a load of goods arriving by truck from Lewisporte.

M. J. Small, the ageing mill-owner, called the road 'the greatest thing that ever happened to this island'. 'Good for business, too,' he added. 'Most of our lumber goes direct to people building new homes. We're selling everything we can cut as fast as it comes from the saw or the planing mill, delivering by truck when the buyers don't call for it themselves. We do a lot of custom sawing, too – cutting logs that people bring to us, you know. We have plans to increase our output, and our only real problem is getting the raw material.'

Born on New World Island in 1883, Mr. Small came from a family of fishermen, worked as a fish-killer and herring-catcher before he began lumbering.

'I used to put up travellers, you know, when you travelled over the ice in the winter, across the frozen runs, by dog team or by boat or however you could get around. We worked hard, and we had to rely on what we could do for ourselves, but times weren't nearly so bad as people say. We hunted all our own meat. There'd be ducks, mostly in the winter, and other sea birds in the spring. Then we'd have seals. In the fall you'd maybe go up-country for a caribou or a moose. Some years there'd be lots of rabbits. We'd have all kinds of fresh fish from June to December, lobsters and salmon. Everyone grew his own vegetables. We lived pretty good, all told . . .

'You know about Coaker? Coaker himself was a farmer, right here in Dildo Run, before he started out along the coast, rousing the fishermen to seize power from the government – and they all joined his union, and took their savings out of socks or banks or wherever they had them, and put them into his company – the Fishermen's Union Trading Company, you know – singing "We are with you Mr. Coaker, and we're forty thousand strong." They thought the millennium had come, or something.'

'Yes, I know, and the bitterness that came after when they thought Coaker had robbed them and sold out to the merchants, and how sure they were of it when he was knighted by the King of England for his wickedness. But Coaker, too, gambled and lost, and took his knighthood as a sort of booby prize. He was a cynical and disillusioned man by the time he retired in the 1930s.'

And later came the rush to the woods – men cutting pulpwood for the Anglo-Newfoundland Development Company (now Price Newfoundland, operating the paper mill at Grand Falls), quarrying limestone at Cobb's Arm, a few of them getting jobs in the mill. But there was always the fishery, even when their union of 40,000 collapsed. And always they came back to it.

'Things were changing, though, even before we had the road,' Mr. Small recalled. 'People were less independent than they were, less able to manage by themselves. No one can kill his own meat any more. The meat they eat here nowadays was killed and frozen up in Canada somewhere.'

As I drove about New World Island's local roads, I was more impressed with the numerous small changes than with the big ones: juke boxes, pin-ball machines, coin-operated bowling games. Where the road makes a T-intersection to connect the villages of Bridgeport and Moreton's Harbour, a sort of cross-roads amusement centre has arisen, with a lunch counter, pool room, and movie theatre.

The people talked about their cars, about the prospects for electricity, about how hard it was to make ends meet, about trips to Grand Falls and St. John's, where they went five or six times a year, for Newfoundlanders have become inveterate gadders-about since the roads were built.

Some of the children were wearing fancy jackets styled in the United States, and cowboy boots. Some of the young men had leather jackets and long hair, like they saw in the movie house. A few of the girls looked cheap and blowsy in ill-applied make-up and ill-fitting clothes six times removed from the fashion centres of New York. They 'jived' with the boys, or, just as often, with each other, in the juke-and-pinball joints, and drank cokes under signs that warned 'Profane Language Strictly Forbidden'. The jive, introduced by Americans in the Second World War, is still the universal dance of Newfoundland outport youngsters. All the girls learn to do it, but only a minority of the boys dance at all.

Remnants of an older culture mingled with this imported American product, but did not mix: kids in rolled-up bib over-alls of blue denim, young men in sea boots and navy guernseys, girls with straight hair looking strangely pale because their families still regarded make-up as one of the Whoredoms of Babylon. About half the people of New World Island are fundamentalists of one brand or another.

'You could never preach the New Curriculum here and get away with it,' United Church minister Harry Harris told me. 'The older people, especially, want the old ways. They expect evangelical and fundamentalist attitudes from their pastors. You wouldn't dare mention such a thing as church union.'

He believes, though, that roads bring increasing sophistication. New World Island, like all northern Newfoundland, is still cursed with sectarianism, with various small fundamentalist sects all thriving on isolation and preaching their own special brand of the Hot Gospel. But, as people mix more with outsiders, they are beginning to accept the facts of modern life.

'Are they better church-goers than people in the cities?'

'No,' the minister said. 'Attendance runs to about one person per family, or a little less, on the average.'

Those in more isolated parts of his parish were 'almost pathetically grateful' for the road, he said, but its social effects were profound, and hard to sum up in a few words.

Even Premier Smallwood, who started it all, is not sure about the effects. In a CBC interview he admitted that there was 'a lot of plus and a lot of minus' to the ending of a people's isolation.

'One has to make a choice,' he said, 'but you fear that there will be a coarsening of the people – that they will lose the quiet dignity, the sweetness of character that they had. There was much that was attractive in our traditional way of life in Newfoundland. But do you have the right to say that people shall remain isolated, cut off from the world, just so as to preserve their uniqueness, their quaintness? And you look at our new hospitals, and our splendid new schools, and you realize that there is a lot on the plus side.'

Just a few years ago, the Premier threatened to 'drag Newfoundland kicking and screaming into the twentieth century'. Now he has done it, and, for good or bad, or for both, the whole way of life in places such as New World Island is changing.

Fishing, once a season-long gamble, is now a day-to-day cash enterprise, and thousands of men who had left the fisheries have gone back to them on those terms. Numerous small service industries such as restaurants, garages, and theatres are thriving. The rural population, which was declining rapidly, is now increasing, but mostly in larger rural centres. Families have become more dependent on the broad structure of society, less dependent on neighbourly co-operation. In disaster, now, you go to the welfare officer, instead of to the family next door.

Now that their daily business connections are as likely to be with Charlottetown or Halifax or Montreal as with St. John's, thousands of Newfoundlanders, especially young people, feel for the first time that they are Canadians. This feeling could never have developed in a small community surrounded by the sea and connected to the outside world by the once-a-week visit of a motor vessel from the provincial capital.

Before leaving New World Island, I went up to an old grave-yard overlooking the ocean, thinking about the way of life that these people had made for themselves out of the savage begin-nings of the Indian-hunters in the seventeenth century: how they had hewn the timbers for their own ships out of the forests, and sailed them to Gibraltar and Greece, and Pernambuco and San Salvador, treading salt water 'with a bone in their teeth' and making record runs, some of them, across the oceans, daring the loneliest reaches of the earth. Now they sail no more. They are lying, those ships, with star-whitened ribs on all our coasts, kelp in their holds, sand clogging their guts. The chanties the seamen sang, in the days when every Newfoundlander went to sea, are changed to the brassy ringing of the paper bells in the juke boxes, and the tinny squeak of the transistor radios in the pockets of the children. Those who are growing up today, with such magic toys in their hands, may never know hunger, as their fathers knew it sometimes, or stark fear under the shadow of the angel of death as pestilence or natural disaster walked abroad. But neither will they know glory, as their forebears knew, tearing down the outside passages with sails 'wung out' before a roaring nor'-wester, or beating up to harbour at the fall of night, with Christmas snow sifting over the deck.

Here too, as at Sandy Point, was written the price of glory, plain for all to see: girls and boys who died before reaching their twentieth year, children buried in infancy, as toddlers, as grade-schoolers. Here on stones eroded by salt air was written the long record of their tragedy, of young men and women who died early in the struggle, of brides who failed in the effort to give birth to their first child. Here beneath broken stones lay the Culls and Smalls, the Nippers and Nobles, most of them children, some of them with small rows of wooden crosses, marking the place of a whole family in a common grave.

The price of glory. Was it worth it? Perhaps it was. For though they walked daily with death, they were finer and gentler people than those who are being raised on popsicles and Montreal jelly-roll and have never known the need for compassion.

There are minus as well as plus factors in the equation of progress.

11. The First and Last of the Red Men

This is true Indian country, for it was here, in Notre Dame Bay and the wilderness that lies inland along its great rivers, that the tragic Beothuck tribe made its last stand before vanishing from the earth.

Newfoundland's Beothuck Indians have been described as 'the people who were murdered for fun'. The white trappers and fishermen who began penetrating the island's forests in the seventeenth century must bear the major blame, though Micmac Indians, immigrants from Nova Scotia, also had a hand in the massacre. The story of the Newfoundland Indian-hunters is one of the most brutal chapters in the history of Canada.

Beautiful Alexander Bay, lying partly within Terra Nova National Park on Newfoundland's east coast, is a spot where Beothuck stone tools may still be dug from the sands by souvenir-hunters. Until recently, this serene stretch of landlocked water was known as Bloody Bay because it once ran red with the blood of Indians slain there by white men.

The Beothucks, never armed with any weapon more potent than the bow and arrow, were hunted first because they were considered a nuisance, and later for the sport of pursuing and killing such elusive game (as well as the occasional profit provided by looting their *meoticks* of furs and hides).

During the early years of the Indian-hunting period northern Newfoundland was settled by outlaws. The sketchy colonial government was arranged to favour a floating population of fishermen, mostly English in the east and south, mostly French in the north and west. Fishermen were forbidden to remain as settlers, and ships' masters were subject to fines if they failed to bring them back to Europe each autumn.

These ships carried women crew members as well as men – usually four to six. Many of them, men and women, lived lives of semi-slavery under indenture to fishing masters, and were often glad to escape to the wild life of the Newfoundland coast. In this way the island was gradually populated with the families of deserters. English naval ships were sometimes sent to round them up, and as late as 1800 a few of them were caught and hanged from the yard-arm of a man-o'-war.

In the wild northern parts of the island, to which some of these people fled, there was for more than a century no law whatsoever – no courts or police or churches or schools. The settlers lived by catching salmon and trapping fur, much as the Indians had done, except that they maintained a sketchy trade with the outside. They dressed in sealskins, making their own boots, mitts, and caps. There are people still living who wore nothing but sealskin trousers as children. They lived by their guns, shooting their own meat at all seasons: seals in spring, ducks and geese in summer and autumn, caribou, hares, and ptarmigan in winter.

Trouble was inevitable between people so rough and lawless as the settlers and people so simple and unsophisticated as the Beothucks. There were clashes almost from the beginning, and organized killings from 1613 to 1823. For the first 156 years the killing of a Beothuck was not even punishable by law, and even after the colonial government declared it a breach of the King's peace, punishable by hanging, the Indian-hunters continued to operate with complete impunity. No one was ever punished for killing a Beothuck.

It started shortly after John Guy of Bristol founded his colony at Cupids in Conception Bay in 1612 and established friendly trade with the Indians, agreeing to exchange European goods, the following summer, for all the furs that they could collect that winter.

In the summer of 1613 several hundred Indians collected at the appointed place in Trinity Bay. About a week after Guy's expected arrival, a ship sailed into the bay and hove to in the lee of the point where the Beothucks were gathered. They immediately began a wild celebration, dancing on the shore, launching their canoes, and paddling excitedly toward the vessel.

Into the midst of this rejoicing fell sudden death. The Indians were met with a broadside of grape-shot which ripped their boats, killed some of them, and sent the rest fleeing into the forest in panic. Ever afterwards they had an almost superstitious dread of firearms, and one or two whites armed with muskets could easily put a hundred of them to flight.

The ship had no connection with Guy. The men on board interpreted the dance as a war dance, and the launching of the canoes as an attack. They reported that they had beaten off an assault by 'murderous redskins'.

But things might still have been put right except for the widely divergent views of the Europeans and the natives respecting personal property. To the Indians, personal property meant only clothes, fire stones, and amulets. All hunting gear was held in common. To the Europeans, hunting and fishing gear were jealously guarded personal possessions. So when the Beothucks began 'borrowing' such gear from European stages and stores, just as they might borrow it from any *meotick,* the fishermen began shooting them in reprisal. Soon they were organizing regular expeditions into the woods to raid Indian camps and recover their lost property. To the fishermen it seemed almost a law of nature that a man had a right to kill anyone who stole from him.

So the organized Beothuck-hunts began, and what began as a feud over property soon turned into a bloody and cruel sport. Settlers used to refer to the number of 'head of Indians' they had killed, and the phrase 'go look for Indians' became a sporting by-word, similar to 'go look for partridge'. Successful hunters notched their guns to keep tally of their kills, and counted a woman or a child equally with a man.

Some of the hunters rolled up an impressive total. One man named Rodgers, living at Twillingate, boasted that he had killed sixty Beothucks down to 1817, when he and two other white men ambushed a party of nine. They maimed all but one of the Indians by discharging loads of buckshot 'into the thick of 'em'. The one who was still able to run dived into the water and tried to swim to an island. But Rodgers launched his canoe, gave chase, and killed the man in the water with his axe. Meanwhile, Rodgers' friends used their axes to finish off the Indians on shore. The nine corpses were left in a heap, and the bones later viewed by a government agent, to whom Rodgers recounted the adventure. He was not punished, or even brought to trial, for his part in the atrocity. A Micmac trapper named Noel Boss claimed ninety-nine Beothucks, and almost killed his hundredth: a little girl named Shananditti, whom he struck with buckshot, but who recovered to become famous some years later as the 'last Beothuck'.

Until recently, most stories of the Red Indians were based on oral traditions, but, when the archives of the First Earl of Liverpool went on sale a few years ago, Mr. N. C. Crewe of St. John's, Newfoundland, a collector and archivist, purchased a long manuscript for another collector, Mr. Andrew Murray. Mr. Murray put it into a drawer among old calendars and photographs and completely forgot about it. I found it there while doing research in his library and persuaded him to present it to the Newfoundland Archives. Now known as the 'Liverpool Manuscript', it is by far the most important contemporary evidence ever written on the subject of the Beothucks. It was compiled by a magistrate travelling in northern Newfoundland from first-hand accounts of Indian-hunts given to him by the Indian-hunters themselves, and the stories it tells are blood-curdling.

A fisherman and his shareman once surprised a Beothuck mother on a beach as she carried her four-year-old boy on her back. They both fired at once, the double load of swan-shot hitting her in the loins. She collapsed and crawled into the woods, holding one hand over the mortal wound. The fishermen then made off with the child and sold him to a merchant, who sent him to England where he was exhibited at several fairs in Poole and other towns for an admission price of twopence. Named John August (after the month of his capture), he was later returned to Newfoundland and grew up to be the master of a fishing boat. He died of tuberculosis at the age of thirty-eight.

This example of sparing a child's life was the exception, not the rule. Most fishermen, who believed in 'killing the nits with the lice', after shooting a party of Beothuck men and women would round up the children and cut their throats. The Indian-hunters seem to have been totally indifferent to suffering.

John Moore of Trinity and a hunting party 'surprised' a woman and two children in the woods. The woman knelt and exposed her breasts – the traditional gesture of submission – but the hunters killed her and wounded the two children, who ran into the bushes and hid. They made a search and found one child, 'which died on one of the men's shoulders before they reached the brook'. The second child was left to die in the woods.

On another expedition by Thomas Taylor, Richard Richmond, and William Hooper, a man, two women, and a small boy were ambushed. The women escaped into the woods, the man was killed, and the child was shot in the legs as he tried to run away. In the *meotick* they found a young girl, whom they later sold to a merchant in England, but, according to their own account, 'the little wounded boy we left to die, because we thought he would not recover of his wounds.'

There were also some full-scale massacres. In one of them, more than a hundred Indians, surprised while they were asleep, were driven out naked or nearly naked on the ice in the winter, while their encampment was totally destroyed by fire. In another massacre at Hants Harbour, Trinity Bay, a group of fishermen trapped a party of Indians on a peninsula and drove them into the sea. They reported 'about four hundred' killed.

Except for one very early account involving a raid against French fishing crews in the north, there is no record of the Beothucks fighting back in any organized way. They sometimes took a fisherman by surprise and cut off his head. In most if not all cases the men they killed were notorious Indian-hunters. The heads were taken to their camps and used in skull worship. A number of white women were taken prisoner by the Beothucks, but were always treated as guests, and later allowed to return home. They apparently had a total taboo against harming women, and there is no case on record of a Beothuck ever attacking either a woman or a child.

Late in the eighteenth century the colonial government adopted a 'save the Beothucks' policy, but apart from issuing proclamations, did nothing further until 1800, when a reward of fifty pounds sterling was offered to 'him that shall bring a Red Indian captive'. The plan was to entertain the captive at St. John's and send him back to his tribe loaded with good-will gifts, but the effect was to trigger still further killings. Fifty pounds seemed like a fortune to the wild men of the north, and they renewed their expeditions and their massacres in an effort to take at least one woman alive. Five women, in fact, were captured in this way, but no man was ever taken alive, and none of the women ever got back to her tribe. One was murdered by her captor after he had received the reward and was commissioned to oversee her safe return. The others all died of tuberculosis in captivity.

The government policy was even made the excuse for killing

the last important Beothuck chief and his brother at a time when their leadership seemed likely to save the tribe from extinction. John Peyton, Jr., of Twillingate, whose father had been a notorious Indian-hunter, led an expedition to Red Indian Lake to take captives, and succeeded in seizing the chief's wife, Demasduit, later called Mary March. The husband, Nonosbawsut, and his brother, came to her aid, but one was shot through the chest, the other stabbed in the back with a bayonet. The chief was a magnificent, bearded giant of a man. His killers, who measured him as he lay dead on the ice, reported that he was six feet seven and a half inches tall. The chief's little son died a few days later, and his wife died in captivity in less than a year. Peyton and his gang were brought to trial for this murder and abduction, but the jury ruled that they had acted in self-defence. Peyton was appointed a magistrate, held court in Twillingate, and lived to a ripe age as 'the first citizen of the north'.

The last killings took place in 1823, when the last known band of the tribe was reduced to seventeen. The starving remnant split up, looking for food. A man and his daughter, his sister, and two nieces set out for the coast, looking for white men to whom they planned to give themselves up in the hope of succour. On the coast they again separated, the father and daughter going one way, the woman and her two daughters the other. The man and girl met two trappers named Curnew and Adams near New Bay. The man approached them in an attitude of supplication, was shot through the chest, and died on the snow without a sound. The girl then came forward slowly, opening her deerskin robe to expose her breasts. She sank to her knees and tore her dress to the waist, then remained in this attitude, hands holding back the torn flaps of deerskin, while the two men drew nearer, raised their guns, and shot her through the heart. Like her father, she died in silence.

Meanwhile the other three women met a second hunting party headed by a notorious Indian-hunter named William Cull. Cull, however, had learned that a live Beothuck was now worth much more than a dead one. He took the three of them captive and claimed the reward. The woman and her elder daughter died that summer, but the younger girl lived to become a domestic servant in the home of John Peyton, Jr., at Twillingate, where she spent five years. Then, on the eve of her death from tuberculosis, Shananditti was taken to St. John's, where, between bouts of desperate illness, she recorded what she knew of the history, customs, and mythology of her people. She died in hospital in the spring of 1829, and though, like all other Beothucks, she had lived and died a pagan, she was given Christian burial in the Church of England graveyard. But her grave was later dug up to make way for a new road, and even her bones were lost.

The fate of the twelve Beothucks left in the woods is not known, though traditions among the Micmacs indicate that a few Beothucks may have survived into the 1850s. At least one Beothuck boy was adopted into the Micmac tribe (as a few had been adopted earlier), and grew up speaking his native, as well as his adopted, language. This boy, named Hop, has descendants living today among the Micmacs of Nova Scotia, and though a few other Micmacs also claim Beothuck descent, these are the only people for whom there is clear evidence of descent from even one of the original Red Men, who, because of their attachment to red ochre, gave their nickname to all the other native tribes of North America.

12. The North-east Coast

The large towns of central Newfoundland, Buchans, Grand Falls, and Gander, specialize respectively in mining, paper-making, and service industries. They are all twentieth-century creations. Buchans produces silver, lead, zinc, and gold. Grand Falls manufactures newsprint. Gander was built after Newfoundland joined Canada in 1949, to replace the shack town of war-surplus buildings that had grown up around the big international airport. It is a spick-and-span town of modern apartments, bungalows, and public buildings, created by the Central Mortgage and Housing Corporation from a master blueprint. It thrives on service industries, transport, and distribution: Notre Dame Bay, Bonavista Bay, and almost the whole of the north-east coast lie at its doorstep. It is a refuelling and freight transfer point for airlines from all over the world.

Twenty-five miles east of Gander on the Trans-Canada Highway you arrive at a hill overlooking Gambo, with a splendid view of the town, river, and bay spread out beneath you. This is the beginning of Bonavista Bay and the really ancient part of Newfoundland, where there has been continuous settlement for at least four centuries, and the people fish for cod by traditional methods going back to the days of the Bristol merchants, the Cabots, and the Corte Reals.

The roads out of Bonavista Bay serve more than a hundred little towns on the Wesleyville, Salvage, and Bonavista peninsulas, most of them devoted to the in-shore fishery.

From Gambo, a wide loop of road takes you along the north shore of Bonavista Bay, past Cape Freels into Notre Dame Bay, and back to Gander. Including the twenty-five miles of the Trans-Canada Highway from Gander to Gambo, this loop is 182 miles long, most of it a narrow, winding, unpaved gravel road. The surface is kept in good repair, but numerous sharp curves and blind hills demand great care and patience. Logging trucks use the road, some of them enormous vehicles that can be passed only when the drivers pull over to let you by, but most of them are very obliging about this, and will help you pass at the first opportunity.

From Gambo you follow the shore of Freshwater Bay past excellent fishing waters and attractive little towns to Hare Bay. Freshwater Bay is an old and well-settled region, the former home of the Smallwoods, who rose from boot-makers and pig-farmers to become the first family of the province. From Hare Bay it is sixteen miles to Indian Bay (called North West Arm on the road maps), where there is a salmon river with a good supply of small grilse, a pulpwood operation, and the most popular trout waters in Newfoundland.

Wesleyville, sixty miles from Gambo, is an important centre of the commercial fishery. In this large, prosperous town, with numerous willow trees and a mercantile air, one senses a past in which money talked a great deal. Many of the houses are impressively large, built by men who prospered as shipowners, mercantile captains, and small merchants. Some of the world's greatest seamen in the nineteenth century came from this region.

At Cape Freels, which you can visit by a short side road or by-pass as you choose, this drive begins to take on its truly distinctive character. From this point along the Straight Shore to Lumsden and Deadman's Bay there are mountains of sand: sand beaches that go on for more miles than you can count, sand dunes climbing up over the land to mix with the forests, sand hills topped with grass, and sand flats through which brooks wind to the sea.

Windmill Brook, just beyond the cape, is an attractive little resort – a trout and salmon river emptying into a barachois with a huge sand beach from which you can swim in comfort, since the water is cut off from the sea. Most parts of the barachois are very shallow, but there is a depth of ten feet or so near the gut. A grass flat has space for a few tents, and the sand flats space for numberless cars. Outside the barachois a great, curving sickle of sand beach, flanked by ragged rocks and cliffs, takes the north-easterly surf rolling in from The Funks.

The surf at Cape Freels can be truly impressive. It has the

whole of the North Atlantic behind it, and waves of fifty or sixty feet sometimes appear on this shore. As they run into shallow water they get higher and steeper, finally breaking on the off-shore shoals in spectacular pillars of spray. There is shoal ground, with a spatter of islands and sunken rocks, for many miles off the cape. This shallow water is a favourite summering place for fish, and the in-shore fishery in small boats extends, here, all the way to Funk Island, thirty-eight miles north-north-east of the cape.

This hard and dangerous shore has produced one of the toughest, most courageous breeds of men to be found anywhere. Nothing that happens at sea can daunt them. They are more at home in small boats than you or I in a house ashore. If you are lucky, they will take you cod-jigging for sport. If the weather is calm, you can hire them to take you to The Funks, to see the greatest sea-bird sanctuary in the western Atlantic. In any case, you can always find a crew willing to take you on a visit to a trap berth, and, if they happen to feel in the mood, they will do step dances in their rubber sea-boots on the tossing gunwales of their boats to the strains of an old mouth-organ. (No self-respecting Newfoundlander would call it a harmonica.)

Trap berths are places where cod traps are set to moorings, in rather shallow water. The moorings are sometimes attached to a headland or a dry rock rising from the sea, but the traps are just as often moored to the bottom with killicks – home-made wooden anchors weighted with large stones. The cod trap, invented by a Newfoundlander in the last century, is the most efficient mass-producer of in-shore fish ever devised. It is a big, box-shaped net with four sides and a bottom, its edges held up by floats, a set of inward-slanting doors in one end with a long leader running into the opening. The fish meet the leader, follow it past the doors into the trap, and then are unable to find their way out again. I have seen traps filled with so much fish that two or even three big boats could be loaded from one of them.

When you go to haul your trap, you lift one edge and keep taking it in over the side of the boat until the fish are brought to the surface. Then you simply bail them out of the trap with a big dip net into the fish hold of the trap boat, where they squirm about in a wriggling mass. Soon you are knee-deep in live fish. But codfish do not have a very firm hold on life. They give up and die rather quickly.

At the wharf or stage you throw the fish out of the boat, or hoist them out in tubs on pulleys in places where there is no landing close to water level. Then you slit them open on a wooden table with a splitting knife – a curved, square-ended, exceedingly sharp instrument a little like a cobbling knife – taking out the guts and a large piece of bone with a single sweep, and push them off the table into a barrel or tub to be taken to the salting shed. A good splitter can keep a steady flow of fish moving across his table, spending no more than four or five seconds on each.

The traditional Newfoundland way of making fish, inherited from the Bristol men, to whom salt was an expensive commodity, requires light salting, very careful handling, washing, pressing, and prolonged sun-drying to achieve the aromatic, amber perfection of a good 'shore cure'. (Ship-cured fish had to be heavily salted because there was no space to dry it.)

Only part of the shore cure is achieved by salting and drying. Bacterial action, akin to that in cheese-making, is also involved. Not much fish is cured nowadays by this prolonged, laborious, and superior method. Most fish today is heavy-salted, to produce a somewhat inferior but cheaper product that lends itself to mass-production, and is in great demand in the Mediterranean, the West Indies, and some other warm countries.

Ten miles past the cape, just beyond the sand hills of Lumsden and Deadman's Bay, there is a barachois into which run the waters of Deadman's Brook. If you follow this stream up-country, you will come very soon to a chain of trout ponds every bit as good as those at Indian Bay, but not so well known because of their great distance from major populations.

Thirty-four miles beyond Wesleyville you reach Ragged Harbour, and, at the head of its inlet, Ragged Harbour River, an excellent small salmon stream that 'comes in' by early July and provides continuous good fishing for several weeks.

From Carmanville the road plunges across a neck of land to Gander Bay, then follows the Gander River for about half its length, trending eastward through a fine hardwood forest to Joniton's Pond Provincial Park, and thence to the Trans-Canada Highway at Gander.

The speech of some of the people of the north-east coast may tend to throw you at first. When they wish to do so, they can all speak 'radio talk' for the benefit of visitors, but they can also speak the ancient Cornish and Devon dialects that they brought to Newfoundland in the seventeenth and eighteenth centuries.

To the uninitiated, these can be just as unintelligible as any foreign language.

When you hear a fisherman complain about the necessity of spelling yaffles of starrigans and spring var out of the droke, you may well imagine that your ears are playing tricks. Not so. This is the dialect speech of the time of Shakespeare preserved in all its purity. He is complaining about having to carry firewood on his back.

A word used for larger chunks of deformed wood is 'crunnicks'. A city man, hearing it for the first time, asked what it meant.

'Why, sir,' said the fisherman, 'they be jest big, ye know, an' twisty.'

'Well . . . ,' the unenlightened visitor pursued, 'if you can't tell me what it means, how do you spell it, then?'

'Oh, sir, we don't spell it,' the fisherman explained, 'we hauls it, with a catamaran, ye know.'

This, in turn, conjured up visions of large, twisty objects, being hauled by a twin-hulled boat. But in Newfoundland a catamaran is not a boat. Here the word still has its original meaning – a heavy, twin-runnered wood sled, hauled by a pony or a dog-team.

Sometimes men from the oldest fishing settlements still ask, 'Wilt have thy grog?' meaning, of course, 'Would you like a drink of rum?' Other seafaring terms reflect the nautical tradition: sweaters are 'guernseys'. The back part of anything is its 'starn'. Anyone who is worsted is 'taken by the wind' like a sailing ship, while one who succeeds in spite of difficulties has managed to 'beat it out', like a ship that has beaten her way out of a harbour on a lee shore.

The ordinary terms used around a fishing harbour have their own special flavour. The anchorage is the holdin' ground. The strip of shore between high and low water is the landwash, and the shore above it is the foreshore. Beyond the headlands lie the offer islands, threaded by tickles of narrow water.

From the landwash, the stages project, often spindly wharf structures made of spring var, or small fir sticks cut in the woods. Above the stages rise the table-like flakes, used for drying fish. Out in the harbour are the mooring collars for the trap boats, though some may be anchored temporarily by their own grap-lins – small anchors with multiple hooks.

Seals on the north-east coast are called swiles, and the guns used for hunting them are swilin' guns. The drift ice where they give birth to their young is the whelping ice. Half-grown seals are bedlamers, from the French *bête de la mer*. By transference, a bedlamer is also a half-grown boy, or one who, in Shakespeare's phrase, is 'in standing water between boy and man'.

Some of the phrases are highly picturesque. You 'pick the rames' when you eat the last bits of meat from a turr or other bird, and if you have little flesh on your bones, you may be 'all rames' yourself. When you travel by hopping from pan to pan over ice so small that the individual pieces will not bear your weight, you are 'coppying over the ballycaters', but only if it's shore ice, because a ballycater has to make along shore. When icicles hang by the wall in Newfoundland they are conkerbells. And my old grandmother, running short of bread with the new batch not yet ready to bake, often made damper devils by cooking small pieces of risen dough like pancakes on top of the stove.

Chunks of firewood in Newfoundland are junks, unless they happen to be *birch* junks, when they become billets. If you don't have a decent house you may have to live in a cubby hole, a small, despicable place, often situated close to a bawn, which is any natural substitute for a fish flake, sometimes a meadow. In Newfoundland, a gulch is what mainlanders call a gully. A gully is what mainlanders call a pond. A pond is what mainlanders call a lake.

Fun, isn't it? These verbal musical chairs could go on almost all day.

The place names as well are unique. Off to your right as you drive into Wesleyville are Silver Fox Island and Shamblers Cove. Famish Gut has unfortunately been abolished in favour of 'Fairhaven'. God Almighty Cove was an earlier casualty when some Puritan official, unable to endure the sight of it staring up at him from the charts, persuaded the Admiralty to abolish it. But we still have Peggy's Bag and Joe Batts Arm, the Horse Chops, and Seldom-Come-By.

Many of the loveliest place names are now just markers for abandoned villages: Ireland's Eye, Little Bona, Sagona, Cul de Sac, Iona Island, and Rose-au-Rue. Others are still inhabited, even flourishing: Spout Cove, Hibbs's Hole, Upper Gullies, The Goulds, Spanish Room, Bareneed, and Witless Bay.

For a short drive to a group of charming and well-named villages, take the road to the Salvage Peninsula. It leaves the Trans-Canada Highway eleven miles east of Gambo, at the Glovertown

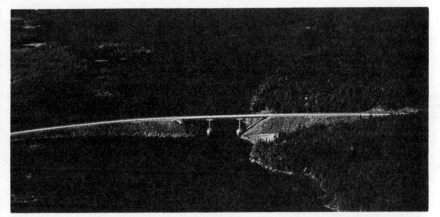

17. Humber Arm, with a part of the city of Corner Brook and the mill that gave it birth

2. St. John's harbour, about sixty years ago

3. Part of downtown St. John's. This is the
   wooden city, Victorian in concept and
   architecture, that survived unchanged until
   the Second World War.

4. Ships of the Portuguese White Fleet

5. Mending nets at Burgeo, on Newfoundland's south coast

6. This marine biology laboratory at Logy Bay was created by its director, Dr. Frederick Aldrich, on the model, internal and external, of a sea anemone.

7. These large, square, two-storey, box-shaped houses are typical of the thousands built by fishermen in little settlements all around the coasts of Newfoundland.

8. Lobster boxes in the small fishing harbour of Salvage in Bonavista Bay. The bright boxes hold lobsters alive for weeks if necessary before they are shipped, still alive, to market.

9. These fishermen, at Portugal Cove in Conception Bay, are gutting a
   boatload of cod that will go from their knives to the plant a few
   yards away.

Strait of Belle Isle

L'Anse-au

St. Antho

Hare Bay

73

Roddickton

Port-au-Choix
Port Saunders
River of Ponds

Fleur de Lys

La Scie
Gull Is
Tilt Cove

Notre Da

Twill

Brighton

GULF OF ST. LAWRENCE

LONG RANGE MOUNTAINS

White Bay

BURLINGTON PEN.

Baie
Verte

Daniel's Harbour
Portland Creek

Parson's Pond
Cow Head
St. Paul's

Rocky Harbour

Trout River

Norris Point

Sheffield
Lake

South
Brook

Bay of Islands

Lark Harbour

Deer
Lake

Cox's
Cove

Sandy
Lake

Howley

Corner
Brook

Grand
Lake

Buchans

1

Botwood

Badger

Grand
Falls

Bishop
Falls

Long Point

Lourdes

PORT-AU-PORT
PENINSULA

Mainland

Cape
St. George

Point-au-
Mal

Red Indian
Lake

TRANS-CANADA

HIGHWAY

Stephenville

BARACHOIS
POND PARK

1

LONG RANGE MOUNTAINS

ANNIEOPSQUOTCH MTS.

Meelpaeg
Lake

St. George's Bay

Victoria
Lake

Round
Pond

ANGUILLE MTS.

Cape
Anguille

South Branch

Doyles

Red Rocks

Grand Bruit

Long
Pond

St. Alban's

Pushthrough

Gaultois

Belleo

Cape Ray

Port-aux-
Basques

Rose Blanche

Burgeo

Ramea

Cape
La Hune

François

Hermitage Bay

Pass

Island Harbour
Breton

L'

Fortune
Bay

CABOT STRAIT

Grand
Bank

MIQUELON
(FRANCE)

Fortune

St. Lawrence

BURIN PENIN

L'ANGLADE
(FRANCE)

ST. PIERRE
(FRANCE)

Point-au-Gaul

Hebron

ATLANTIC

Nain

Hopedale

OCEAN

Indian Harbour

LABRADOR

Churchill Falls

Cartwright

Labrador City Wabush

Goose Bay

Battle Harbour

NEWFOUNDLAND

QUEBEC

FOGO I.

Ragged Hbr

Lumsden

NEWFOUNDLAND

Cape Freels

Wesleyville

Bonavista Bay

St. Brendan's

Burnside
Salvage

Bonavista

Catalina

Trinity

CAPE BRETON I.

Grate's Cove

0   100   200
MILES

Hant's Hbr

Bay de Verde

Conception Bay

Pouch Cove

Carbonear

Torbay

Spaniard's Bay

BELL I.

Topsail

ST. JOHN'S

Harbour Buffett

Whitbourne

Bay Bulls

Argentia

Witless Bay

Placentia

Colinet

Salmonier

LaManche

Aquaforte

Ferryland

Bride's

Branch

Renews

Mary's

Biscay Bay

St. Mary's Bay

Cape Race

St. Shott's

Trepassey

NEWFOUNDLAND

0   20   40   60   80
MILES

10. Michael Reardon of Portugal Cove, retired fisherman

A View of a Stage & a,
A. The Habit of y Fisher
which they throw y Cod whe
to extract y Oyl from y Cods
the Oyl. M. The manner of Dr

11. A trapskiff on the stocks at Burnt Cove

12. Detail from **Eric Mill's map** of North America, published 1712-**14**. This ancient drawing – a favourite of editors and **historians** – is remarkable mainly for its inaccuracy.

nner of Fishing for, Curing & Drying Cod at NEW FOUND LAND.
Line . C. The manner of Fishing . D. The Dressers of ỹ Fish . E. The Trough into
Salt Boxes . G. The manner of Carrying ỹ Cod. H. The Cleansing ỹ Cod. I. A Press
asks to receive ỹ Water & Blood that comes from ỹ Livers. L. Another Cask to receive

13. Codfish spread to dry on the beach without the use of flakes

14. Stages, flakes, and fish stores at Bay de Verde. The flakes, trademark of the Newfoundland outports, áre little used today when most fish is sold fresh or in saltbulk to processing plants.

15 & 16. The mighty Churchill Falls (left), where a great river cascades over a series of slides and sheer drops with a total fall of 1,080 feet. At this site in central Labrador, the world's largest power-house is being built more than a thousand feet underground in the heart of a mountain to produce six million horsepower of electricity. Below is one of the two tunnels under construction in the base of the mountain to carry the water from the turbines back to the river at a point well below the falls.

1. The Road to the Isles skips by bridge and causeway from island to island in Notre Dame Bay, linking the important fishing settlements of New World Island and Twillingate to the province's main road system.

intersection. Seven miles of pavement, followed by twenty-two miles of roller-coaster dirt road, take you to Salvage. On the way, there are connections to Saunders Cove, St. Chads, Burnside, Sandy Cove, and Happy Adventure. On the main road are Glovertown, Traytown, Sandringham, and Eastport.

Many of those places have splendid sand beaches, all of them are in fine seascape settings, and Salvage itself is perhaps the most picturesque of all Newfoundland fishing villages, in a perfect little gem of a harbour among bare headlands and surf-washed islands. Just north of here, reached only by boat, are Shalloway Cove, St. Brendan's, and Offer Gooseberry Island. (If anybody wonders what an offer gooseberry is, it's a gooseberry that's farther off than one that's nearer by.)

The Salvage Peninsula is a great place for doing very little – lying in the sun, catching a few caplin, or just chasing around over miles of sand beaches in your bare feet. The beaches are clean and empty, with none of the litter, the tin cans, and the broken glass so often found on beaches close to cities. The protected bays on the inner parts of the peninsula also offer good swimming in warm salt water.

Part of the Salvage Road runs through Terra Nova National Park, and the Trans-Canada Highway from Glovertown to Port Blandford (thirty-five miles) cuts right through the middle of it.

Except for caribou and arctic hares, the park has all the animals common to Newfoundland, many of them now accustomed to visitors. The score I compiled in a three-day visit included seven bears, three foxes, an undetermined number of beaver and muskrats, a fair-sized bull moose that could be approached within thirty feet and that walked right across the camp-ground, and dozens of species of birds, including some rare ones. Visitors often also see lynx, weasels, otters, and varying hares.

The bears are wild and shy. They have never been fed by visitors, as in some mainland parks, and you are strongly advised not to try it, or to approach them too closely. The bull moose that crossed the camp-ground was so tame that even a crowd of forty spectators failed to upset him, and it took a troop of shouting children to make him move. Even then, he just sauntered off sedately, nibbling leaves as he went. The lynx, also, are tamer than anywhere else in Newfoundland. These big cats will sometimes stalk people for fun, though they never attack. They look like handsome, overgrown pussy cats, but they are suspicious and unfriendly.

The campsites at Terra Nova National Park are filled to capacity almost every day in summer. You have to queue up early in the morning for a campsite, and you have to reserve cabins well in advance. The camping park is well serviced, but in natural setting and privacy it is far inferior to those in the provincial camping parks, of which there are seven on the east coast.

But Terra Nova National Park has fine tidal flats and marshes, many miles of inland salt water, and access to some of the finest boating in eastern Canada. There is an excellent dock on Newman Sound, and if you do not have your own boat you can rent light outboards from a concessionaire. The dock is also popular for swimming and fishing. There is a fresh-water swimming beach, a restaurant and canteen in the cabin area, hiking and nature trails, and some fairly good fishing for sea trout and brook trout.

The Ochre Hills Lookout is a disappointment, but the Blue Hills Lookout is well worth a visit. From the car park near the end of the winding road, or from the fire tower above, the visitor sees a panorama of forest and lake, seashore, island, and mountain, with the distant lands of Bonavista Bay piled one above another, falling away in diminishing shades of blue like the hills in a traditional Chinese landscape painting.

Charlottetown, the park's pet village, is a still-unspoiled little Newfoundland outport with white houses and picket fences, a motel and restaurant, boats that you can rent, and horses that you can ride. (They are very safe, slow, sweet-tempered old plough horses that any experienced rider would find amusing if not infuriating, but are fine for small children or those who have never been on a horse before.)

Well-equipped children's playgrounds share campsites and picnic grounds. At the western end of the park, near the entrance from Port Blandford, on a bluff above a Clode Sound sand beach, they have built a large open-air kitchen shelter for those who want to do a real cook-out. It stands in an improved woodlot beside a lawn with swings, picnic tables, fireplaces, and grills.

The Bonavista Peninsula (the land you see when you look across Clode Sound from the National Park) lies between the bays of Bonavista and Trinity, and is served by roads along its north and south shores, and by others that cross it at four points. Just outside the park, at Port Blandford, you can cross the end of the sound on a causeway, and take a road that skips from one small bay to the next along the north shore to the town of Bonavista, near the cape, a distance of seventy-three miles. You pass, en route, five of the arms of Bonavista Bay: Clode Sound, Goose Bay, Sweet Bay (not to be confused with the Sweet Bay on the other side of the park), Southern Bay, and Blackhead Bay.

The people on this shore are woodsmen, boatbuilders, and carpenters. Most of the men work far from home, in cities or on construction jobs. Some of them drive hundreds of miles every week-end to spend two days with their families. Some work so far away that they get home only for Christmas and vacations, or during winter lay-offs. They have been living this way since the Americans began building their bases in Newfoundland in 1940, when there was a sudden demand for construction workers, to which the boatbuilders of Bonavista, Trinity, and Conception bays promptly responded, setting up a pattern of life that has survived for thirty years and promises to continue indefinitely. They work across the province from St. John's, a few hours' drive away, to Labrador City, a thousand miles by road and air; or even in Montreal or Toronto, while their home towns are populated by their women and children.

People on the outer parts of the peninsula, toward the cod banks, are fishermen. Bonavista, with 6,000, is the largest all-fishing town in Newfoundland. Here, as in all the larger fishing towns, they have abandoned the traditional methods of salt curing in favour of a fresh-fish industry that depends on filleters and flash freezers and deep-sea boats that can fish far from home when necessary. Only the surplus that the plant cannot handle in times of glut is put into salt.

Bonavista is one of the oldest fishing towns. According to a long-standing and hardy tradition, it was the landfall of John Cabot in 1497, but the tradition has not stood up under the attack of historical research. The cape was, in fact, the major landfall for fishing fleets arriving from Europe in the sixteenth century, just as Cape Race was the major point of departure. This may well have led to the Cabot tradition.

In the early sixteenth century, if not before, the Basques used Bonavista as a whaling and sealing station. But it had fallen into English hands before 1600. When they drained a pond at Bonavista in 1926 an old longboat of black oak was dredged up from the bottom. It bore a brass disc with a double-headed eagle, the letter 'G' inscribed between the heads, and the date 1583. The date suggests that it belonged to Sir Humphrey Gilbert, who came to Newfoundland with Queen Elizabeth's commission that year, and who, perhaps, had it built especially for his voyage. Fishing crews must have continued to use the boat for the next thirty-seven years, at least, for a French copper coin, dated 1619, was found wedged between its planks.

During the hundred years of the colonial wars, the French attacked Bonavista repeatedly. In 1704 the town (then having some thirty fishing 'rooms' with six hundred people) was successfully defended by a Yankee skipper, Michael Gill, of Charlestown, Massachussetts.

Gill had begun trading between New England and Newfoundland in 1698. By 1704 he owned a 150-ton Boston trader, mounting fourteen guns and carrying a crew of twenty-four men. He was at anchor in Bonavista on August 18 with three English ships, two of them armed, mounting fourteen and twenty guns, respectively, when the French attacked at two o'clock in the morning.

To gain surprise, the raiders left their ships at anchor and stole into the harbour in boats. They boarded and captured the two armed English ships, and the smaller unarmed merchant ship. But the alarm had been sounded on Gill's barque, and, discovering this, they trained the guns of the two captured ships on her and began a naval battle that continued for six hours.

During the battle two of the captured ships were burnt – used as fire ships against Gill – but by smart manoeuvring he got clear of them. His vessel was riddled with shot, but he kept her under way and continued firing until, about eight o'clock in the morning, the fishermen who had fled to the woods appeared in a body on shore with their guns. The French then escaped to sea, taking the crews from the three ships as prisoners, but released them a little later and gave them a boat in which to return to Bonavista.

The release of the prisoners was not an unusual incident, but typical of the mutual courtesy and good manners with which both sides fought. There was a lot of manoeuvring and property destruction, but no wholesale bloodshed and little needless cruelty during the clashes between English and French in Newfoundland.

Captain Gill's elder son became the first colonel of the Newfoundland militia, his younger son chief magistrate at St. John's, and his grandson a prosperous merchant trading between Newfoundland and the West Indies. He has many descendants living in the island today.

From Bonavista a three-mile road runs out to the cape, which is a bluff, stormy headland with a cruel chunk of rock rearing high out of the sea at its tip. There a fine lighthouse, and a fog alarm that can knock you over the cliff if it starts up behind you unexpectedly, keep company with vast flocks of sea birds and schools of small whales cruising past the point on the way to their feeding grounds in Bonavista and Trinity bays.

From Bonavista you can return by way of the Trinity Bay Shore through Catalina and Port Union to Trinity.

Catalina is an old fishing and merchant town that had achieved a position of importance before 1745. Its neighbour, across the harbour, is new. Port Union, founded by Sir William Coaker, became the centre of his efforts to seize the Newfoundland government, or at least control of the Newfoundland fishery, from the merchants, and place it in the hands of the fishermen.

Coaker was born at St. John's, but was farming in Bonavista Bay when he began organizing his Fishermen's Union in 1908. The fishermen were then in total thralldom to the merchants, who ran the industry by means of a barter system, without cash, and kept their dealers perpetually in debt. Many fishermen can still remember a time when money was rarely handled. Those who ran the government also owned the great mercantile establishment of Water Street in St. John's.

It was Coaker's declared intention to make the grass grow on Water Street. With this ambition the fishermen were in complete sympathy. So bitter were they that year against the establishment that when one of them was jailed at Catalina for appearing drunk in court, they mobbed the jail, rescued him, and tried to pull down the courthouse with a ship's cable. It was part of a long-standing defiance of the law in that region. On at least two earlier occasions mobs had rescued men from the public whipping-post.

Coaker got almost every fisherman on the north-east coast of Newfoundland into his union. But the minority of fishermen on the south coast mostly refused to join, even when locals of his union were organized there. The reason, perhaps, was that most of the southern fishermen were Roman Catholics, and Coaker's union had definite overtones of evangelical Protestantism. This, alone, defeated him. Could he have really organized all the fishermen across denominational lines, they would probably have had to call in the British Marines to stop him.

His most ambitious effort, however, was a nation-wide fishermen's co-operative. But not knowing how to organize a co-operative, he organized a limited liability company instead. His Fishermen's Union Trading Company, a combined producer-consumer organization with thousands of fishermen-shareholders, founded the great mercantile plant at Port Union in 1916.

Meanwhile, Coaker and a group of associates ran for election, and entered the House of Assembly in 1913, wearing their uniform of roll-necked blue guernseys, the badge of revolution. Though the fishermen's party was in a minority, the merchants on both sides of the House trembled in their seats.

They coaxed Coaker into coalition. Though he held complete command of the north and east coasts, and never had a candidate defeated there, he could not elect an outright majority. He chose to align himself with first one, and then another, of the merchant parties. He and some of his followers held portfolios in three different governments, including the portfolio of marine and fisheries, but failed to bring about the revolution that they sought. Governments and oppositions might quarrel over other issues. They were united against Coaker.

In addition to his other schemes, Coaker founded and edited a newspaper, the *Fishermen's Advocate*, which still survives as an emasculated weekly at Port Union.

Gradually the politicians cut him down to size. He got mixed up in graft with the Squires administration, grew personally rich, accepted a knighthood recommended for him by the English governor, became a merchant hardly distinguishable from other merchants, took to wintering in the West Indies, and finally, at Port Union, built a monument to his dog. His own monument is there, too, commemorating a man who died rich, successful, and defeated by time, by circumstance, and most of all by himself.

Trinity, twenty miles south of Port Union, is another very old fishing town, said to have been named by Gaspar Corte Real when he sailed into it on Trinity Sunday in 1500. It is a popular holiday resort in a picturesque, landlocked, maritime setting.

At Trinity the first court ever established by the English in the New World (the first by any nation in Canada) was held on board Captain Richard Whitbourne's ship on June 4, 1615, Whitbourne having been appointed a Judge of the Admiralty under commission from James I, with jurisdiction throughout Newfoundland.

Though it was heavily fortified in the eighteenth century, Trinity was twice captured by the French without opposition, and no important military actions were ever fought there. Its many guns (whose batteries are still to be seen at the town and out on the point) never fired a shot in its defence.

By the early 1700s, Trinity was an important fishing and trading town where fortunes were made. One fish merchant, who had started with a single small ship, retired to England shortly after 1750 with the equivalent of two million dollars in today's funds, as revealed when his will was probated. Others stayed and built mansions. One of them, in a semi-ruined state, is still to be seen on the old Garland property.

The first vaccination in the new world was performed at Trinity by Dr. John Clinch (who was both medical doctor and Anglican priest), using vaccine sent to him by his friend Dr. William Jenner, who had invented the process in England. Since Newfoundland seamen were then sailing in their thousands to all parts of the earth, smallpox was a constant threat and a frequent disaster. Vaccination was quickly accepted, promoted into a public campaign, and undoubtedly saved many lives.

From Trinity the road follows the Trinity Bay shore southward to Trouty, New Bonaventure (with a branch to Old Bonaventure), and Kerley's Harbour. The thirteen-mile gap from Kerley's Harbour to Burgoyne's Cove has not been closed as yet, and one must drive around by way of the north shore through Southern Bay and Lethbridge to Clarenville. Thirty of the eighty miles between Bonavista and Clarenville by this route have been paved.

From the vicinity of Clarenville there are two short drives that I strongly recommend. The one crosses Smith Sound by causeway to a group of villages on Random Island, ending on the north shore at the tiny hamlet of Lance Cove, in a nook of the hills, and on the south shore at the thriving fishing town of Hickman's Harbour, a clean, attractive, and growing community. The other runs out along Southwest Arm to the headland villages of Southport, Gooseberry Cove, and Little Heart's Ease. Little Heart's Ease, in particular, is one of those communities with a postcard setting between two arms of the sea, and the sort of background that you would think had been created by a Hollywood designer.

From Clarenville it is a two-hour drive by the Trans-Canada Highway to the city of St. John's.

13. Canada's Oldest City

If you set your watch by the noonday gun, if turr-shooting is your favourite sport, if your favourite meal is seal-flippers, but cod tongues run a close second, and your favourite dessert a dish of yellow berries called bakeapples, if you love nothing better than a kettle of boiled tea over a fire built of crunnicks on the barrens, if your idea of hospitality is to offer your guest four-ounce draughts of black navy rum straight from the bottle, if you regard all Canadians as foreigners, and still think of England as your Mother Country, then you are a St. Johnsman. Not just a New-foundlander, for Baymen are Newfoundlanders too. But a free citizen of the proudest and oldest European city in the new world.

As you drive into St. John's from almost any direction you will see signs telling you that it is North America's oldest city, and that it has a population of 100,000. Neither of these statements is true.

Almost all North American towns try to pretend that they are bigger than they are, as though excellence lay in mere size: the symptom of an inferiority complex, certainly. But St. John's does not need to ape Kalamazoo in this or any other respect. She has plenty to be proud of without pretending that she is as old as Mexico City or as big as Halifax.

St. John's has a unique atmosphere, a stronger personality, a saltier flavour, and a deeper sense of history than any city on the mainland. It is no accident that the editors of both daily newspapers – Michael Harrington of the *Evening Telegram* and Albert Perlin of the *Daily News* – are both semi-professional historians who have published books and articles on many aspects of Newfoundland history. If an authentic relic of a fifteenth-century voyage were discovered at St. John's, it would probably shunt all other news off the front pages.

The howling of the sirens across the slush of the waterfront on a bleak spring day as the sealing fleet sails for The Front makes every native Newfoundlander in the ageing city catch his breath with a sense of centuries-old excitement. Gathered in groups on the coastal pier of the Southside, they have come to split a bottle of screech with the departing sealers, to wish them bloody decks and holds weighed deep in fat. And they have also come to see the year renew itself. For this is the beginning, the first act in the annual drama of life and death and elemental struggle played out in the mid-ocean setting where the history of Canada began.

The sealers have barely departed for their six-week adventure among the ice-floes of the north when the foreign fishing fleets begin to arrive. Portuguese, Spaniards, Russians, Poles, Faeroe Islanders, Japanese – they come from the ends of the earth to fish the great banks laid down in the sea off St. John's by a succession of ice ages. They crowd into the mile-long harbour seeking bait, salt, water, fuel, ships' stores, or shelter from the storms that have wrecked thousands like them on the hazardous fishing-grounds of the Western Ocean.

First to arrive are the Portuguese, coming around Easter time, as they have come each spring since the days of the Corte Reals almost five hundred years ago. Their fleet of white auxiliary sailing ships and black motor vessels works all the fish banks from the Virgin Rocks to the Greenland Sea, but treats St. John's as its home port in the new world. There is a long-standing friendship between the Newfoundlanders and the Portuguese. They are almost the only civilized nation that we have not fought at some time or other in our history. Their periodic visits become holiday events. Shops hang out signs saying that Portuguese is spoken. Visitors from the city make merry with officers and men on board the vessels. The docksides flutter in a bright array of dory sails dyed scarlet, orange, pale green, or bright blue, each ship having its distinctive colour.

The sailors treat St. John's as their second home, thronging its stores and movie houses, attending parties on shore, knitting nets on the docks, playing their own wild brand of barefoot football in the parks, singing Latin music to the throbbing of guitars, carrying on a brisk if illicit trade in vino (cheap red wine) with waterfront labourers, or visiting the Portuguese shrine of Our

Lady of Fatima in the Basilica of St. John the Baptist, created in 1955 by Portuguese fishermen who had survived shipwreck on the banks. The little flowered shrine with its painted statuary looks oddly out of place among the severe white marble and soaring stained glass of the vast Romanesque church.

The Spaniards, mostly small, dark men in small, dark ships, keep much to themselves, and pass almost unnoticed among the throngs of foreigners on Water Street. They, too, have been visiting St. John's since the days of the Cabots and the Corte Reals, but they often came as enemies, and for long periods were banished altogether from the Newfoundland trade. They do not have the record of half a millennium of uninterrupted friendship enjoyed by the Portuguese.

The Russians and Japanese are late-comers, but have added a further cosmopolitan flavour to St. John's harbour. Their presence, in huge factory ships and integrated fleets able to out-fish anything else in the world, creates a vague uneasiness, for they are already beating us hands down at a game that we were playing before the first Russian ship ventured into the Atlantic, or the first Japanese suspected that there was an Atlantic to venture into. All the foreign seamen are well-behaved, but the Russians are absolutely exemplary. As with all nationalities, there have been three or four Russian deserters, but none arrested for drunkenness, fighting, disorderly conduct, or the other forms of mischief common to seamen all over the world.

One morning after the fishing fleets have squared away for sea and the city is basking in the pale, watery sunlight of spring, a black ship, reeking with rancid oil, comes slipping through the mists at the harbour mouth – The Narrows, as the entrance to St. John's is called – and an hour later word is passed around, 'There's flippers on the docks!'

Mention seal-flippers, and any true Newfoundlander begins to water at the mouth. No Englishman loves his cakes and ale one half so well as the St. Johnsman loves his flipper. Canadians (and other foreigners) often make the mistake of supposing that this famous Newfoundland delicacy consists of the animals' paws. Not at all. The paws are called pads, and are usually discarded. The flipper is the front shoulder, corresponding to a shoulder of lamb or a shoulder of pork, except that it is much tastier than either. It is heavy with rich, lean meat, the colour of red mahogany, so tender that you can cut it with a fork, and of a hearty, gamy flavour like that of wild duck. Flippers are cooked in huge pies with vegetables and pastry. They are the centre of social feasts and family gatherings. The Methodist College Literary Institute, Canada's oldest debating club, which, despite its name, and with true Newfoundland lack of logic, numbers atheists, Catholics, and Jews among its members, calls its entire membership together each April to join in a meal of flippers. Babes in rompers cry for them, and centenarians have been known to cling to life for one more month, waiting until 'the flippers are in' to die with the well-remembered taste in their mouths.

Except for hides and fat, the flippers are usually the only parts of the seals brought to shore. The carcasses are left for the sharks and the flatfish. Men and boys bargain over flippers at street-corner barrel-head sales. The law says that they must be wrapped when sold, but the old newspapers used for this purpose are quickly discarded, and the flippers carried home in triumph, red and raw and dripping, on a string.

Though St. Johnsmen pretend to despise the Baymen (who in turn describe them as Townies), the city is, in fact, the biggest outport of them all, a town with a strongly insular and provincial flavour, where the pre-dawn stillness is shattered each morning by the coughing of motorboats going to haul cod traps at Cape Spear and Sugarloaf and Blackhead, for, in addition to being the capital and the main centre of manufacturing and distribution, St. John's is one of the province's largest producers of fish, with two fishing towns included within its limits. The fishermen's houses are perched on the bare rock near The Narrows. Their settlements are named the Upper Battery, the Lower Battery, and the Outer Battery, for they were fortified almost continuously from the days of the pirate admirals until the Second World War, when the Germans sank ships almost in the harbour mouth and made unsuccessful torpedo attacks on the harbour itself.

The people of St. John's have a long record of fighting their own wars. After they had successfully fought off the pirates in the seventeenth century, they fortified the harbour with their own guns, and formed a fishermen's militia to man the batteries, all without help or encouragement from the King's Government in England. They achieved in the process a sense of independence which they still maintain. St. Johnsmen sincerely believe that they are several cuts above just about everyone else, and that they can lick the world single-handed.

This was their attitude when, in November 1696, they went out with their sealing guns and powder horns to ambush a regular French army under Pierre LeMoyne d'Iberville on the Southside Hill overlooking the city. They hadn't a chance, of course. Half of them were killed on the spot. But they delayed things long enough to organize the defence of the town, and though the French burnt most of the city, they failed to capture the fort. St. John's was burnt three times during the French-English wars, but no fleet ever managed to force the harbour entrance, though it was often tried.

On St. John's' eastern edge is Quidi Vidi Village, a fishing suburb that has changed very little in two hundred years. It includes a colonial-style wooden house built some time before 1750 and used as a dressing station for the wounded when the English recaptured St. John's for the last time, using troops from Halifax, in 1762. Quidi Vidi has a little fort of its own, recently restored, which, during the wars with the French, was not manned by the St. John's militia but by a separate unit of fishermen-soldiers known as the Quidi Vidi Volunteers. The village has its own vest-pocket-sized harbour, barely wide enough, at the gut, to admit a trap skiff. It was considered a dangerous place for small-boat landings in a flanking attack on St. John's even as recently as the wars of Napoleon (when a ship was captured with a plan for a French attack on Newfoundland), and the English authorities wanted to seal it off by dynamiting the hills on either side. The fishermen, however, who had lived there for genera-tions and had a violent antipathy to being moved to St. John's, kicked up such a fuss that the plan was abandoned. But the moun-tain went to Mohammed, and St. John's now encloses Quidi Vidi on all sides except for its narrow access to the sea.

Here, on Quidi Vidi Lake, we hold our annual regatta, the oldest organized sporting event in North America, which was being run off annually even before it became an official national holiday in 1828. It is less like a sporting event than a national festival. Held on a suitable day in August (selected, after an early-morning look at the weather, by the all-powerful Regatta Com-mittee), it combines boat races with various forms of gambling and the sideshows of a fall fair, offers unsanitary food and spruce beer and brass bands as added attractions, and brings out crowds of 20,000 to 40,000.

The regatta began with races between crews of fishermen in

fishing boats, sometimes competing with naval seamen in whale-boats and longboats. Now standard racing shells have replaced the skiffs and dories, and the annual championship usually goes to a crew of truck drivers rather than fishermen, but the cod-killers of Outer Cove still hold the all-time record for the course, set in 1901. The boats they used then must certainly have been faster than those in use today, for no one has come even close to equalling the record in the last fifty years.

For its first four centuries, St. John's was exclusively a fishing and fish-trading port. It was a fishing station at least as early as the Bristol Company Adventurers (of 1503). When Sir Humphrey Gilbert arrived in 1583 to proclaim the first English laws in the new world, St. John's was a substantial town with a floating, mainly seasonal, population, and its harbour was crowded with shipping. It was a free port, used by the ships of all nations, and goods were bought, sold, or bartered there without taxation.

The Upper Path and the Lower Path, which ran between the fish stores and the merchants' rooms in Gilbert's time, are still in use today as Duckworth Street and Water Street, now, as then, the main mercantile streets of the province. Today they blossom with neon signs and bristle with parking meters, but they are still dominated by the smell of salt fish and the thunder of breakers on Pancake Rock.

Though the streets still follow the contours of the hills, the city itself has been renewed time and again. After the French got through burning it down as an act of war, the St. Johnsmen began burning it down for themselves. Substantial parts of it were burned in 1817, 1839, and 1840. In the great fire of 1846 it was ravaged from end to end, more than half its buildings laid in ashes, and 12,000 of its people made homeless. But the 'great fire' still remembered by the oldest inhabitants was in 1892, when the waterfront and the industrial heart of the city roared sky-ward in a mile-square eruption of flame that lasted a day and a night.

Since few buildings antedate the great fires, the older parts of St. John's have a distinctly Victorian look, with gabled buildings, numerous dormer and bay windows fronting directly on the side-walks, and a lot of gingerbread trimming copied on local wood lathes from foreign stonework. The city was dominated by this style of architecture until the Second World War, when it began to spread out in a rash of modern subdivisions. The first, and the biggest, the centrally-planned Churchill Park development, created a second centre of gravity on the north side of the harbour ridge, competing with Water Street. This has recently been reinforced by adding the largest mall-type shopping centre in the Atlantic provinces.

But the modern city with its supermarkets and shopping plazas and tower-style apartment buildings copied from the mainland, its airport, its overpasses, its hundreds of miles of asphalt and concrete, merely sits around the edges of the old town of my boyhood, where 30,000 people clustered around the slope of a bowl that dipped steeply into the sea.

The old town is still there, with its steep streets and stone crosswalks where little boys with brooms once laboured for a shilling a week to sweep a path through dust or litter for pedestrians. Some of the streets dropping down toward the sea are so steep that they have concrete steps instead of sidewalks.

Here and there on a corner in old St. John's, a 'bulls-eye shop' remains to spite the supermarkets. The dingy little store where I bought molasses candy bull's-eyes when I could barely reach over the counter is still there. It has a neon sign now, and a freezer. Otherwise it is much the same as it was when I bought my first half-pints of black Irish porter from the fat, motherly old Irishwoman who allowed that selling porter to twelve-year-olds might be a tiny bit against the law, yet knew she was in the right because porter was so good for growing boys.

The school where I learned my letters is still there, smelling of the very same brand of disinfectant. And the other schools, to the east and west, where children from other divisions of Christendom were taught abominations by agents of the devil, are still there, too. The schools being divided, like the population, into three parts, Catholic, Anglican, and Nonconformist, our interschool rivalry in sports and everything else took on the character of a holy war. The old schools with their old passions are overshadowed, now, by vast 'regional' institutions – which, however, are still divided according to religious denominations, with a few new ones added. The days of this school system seem to be numbered, however. The major Protestant school boards have decided to unite, and there is a strong, growing movement among Roman Catholics to have the church school system abolished altogether.

The dingy streets where schoolboys fought their religious battles were only one part of old St. John's. It had its splendours, too, as befitted the most European city in Canada. Government House was, and is, a true old-world mansion, sprouting innumerable chimneys above its granite walls. The Lieutenant-Governor still lives in this retreat, surrounded by many servants and much splendour, symbol of an empire of which St. John's was once the very cornerstone.

But the seat of real power today is a pile of yellow brick and glass built in 1960 – a monster among buildings, housing 5,000 civil servants and their political bosses. Confederation Building, as they call it, is functional and impressive, but an unfortunate piece of architecture. Only after 1965 did the modern look replace the biscuit-box look in St. John's public buildings. Even the older buildings of the university, dating from the 1950s, look like those of a motor-car factory out of the American Middle West. But its newer buildings are handsome as well as impressive. In them is housed a university that is going to make itself felt in the future, especially in certain fields of natural science, in which St. John's has managed to secure specialists with world-wide reputations.

The court house, on Water Street, is one of the best examples of Victorian architecture in St. John's. Not over-ornate, it is built like a castle, a solid pile of stone, impressive and well-proportioned. The Anglican Cathedral, however, is the outstanding architectural achievement of the city. Begun by Sir George Gilbert Scott in 1847, and completed in 1885, it is universally recognized as one of the finest examples of Gothic in the new world. The Roman Catholic Basilica, with space for 8,000 worshippers, has an awe-inspiring interior and an impressive collection of art work.

Some of the small modern churches are well done, too. Outstanding, but by no means alone in this respect, are the beautiful Jewish Beth El, and the neo-Gothic United Church of St. James.

St. John's is above all a trading city, an overgrown mart. The children who bought bull's-eyes at corner stores didn't play cowboys. They played shop instead. They were surrounded by puncheons of molasses and strings of dried figs from the West Indies, coconuts brought by their fathers or uncles from Brazil, leather boots and bales of cloth from England, chests of tea from Ceylon, oranges from Seville, and barrels of wine from Portugal. St. John's has breathed trade for centuries. The true St. Johnsman never thinks of making something he can use, but only of buying something he can sell. Being 'in business' means being in trade. Until recently the whole province was supplied from this one trading centre, and all exports, from every corner of the land, flowed out over its docks.

From early times the merchant class formed a special aristocracy, but not an aristocracy of wealth alone. Even today the *nouveaux riches* who have made their money selling TV sets and radio advertising cannot enter it. They can join the golf club, or even the semi-exclusive City Club, but the club of the old families is for ever closed to them. The Class has a large group of camp-followers who are almost, but not quite, its members. One of the requirements is that one's grandfather must have been a successful trader with connections in at least fifteen foreign countries. Another – not rigid, but it helps – is that one should have been educated abroad, preferably at an English public school, though Dublin still rates, and some private schools in Canada are starting to gain recognition. Above all, though, one must have the aristocratic outlook – an attitude specific though hard to define. Some of The Families have an astonishing vigour through many generations. There is none of this Faulkner-like collapse from greatness in St. John's. Men whose great-grandfathers cornered the market in seal fat have a stranglehold on the supermarket trade today, and have even forced the national food chains to make deals with them.

Every city as old as St. John's has a special character acquired over many generations. Here it includes an accent – a heavily-modified Irish brogue, even though the population is mainly of English descent. There is a special look and a special manner. One St. Johnsman can spot another in a crowd anywhere in the world. His marks are subtle but obvious to those in the fraternity. His attitudes are practical and hard-headed. He is not a sentimentalist, but he prides himself on his hospitality, and makes a great issue of entertaining strangers. If he has a sentimental side, it is his attachment to the ugly but fascinating town of his birth. He may, and often does, spend his life abroad, but if you meet him in Boston or San Francisco or on the London docks, he will tell you that when he retires he wants to go home to the grimy old city on the rock.

The expatriate forgets the bitter cold of a May morning in a trap boat off Blackhead with a north-easter blowing and salt spray running down his neck. He remembers his turr-shooting trips to the mouth of Freshwater Bay or the annual trouters' holiday on May 24 when the whole town was emptied of able-bodied men and the waters were dappled with trout flies for fifty miles around. He remembers the bumper buckets of berries he gathered from the barrens surrounding the town, the bakeapples (bog-apples, cloudberries) that he picked from the Witless Bay marshes, or the hunting trips with dog and gun and kettles of boiled tea on the partridge grounds to the west.

He may have known hard times. He may have been hungry or out of work. But if he thinks back far enough he may remember coppying out past the Chain Rock light on pans of floating ice, seeking a stray seal or the ducks that collect in spring along the floe-edge. He will remember the scenes at the end of such a hunt, with sea boots, bay wool socks, and guernseys hung to dry behind a red-hot stove, while seal or ducks or turrs simmered in the oven. And he will certainly remember the return of the spring, with the ice thundering and the world erupting, when there were open fires on his home hearth in the evening, birch logs roaring up the chimney, while from the kitchen came the smell of smoking cod tongues and of dandelions swimming in the pot with a slice of salt pork for flavouring.

14. Pirate Government

Newfoundland's east coast has a long history of piracy with literally thousands of her fishermen enlisting (either as volunteers or 'forced' men) in the crews of pirate vessels. Sir Henry Mainwarring, a seventeenth-century pirate who later became an English admiral, described the island as the best of all places for a refit and recruitment. He never had the least trouble enlisting Newfoundland crews, he declared, and always succeeded in getting volunteers.

The world's most successful pirate, a contemporary of Mainwarring's, commanded a whole fleet of ships sailing out of Newfoundland in the early 1600s. While colonists were busy trying to found permanent settlements on our east coast, Peter Easton was making himself lord of the Western Ocean. In a dazzling twelve-year career he rose from an obscure naval captain to become Marquis of Savoy and one of the richest men in the world.

After three and a half centuries, Newfoundlanders 'remember' Easton as though he had sailed away only yesterday. More than 1,500 Newfoundlanders who sailed with him left descendants who still tell of the exploits of 'the great Easton' with affection and respect. He is remembered as a sort of Robin Hood, a popular folk hero who gave the underdog a chance for wealth and self-respect in days when fishermen and common sailors were little better than slaves.

In the old Newfoundland seaport of Harbour Grace, where Easton built his fortress and made his headquarters, you can still hear oral traditions of a naval battle that he fought almost at the mouth of the harbour:

On a bright September day in 1611 Easton's flying squadron of four fast ships rounded Cape St. Francis, and bore up for

Harbour Grace, twenty miles away. Though by then he virtually ruled the seas, and had commanded at least forty ships at a time, he still preferred to fight with small squadrons and to overwhelm his enemies by the fury of sudden assault. From Panama to the Strait of Belle Isle he was respected and feared. This time, his tactics had paid off handsomely: he was bringing home the richest prize ever captured in a sea battle – the treasure galleon *San Sebastian*, laden to the decks with treasures stripped from Spanish America.

As his flagship leaned away from the wind, square sails bellying, he ran up signals to announce his success and scanned the fortress for an answering pennant. But no flag flew from the watchtower that he had built only the year before. Surprise gave way to alarm as a squadron of five warships flying the Basque flag rounded Feather Point and went over on the port tack to try to get to the windward side of the pirates.

Easton grasped the situation instantly, shouted an order that was scarcely needed, and his experienced crewmen, recruited from the Newfoundland fisheries, leapt to halyards and braces and swung the squadron, like a single ship, over on the starboard tack, almost on a collision course with the leading Basque vessel, which they now recognized as the *St. Malo*, flagship of the convoy protecting the French and Basque fisheries.

Though the Basques were more heavily armed, their ships were slower than the pirates', and they should never have attempted to outmanoeuvre the man who had already won the titles of 'the Arch-pirate', 'the Pirate Admiral', and 'the Great Easton', as he is variously described in the books and documents of his time. In a single stroke he had crossed the head of the Basque line, and was raking it with broadsides from his four fighting ships, while his prize crew edged the galleon safely off to windward.

A second clever bit of seamanship by Easton separated the *St. Malo* from her support. Then, while his three vessels dealt with the other four, he fought it out with her, almost rail to rail. Having failed to get to windward, the Basque flagship was caught on a lee shore, where she would be forced to tack into the wind. Easton pressed his advantage, crowding his larger and clumsier rival until white water was breaking on both sides of her. Then he turned nimbly aside as the *St. Malo* struck with a grinding crash and heeled over helplessly.

His leading foe disabled, and her crew marooned on a rocky islet, Easton turned back to the main action to find the other enemies already lowering their flags and begging for quarter. Their ships were taken as prizes, looted, and burnt. Then the pirates landed in force and recaptured their fort. As the sun set, they were once more masters of Harbour Grace. The galleon was beached, her treasure unloaded. The rocky islet where the *St. Malo* was stranded was known for the next three hundred years as 'Easton's Isle'. Forty-seven pirates, killed in the battle, lie buried in the Pirates' Graveyard at Bear Cove near the harbour mouth.

The pirate was idolized by the local fishermen, and even the colonists from near-by Cupids (founded by John Guy of Bristol in 1610) sought his protection for their stores and supplies. But Peter Easton had loftier ambitions than the homage of a few poor colonists.

The career of this strange man began in the golden days of Elizabeth I, when he was a privateer under Drake, Hawkins, and Raleigh, all of whom roved the seas for the glory and enrichment of their virgin mistress, who sat on her insecure throne, jauntily defying the all-powerful fleets of the King of Spain, and sharing his gold with her captains.

Sent to Canada in 1602 as convoy for the fishing fleet, Easton had barely cleared the English Channel when he sighted a Dutch pirate vessel, ran her down, and captured her. To his surprise he found she carried as prisoners the crew and passengers of a small Irish vessel that she had seized, looted, and sunk. Among the prisoners was an Irish girl named Sheila – a daughter, so tradition says, of the Celtic King of County Connaught. Easton's lieutenant, Gilbert Pike, took this girl as his wife, and settled with her at Mosquito, a suburb of Harbour Grace now known as Bristols Hope. There they founded the oldest and one of the largest families in Canada. Thousands of Pikes today trace their ancestry to the English sea rover and the little Irish princess who was known in Newfoundland as 'Sheila Nagira' and is reputed to have lived to be more than a hundred years of age.

While the Pikes remained in Newfoundland, Easton returned to England, only to find himself out of a job. For Elizabeth died in 1603, and James I, her successor, promptly made peace with Spain and disbanded the navy. A number of privateers, including Easton, then turned to piracy.

Peter was outfitted, supplied, and protected by the great Cornish family of the Killigrews – the robber barons of Land's End whose castle of Pendennis, up-river from Falmouth (a city which they founded), was for many years a pirate refuge. While helping Easton seize control of the English Channel (a job that took him just seven years) and collecting protection money from him, the Killigrews also held positions at court. One of them had been Elizabeth's foreign minister. Another was on his way to being an admiral for the Stuarts. A third – one of James's favourites – was a well-known playwright and Master of the Revels. A fourth had tried to sell England to Spain for ten thousand pounds in gold in the days of the Armada, and had been tried for high treason and acquitted, though there is now not the slightest doubt about his guilt. With the Killigrews' help, Easton built up a fleet of forty armed ships, drove all foreign privateers out of the Channel, and collected tribute from every merchant vessel passing through his domain.

But the West Country Merchants, a powerful group whom he robbed mercilessly, petitioned Lord Admiral Nottingham to send a fleet against him. The Lord Admiral commissioned a rising young aristocrat, Captain Henry Mainwarring, to fit out a squadron in the hope of taking Easton by surprise. The ships given to Mainwarring by Nottingham proved to be totally unseaworthy, however, and he fitted out a second squadron at his own expense. Then, at the age of twenty-three, a seasoned world traveller, sailor, lawyer, and scholar, with two degrees from Oxford under his belt (a typical Elizabethan, in fact), Henry Mainwarring sailed to do battle with the pirate admiral.

But the delay had given the Killigrews ample time to carry word to Easton. Even though he could have made short work of Mainwarring, he had no intention of fighting a battle with a commissioned British squadron (an act of high treason), so he quietly disbanded his fleet, took the ten strongest ships, and emigrated to Newfoundland. He arrived in Conception Bay early in 1610 and fortified Harbour Grace while Mainwarring was still seeking him in the Channel.

Finding no pirates whose capture would pay his expenses, Mainwarring got an enlargement of his commission, allowing him to hijack the cargoes of loot which Spain was then collecting from her rape of the Aztec and Inca empires. He made his headquarters on the Barbary Coast of the Mediterranean, where he could prey on the Spaniards and build up a fleet strong enough to pursue Easton across the Atlantic. The plan worked well. He grew wealthy on Spanish gold, made periodic visits to Ireland to recruit crewmen, and, by 1612, was ready for his great leap westward.

Meanwhile, in Newfoundland, Easton was growing even richer. He not only made forays into the Caribbean, but collected tribute from the world's fishing fleets, which converged annually on the Grand Banks. Captured vessels not needed in his expanding armada he sold in the French free ports, and also dealt in cargoes of wine and fish taken from the Portuguese and the Basques.

With more than a hundred captured cannon he not only fortified Harbour Grace, but built a second stronghold at Kelly's Island on the other side of Conception Bay, where the settlement of Killigrews was named for his Cornish patrons (and, even today, boasts a large population of Eastons, probably descendants of the pirate crewmen who adopted their captain's surname, as was a common custom of the time).

Learning of Mainwarring's success in the Mediterranean and of his intention of following him to Canada, Easton began negotiating with King James for a pardon. So far, he had done nothing that might not be forgiven, provided the price was right. He dispatched a ship under Captain John Harvey to Ireland, with a message to be passed on, through the Killigrews, to the King. He opened a second channel of negotiation through Captain Richard Whitbourne, the admiral of the Newfoundland fishing fleet. When Whitbourne arrived in London, the pardon had already been granted. But just to be on the safe side, King James (who had a keen eye for a fast buck) issued the pardon a second time, and copies of both pardons are preserved in the Public Records Office.

Meanwhile, with the threat of Mainwarring's fleet sailing against him, the arch-pirate decided to move from Conception Bay to Ferryland, fifty miles to the south. He was the first to recognize the importance of this natural fortress, later to become the English capital of Newfoundland, which, through a century of French-English conflict, was never successfully attacked from the sea. In Ferryland, Easton built a large house in a commanding position on Fox Hill, fortified the headlands, set up a battery on Isle au Bois, which sits like a plug in the harbour mouth, and then sent out his squadrons to prey on all the traders of the Western Ocean.

His most daring venture was a raid on Puerto Rico, with its Spanish colony founded by Ponce de León. He sailed right into the harbour of San Juan, bombarded the shore batteries into silence, then led a landing party which stormed the famous fortress of Morro Castle and captured the governor's palace. He collected what tribute the colonists could scrape together, took the stockpile of gold from the local mines, and then sailed back to Ferryland. He thus avenged the failure of Sir Francis Drake, who had been defeated in his attempt to do the same thing thirteen years earlier. The capture of this bastion of the Spanish empire, more than any other feat, gave Easton his aura of invincibility.

He ruled his private kingdom from Ferryland until 1614, and, if he ever received the pardons issued by King James, he never acted on them. Mainwarring arrived with his fleet and took over Easton's old forts in Conception Bay, but so far as we know the two pirates never met, though their subsequent careers were very similar. It was not Mainwarring's arrival that hastened Easton's departure, but news from the Caribbean that the Spanish Plate fleet was preparing to sail for the Azores.

Easton quickly divided his enormous treasure among the ships of his fleet, and, with his private squadron of ten ships, hastened off to the Azores, where he deployed them in a wide arc to the west and south, awaiting the Spaniards.

None of the details of the ensuing battle have come down to us. We know only that Easton arrived in Tunis a few days later with four captured Spanish galleons as prizes. The Bey of Tunis, recognizing Easton as perhaps the greatest sea-fighter who ever lived, entered into an alliance with him, and together they fought a very profitable war against Spain. He also served under the Duke of Savoy in an attack on the Duchy of Mantua, distinguishing himself as the officer in charge of artillery.

He then settled in Savoy, purchased a peerage, and built a great palace. His personal share of the spoils, after he paid off his captains, was reported to be two million pounds sterling, the equivalent of about a hundred million dollars in today's funds. He ended his life as the Marquis of Savoy, in great splendour and wealth.

On the Riviera, Mainwarring finally caught up with him, but

by now had given up any plans for Easton's capture, and, with a fleet manned entirely by Newfoundland fishermen, was waging a private war against Spain.

The Bey of Tunis offered Mainwarring, in his turn, command of the Tunisian navy and a share in the kingdom, but he rejected all foreign offers and returned to England where he was granted a pardon, a knighthood, and a naval commission. He was elected to Parliament from Dover, and was received at court. He was then recommissioned – this time under pay – to police the North Atlantic, and sailed just in time to rescue the Newfoundland trading fleet, which, loaded with export fish, had been seized by a group of Easton's former captains.

Mainwarring later rose to become an Admiral in the English fleet. He spent much time at court and became one of the King's boon companions. He was still under thirty when he arrived home with fabulous wealth that he shared with the King. He was not only the foremost English seaman of James's reign, but commanded a fleet under Charles I and fought in the Civil War against Cromwell. He lived into old age, but fell on evil days. His last action took place at Pendennis Castle, the stronghold of the Killigrews, in Cornwall, which withstood a five-month siege after the rest of England had capitulated. With other Royalists he then escaped to the Isle of Jersey, but, in 1651, petitioned for a pardon and permission to return to England. His estate was valued at eight pounds, and his fine fixed at one pound, six shillings, and eightpence, being paid on December 18, 1651. He died a year and a half later, and was buried at St. Giles in Camberwell.

Meanwhile, Newfoundland fell under the dominion of other pirates. Some of Walter Raleigh's 'erring captains' levied regular tribute and enlisted crews from the fishing settlements. Altogether, according to an estimate by Sir William Vaughan who lived at Ferryland in the 1620s, more than 1,500 Newfoundlanders had sailed away in pirate ships 'to the great hurt of the plantations'.

Captain Jacob Everson, a Dutch privateer, attacked St. John's with four armed ships in 1673. Captain Christopher Martin, admiral of the fishing fleet that year (the 'admiral' being the first captain into port in the spring, and having charge of all port activities), organized the first known defence of the harbour.

With assistance from twenty-three other fishing masters he erected batteries at The Narrows and drove off the Dutch.

Shortly after this the French imposed a Gallic Peace in the western Atlantic, but piracy flourished once more when France was defeated by England and several of her colonies taken from her by the Treaty of Utrecht. The notorious Captain Anstis and the Welsh Puritan pirate Bartholomew Roberts both visited Newfoundland in 1721, the latter sinking twenty-one of the twenty-two vessels then in harbour at Trepassey, and sacking the town.

John Phillips, an unemployed shipwright who emigrated to Newfoundland from England that same year, began his career as a pirate in Newfoundland and ended it a few months later off the coast of Massachusetts. He entered into a conspiracy with a group of fishermen at St. Peter's (St. Pierre) to seize an American ship then in port. Five of them put to sea, captured a number of fishing vessels on the Grand Banks, refitted a captured ship, recruited crewmen from the fishing crews, then sailed for the West Indies to seek their fortune.

In the following eight months they ran down and captured at least thirty-three ships, some of them armed, and one that was actually fitted out for war, mounting twelve guns. But in the end Phillips and his friends were overpowered by a mutiny among captured men. Most of the pirates, including Phillips himself, were killed in the battle, and his head was pickled and taken to Boston to be exhibited on the dockside. Those not killed in the battle were tried and hanged – but one of them, William Taylor, who had joined Phillips' crew while on his way to a Virginia plantation where he was to serve a term as a bond slave for debt, was pardoned, and later came to Newfoundland to found a family that still survives.

Eric Cobham and his common-law wife, Maria, perhaps the most ferocious pirates in history, operated on Newfoundland's west coast for about twenty years, finally retiring with great wealth and honour to enjoy long years of aristocratic tranquillity.

Cobham, born in Poole, went to sea as a boy, and was a smuggler in his teens, being involved in one 'trip' when ten thousand gallons of French brandy were landed at Poole. But he was caught, flogged, and sent to prison at about the age of nineteen. After two years in Newgate he got a job as a clerk at an inn in Oxford, where he succeeded in robbing a guest of a bag of gold and escaping with it while the innkeeper was hanged for the theft. He bought a ship, recruited a crew, and promptly captured an East Indiaman with a gold cargo valued at 40,000 pounds. He scuttled the ship, drowned the crew, took his girl-friend, Maria Lindsey, from Plymouth, and sailed for Nantucket, then northward into the Gulf of St. Lawrence, making his head-quarters at Sandy Point in St. George's Bay.

This harbour, later the 'capital' of western Newfoundland and an important naval station, centre of the gulf and Labrador fisheries, was then unoccupied except for a few Indians and a few Acadian refugees.

Eric and Maria Cobham specialized in seizing ships bound up and down the St. Lawrence (many of them carrying cargoes of furs). They disposed of their loot through the black markets in the French free ports, as Easton and Mainwarring had done more than a century earlier, and, since they followed a policy of murdering every man who fell into their hands, their crimes went undetected. The ships were simply listed as 'missing with all hands'.

After twenty years of this they sailed to France, bought a large estate near Le Havre from the Duc de Chartres, and founded a family which was soon elevated to the nobility. Cobham, now a wealthy squire and land-owner, was appointed a magistrate and a judge in the French rural courts – a position that he held for twelve years. But Maria (who had always been an insane sadist whose greatest delight was killing) finally took poison and jumped over a cliff.

Cobham lived on to a ripe age, but on his deathbed made a full confession of his piracies to a priest, adding the request that it be published. The priest complied, but the Cobham family promptly bought the entire edition of the book and had it burned. Somehow or other one fragmentary copy escaped the flames and was lodged in the French archives, where it is still available to researchers.

There were many other pirates, before and later, in New-foundland, but these are sufficiently typical of the breed. They have left a permanent mark on the island in numerous stories of treasure, and some authenticated finds of Spanish gold. They also contributed greatly to Newfoundland nomenclature. Some of the most picturesque place-names came, originally, from pirate ships – among them Happy Adventure, Heart's Desire, Bonaventure, and Black Joke Cove. Others were named for the pirates themselves: Kelly's Island, Turk's Cove, and Turk's Gut – the latter because all pirates were known indiscriminately as 'Turks' in the seventeenth and eighteenth centuries.

15. Rum-runners and Masterless Men

Southward from St. John's, then northward along Trepassey Bay, St. Mary's Bay, and Conception Bay to St. John's again runs the most interesting loop drive in Newfoundland, two hundred miles with Trepassey at the mid point, one hundred miles from St. John's by either the eastern or the western route. Approximately half this road is paved, and the pavement is being extended each year.

Every cove along the road to Cape Race has stories of pirates and buried treasure, of battles between French and English, or of great wrecks in the days of sail.

Bay Bulls, twenty miles from St. John's, is one of the oldest towns, named for the bull walrus that used to be hunted there, though now you must go a thousand miles north to find one of these huge beasts. A single walrus showed up at Bay Bulls, though, in the summer of 1967, as though looking for its vanished ancestors, and took up residence on a rock. It stayed only a few days before starting back toward the Arctic.

Polar bears that land somewhere along this shore almost every year, having come south from Greenland or Labrador pursuing seals, never return to their icy habitat. Without exception they are tracked down and shot by one of the fishermen.

Bay Bulls was the site of the last French attack on Newfoundland, during the wars of Napoleon. A naval force landed there, intended as a flanking movement against St. John's, but abandoned the plan when a prisoner told them the city was defended by 5,000 regular troops. (It wasn't.) They then sailed off to harass the coast of Labrador. Bay Bulls had been fought over many times before that. Four big cannon now serve as gate-posts for the church and as pedestals for its statuary. Near by are the ruins of a battery used to defend the town against pirates in the seventeenth century, and the abandoned installations of the anti-submarine base from the Second World War.

Forty miles from St. John's a short side road leads to La-Manche, now almost deserted between its towering hills. Here houses, flakes, and the local road were all built on stilts over the harbour or along the mountain-side. The catwalk that carries the road crosses the tossing white plumes of LaManche waterfall on a swaying suspension bridge from which you can watch the big sea trout, far below, playing with the fresh water at the river-mouth. Lake and river leading to LaManche are passable by canoe through the fine valley of LaManche Provincial Park to within half a mile of the settlement, but that last half-mile is impassable at any time.

Just south of LaManche is Cape Broyle Bay, once a great haunt for gentlemen adventurers, with concealed moorings where a pirate ship could hide in safety. You may still see moor-ing rings by which ships were secured fore and aft to the cliffs in a little cove too small for any ship to swing at anchor.

Here, too, on a bold headland, is the Devil's Staircase with the skeleton of a big boat perched at the top, 300 feet from the sea. The Devil himself, according to local superstition, put it there. Its actual story is a complete mystery. There is no reasonable approach from land, no reason why anyone would build a boat on a cliff top. Any sea or tidal wave which could have lodged a boat in such a place would have drowned half Newfoundland at the same time. It must have been winched up to its perch by blocks and tackle, with enormous labour. But why?

After the pirates came the whalers and the rum-runners. They ran the rum from St. Pierre, the French island a day's sail to the south and west of here. John Hawkins, a retired smuggler who had spent his life in the trade (and has since passed to his eternal reward), described some of the tricks of the trade to me.

'We used to sell rum to every licensed house along this coast – there was a lot of public bars in them days – they'd buy one gallon of rum from the government bond store and three gallons from the rum-runners.

'But the stuff they got from me was always watered a bit. Not enough to hurt, mind ye. We'd have an empty ninety-gallon puncheon in the hold, and we'd run into a little harbour called Shoe Cove and drop anchor. There we'd fill up our puncheon by taking a bucket of rum out of each one of our customers' casks, and replacin' the same with a bucket of sea water. The customers never knowed the difference. Mind ye never put fresh water in yer liquor. It rots good rum. But salt water presarves it.

'Had some mighty close calls,' he admitted with a cackle of mirth. 'I mind the time we was runnin' fourteen puncheons of rum into St. John's harbour in a little jack boat under sail. Almost in, we was, when here comes the revenue cutter, full steam astern. Well, we had to beat in agin' the wind, ye see, couldn't possibly heave to where we was. Fourteen tacks we made, gettin' in through The Narrows, and every time we went over on the port tack our deck was hid from the revenue boat, and here goes a barrel of rum over the side. When we come up to the wind and dropped sails and the customs officers come aboard, we was as clean as a cut cat.

'The fishermen from the Lower Battery seen us dump that rum, and that night out they goes with graplins and jiggers and hooks up every one of them barrels of rum just as nice as you please.

'There was the time, too, when we tied up alongside the *Eugene B. Macmillan* in St. John's, and she takin' water ballast in puncheons out of our hold, with the customs men lookin' on. And her skipper sings out, "Hurry up with that God damned water ballast, ye lubbers!" and sure every puncheon was a puncheon of rum which she was goin' to peddle to the outports down north – Notre Dame Bay and them places. Nobody thought we'd have the face to do it like that, ye see. And after the water ballast was all out the customs men looked us over and give us a clean bill o' health.

'The cops knowed what was goin' on, o' course, but we was always a jump ahead. One time we had six cases o' fancy liquor for some big shots in St. John's – I'll not mention their names – and just as the customs men come alongside one of our men jumps over the bow with a big sack on his back and takes to his heels as fast as he can go up the dock. Well, naturally every law man in sight takes out after 'im, an' when he's finally caught, half a mile or so up Water Street, they finds a sack full of empty bottles, and by the time they gets back, our six cases of whisky are all safely stowed ashore.'

There is still a lot of St. Pierre liquor drunk and sold on the Newfoundland black market. The R.C.M.P. runs an elaborate anti-smuggling patrol, and sometimes seizes big cargoes of hooch, but by ship, by boat, and by small plane the flow of booze from the French islands continues. It's tax-free, you see.

But smuggling is no longer a paying occupation. Nobody does it full-time any more. Whaling, too, was a passing phase in the history of Cape Broyle, and today the old town has settled back peacefully to its original trade of catching and curing codfish.

Ferryland – six miles away over the Cape Broyle Barrens – consists of a little bay, a remarkable peninsula and a series of islands, an outer harbour, and a tiny inner harbour called The Pool, the whole presenting a hauntingly beautiful seascape, especially when viewed from The Gaze, a grassy hill where settlers once kept sentries posted to watch for attacking ships.

Ferryland was used as a fishing station by the Portuguese in the sixteenth century. Then it was settled by a few fishing families – mostly English, who, because of their habit of light-salting the fish, had to maintain shore stations with a few permanent settlers to protect their property. These scattered families were living there in 1612 when the pirate admiral Peter Easton arrived with a fleet of armed ships, built his mansion on Fox Hill, fortified the town, and made it the capital of his maritime empire. He sailed away in 1614 to found a pirate kingdom in the Mediterranean, but his old forts were rebuilt by the settlers and used against pirates, privateers, and the naval squadrons of France.

Lord Baltimore's settlers arrived with a Royal Patent in 1621 and evicted at least some of the original residents as squatters. Baltimore later built a great house fronting the sea – a pretentious colonial plantation – and brought in hundreds of settlers from Britain. Ferryland then became the English capital of Newfoundland, first under Baltimore, then under Sir David Kirke. There were other royal plantations, too, but none of them succeeded in enriching their founders. The colonies were abandoned, and the fishermen returned. They have been there ever since, a permanent part of the land that the aristocrats tried, unsuccessfully, to coin into gold guineas and sovereigns.

During the French-English struggle for Canada, Ferryland was repeatedly attacked and on two occasions captured by the French, though never in an attack from the sea against fortified positions. Easton was right when he judged the harbour safe from any assault by ships.

Even today, French cannon balls are frequently dug from Ferryland's potato patches. Occasionally other oddities are found there, too. At the mouth of a brook that runs through Easton's old property, William Morry, who owns a fish business in the settlement, found a beautiful ring of the reign of Queen Anne, a ring that his wife, Pat, wears today. There have been a number of reports of small treasure caches, probably family heirlooms and valuables buried during the French attacks and occupations. There is no reason to believe that Easton or any other pirate left treasure there.

From Placentia, opposite Ferryland on the other side of the Avalon Peninsula, the French launched an offensive by sea in 1694, intending to capture or destroy all the English settlements. The offensive was stopped at Ferryland by a home guard of settlers who took guns from their ships and fortified the old earthworks that had been used by Easton eighty years before. In the battle between the ships and the shore batteries the little settlement lost ninety of its men, but they saved the English colony from conquest.

Two years later the French attacked again – this time by land as well as by sea, their forces being commanded by the two d'Iberville brothers. They captured Ferryland from the rear, and took all the other English settlements too, but the d'Ibervilles had no troops for garrison duty, and were forced to withdraw after burning the English plantations. The settlers simply came out of the woods and rebuilt their homes. The Ferrylanders then successfully beat off two other French attacks.

In 1709 the Governor of New England, hearing that the settlement was once more under French siege, sent a ship to its relief, and offered to take the entire population to the safety of the American colonies. The settlers politely refused to go, declaring that they were willing and able to manage their own defence. Their letter, signed by thirty masters of fishing establishments, is preserved in the archives at St. John's.

Ferryland's most famous battle was in 1762, almost a century after the original French assault. In this battle the great-grand-mother of Newfoundland's prime minister Sir Frederick Carter (who was a delegate to the original Confederation negotiations of 1864) is credited by tradition with wrecking a French warship.

At that time Robert Carter had a grant to Isle au Bois at the harbour entrance. With the help of the fishermen he had fortified the island against attack by pirates or foreign ships, and when the French made a determined effort to conquer Newfoundland in 1762, it was successfully defended by two hundred fishermen under Carter's leadership. The men handled the guns while their wives brought up ammunition and swabbed down the guns to keep them cool. Mrs. Carter, however, was in charge of a gun crew herself, and a shot from her gun turned the tide of battle, bringing down the mainmast of the leading ship in the French squadron.

Though the French continued the attack throughout the day, they did not succeed in landing a man or a gun or in silencing any of the settlers' batteries, and they abandoned their whole scheme for conquest by sea.

Ferryland has been at peace for many years now, battling only the storms that roll in continually from the vast and brooding ocean. But the visitor may still see the great guns that lie under water, the old earthworks at Isle au Bois, the remains of barracks and magazines, and the cannons that came to rest in the crannies of the cliffs, when time accomplished what the brave French seamen could not and reduced the English forts to dust.

In the late eighteenth and part of the nineteenth centuries, Ferryland was more or less constantly under naval rule, with British frigates stationed in the harbour and marines patrolling the town. It was a brutal form of government. One night a frightened boy came to the door of the house on Ferryland beach now owned by Howard Morry. Morry's great-grandmother answered the knock and gave shelter to the youngster, who had deserted a warship to escape constant ill-treatment. When a naval detail came to search she hid the boy in the cellar and kept him there for six months, letting him out only at night. But word leaked out, another search party was sent, and the boy was seized, taken on board ship, and flogged to death. The woman herself barely escaped banishment, and would, in fact, have been transported as a bond slave to a plantation except for the intercession of powerful friends who had the governor's ear.

The law on land was almost as harsh as at sea. Ferryland had a court house, a magistrate, and three whipping posts in three separate regions of the town. Men sentenced to be flogged for such crimes as stealing a jug of rum or refusing to work for the fishing masters were taken to all three places in turn so the whole town could view their punishment. In the circumstances, many young men simply ran away from the plantations and took up the lives of outlaws. They were known as the Masterless Men, and the best-organized band of them lived near Ferryland at the Butter Pot Barrens.

Inland, and just south of the town, you can see a bold peak of red sandstone, standing almost a thousand feet above the low coastal plain. This is the Southern Butter Pot, an outlying buttress of the high caribou barrens. Here in the late eighteenth century the Masterless Men built a settlement of log tilts, declared their independence from the rest of the world, and defied the laws of England for a generation and a half.

The Butter Pot is nine miles inland from Ferryland in a wilderness of lakes, rivers, and forests where, even today, a herd of some five hundred caribou exists under government protection. In the days of the Masterless Men the herd may have been ten times that size, and provided them with a ready source of meat. Small game and furs are also plentiful in this region.

To this virgin wilderness, some time after 1750, came Peter Kerrivan, a deserter from the English navy. Scarcely more than a boy, but a most resourceful one, he was already the leader of a band of young companions who had escaped from the intolerable life of the fleet, or the scarcely more tolerable life of the plantations, to take their chances like Indians in the backwoods.

Kerrivan had been impressed into the navy, where he was half-starved, forced to work under deck officers who drove the men around with canes or quoits like cattle, and threatened with flogging, keel-hauling, or ducking from the yard-arm for any show of insubordination.

The men who worked ashore for the fishing masters were mostly indentured servants – the so-called Irish Youngsters, who were abducted from Ireland either by force or guile and literally sold by the head to the owners of the Newfoundland fishing establishments. They could be hanged for running away, but nevertheless many of them did, and during the French-English wars they deserted, wholesale, and joined the French army.

The Masterless Men built their tilts at the Butter Pot because it was a first-class lookout in case of pursuit. Then they turned to hunting, to stealthy raids against the fishery plantations, and to surreptitious trading with the settlers in the more remote villages along the Southern Shore.

Their fame soon spread, and their numbers grew, as indentured men and apprentices deserted their ships or their fishing rooms and made their way to the Butter Pot. Within a few years they were an acknowledged scandal in an otherwise docile colony. Outraged officials with no police or militia of their own called on the navy to capture them and make a public example of them.

Some years passed, however, before the first expedition against the Masterless Men was organized. By that time Kerrivan was no longer a callow youth, but an expert woodsman. Anticipating an attack, or perhaps having actual word of it in advance, he and his followers had constructed a number of blind trails, well cut and marked, but ending in bogs without exits, or petering out in thick bush.

As the marines advanced, the Masterless Men retired to the west and north, where they had roads leading all the way to St. Mary's and Trinity bays. After exploring the false trails for some days, the expedition finally reached the Butter Pot only to find the settlement totally deserted, with every rag and chattel removed. They set fire to the village, but had to retire without a single prisoner.

Several subsequent expeditions were sent over the hills toward St. Mary's Bay in an effort to round up the Masterless Men. Three times they burnt the tilts at the Butter Pot, and three times they were rebuilt. Only once did they succeed in capturing anybody — four young recruits from Ferryland who had joined the band only a few weeks before. These luckless Irish Youngsters, taken by surprise away from the main body of outlaws, were seized and marched back to Ferryland. They were taken on board the English frigate, tried, sentenced, and hanged with great dispatch.

You can still hear an orally preserved account of this incident from Howard Morry in Ferryland, who had a first-hand description of the hanging from his own great-grandmother. As a small child she lived in Aquaforte, a few miles to the south, and was taken by her mother to visit Ferryland, there to see the outlaws hanging from the yard-arm of the frigate as an example to all who might be tempted to flout authority.

But the only result of the execution was to make the outlaws more cautious. None was ever captured after that. They remained as popular and successful as ever, and carried their road-building to the point where they had a regular system connecting the various small settlements of the Avalon Peninsula. I have talked to old men who used those roads often in the nineteenth century. Later they were used by the government mail-carriers who, in the early days of the mail service, travelled the length and breadth of the Avalon Peninsula – distances of some hundreds of miles – on foot, their mail sacks on their backs. Some of the old roads exist as woods trails, even today.

The independent fishermen in the small settlements traded with the Masterless Men, and some of them, including Kerrivan himself, even married girls from the coastal villages. He never returned to civilization, but lived to a ripe old age as the patriarch of the Butter Pot – a veritable Old Man of the Mountain and a legend in his own time, so well known that oral accounts of his exploits are preserved in the fishing settlements today, a century and a half after his death.

Only the changing times brought an end to the society of Masterless Men. During the nineteenth century the military forts in Newfoundland were abandoned, and the visits of the Royal Navy became fewer. Civil laws, though still harsh, were less brutal, and even indentured servants began to have legal rights. The right of small-holders, or even men without land titles, to live and work apart from the fishing masters was gradually sanctioned by tradition, and finally by law.

Kerrivan's sons and others of his followers then gradually drifted out to the coast, settled down in small coves never visited by the navy, married the daughters of other outlaws who had settled there generations earlier, and raised families who, in time, became perfectly solid citizens. There are hundreds of Kerrivans living in the small fishing settlements today. Some of them, at least, are proud to trace their ancestry to the Robin Hood of the Butter Pot who defied the King of England in the seventeenth century.

16. A Land of the Prophets

From Ferryland the road climbs over a hill and drops down to the tidy little fjord of Aquaforte – another favourite haunt of Easton and of later adventurers. At least one scuttled ship still lies sunken in the inner barachois, where it can be seen through the clear water at low tide. A peaceful village, Aquaforte has a turbulent sea-trout river plunging into the end of its fine harbour, and numerous little waterfalls trailing, lace-like, down its hills.

Long after the pirates vanished, Aquaforte became a whaling centre, with a factory; the Windsor family, who were master whalers, built a fine house that still stands on a small, steep peninsula, like a castle on a hill, commanding the centre of the harbour. The people who live there today trace their family to the first Windsor, a tough and able fisherman who staked off a large tract of fishing-grounds for the exclusive use of his clan, and defended it at gun point against all comers.

The family history, recorded in a huge old Bible, has a gap of twelve years during which the Windsor who then headed the clan sailed to Europe, fought Napoleon, and was taken prisoner. After Napoleon's defeat he was set free, returned to Aquaforte, and took up once more the begetting of sons and daughters by the woman who had kept his family together through the intervening years.

The whalers have now followed the pirates into history, and the peace of old age has settled over Aquaforte. Even the fish flakes lie idle, for most of the fish is sold fresh or in saltbulk. It would be an ideal 'summer place' except that it lies just a little too far from St. John's for convenient commuting.

South of Aquaforte is Fermeuse, with its fish plant, and

beautiful Admiral's Cove, choice of the fishing admirals who, on first arrival, not only had the annual pick of fishing berths, but administered the law among the foreign fishermen for the season.

Here, again, are legends of pirates and stories of wrecks and disasters – and no shortage of people to tell you about them. Mostly of Irish descent, the people have a traditional gift for conversation and for story-telling, as well as for hospitality; you can go to any door and be invited in for a yarn and a cup of tea, maybe something stronger if there's a drop of it in the house. The people here are not surprised to find that the visitor is interested in their history and their folklore. They are interested in it themselves, and have taken care to preserve it, in stories told around their firesides, generation after generation.

Not far from here lived Peter Kelly the Prophet, a village magician with a reputation for casting out devils, curing diseases by spells, bringing fish to the nets, and entering houses through keyholes.

It started one day when he was locked into a house by mistake. The housewife, returning, found him there, believed his story that he had gone in through the keyhole ('I'm a kind of a prophet, you know,' he said. 'I can go in and out through a crack that would scarcely admit a knitting-needle. God save all here.'), after which his reputation was made and he was known everywhere as Peter Kelly the Prophet.

When the fish failed, Peter was called upon to take off the evil. He was especially good at casting evil spirits out of fishing boats so that the owners got bumper catches. He did it by taking large stones out in the boat, forcing the spirits, by incantations, to enter the stones, and then dropping the stones overboard. The very first time he tried this, the fish arrived in dense shoals the next morning (as they so often do), and Peter was able to make a comfortable living as a miracle-worker without having to lift his hand to an honest day's work for the rest of his life.

The quiet little village of Admiral's Cove, just off the main road near Fermeuse, was the birth-place of a more successful prophet than Peter, though one equally mad. He was the founder of the world-wide British-Israel movement, which once had millions of followers, and still has many adherents today.

His name was Richard Brothers, and his titles included 'Prince of the Hebrews, Lion of the Tribe of Judah, Nephew of the Almighty, Cousin of the Lord Jesus'. He was born on Christmas Day 1757, and fished in Admiral's Cove as a boy. But at the age of ten or eleven he was sent to school in England, and at the age of fourteen he entered the navy as a midshipman.

Brothers fought in a number of battles, retired from the navy as a lieutenant, then entered the merchant marine and sailed to all parts of the world. He was only thirty-three when he retired on a government pension, and began having visions.

He was told by his voices that he was the rightful heir of King David, and ought to be sitting on the throne of the New Jerusalem, then wrongly occupied by the King of England. He forswore his allegiance to the Crown and publicly claimed the throne for himself. The authorities ignored these claims, but cancelled his pension and imprisoned him for debt. In prison his visions increased fourfold, and upon his release he started publishing a series of prophetic letters addressed to the Prime Minister, the King, the Queen, and other notables.

He said he had ascended into heaven and spoken directly with God. His claim to the throne was based on his descent from King David through James the brother of Jesus (hence his surname, Brothers), and since England was the successor to Israel, and the home of the Ten Lost Tribes, he was the rightful heir to its throne.

Next he published a series of books interpreting Daniel and the Apocalypse in terms of the Anglo-Saxon race as the Ten Lost Tribes of Israel. He was to become the king of all the Anglo-Saxon peoples, on both sides of the Atlantic, lead them back to Palestine, and there 'subdue all things under his feet'. In a very few years he had tens of thousands of followers on both sides of the ocean.

Brothers was a typical, very advanced case of paranoid-schizophrenia. Today he would be treated with drugs, and probably with electric shock. In 1795 he was simply imprisoned as a criminal lunatic, with a charge of high treason waiting to be heard, should he ever recover his reason. Luckily for himself he did not, or he might have been drawn and quartered, as was the picturesque custom of the time. He languished in an asylum, persecuted for righteousness' sake, while his followers multiplied, his books ran through numerous editions, and even scholars and members of parliament became converts to his cause.

After his death his following increased, branched out into

various directions and subdivisions, and is still very large today in Britain, Canada, and the United States. The only place where Brothers made absolutely no impression on the Anglo-Saxon Israelites was in Newfoundland. At Admiral's Cove, where the Brothers family still lives, you had better not mention the name of Richard. They regard him as a dark stain on the escutcheon.

Renews – the next settlement after Admiral's Cove – has one of the most detailed stories of buried treasure. It is supposed to be in the graveyard.

Eighty years ago a ship's crew rowed ashore in a boat at Renews bringing a coffin with them. They hired a man named Jim Devine to take the corpse of their departed ship-mate to the burying-ground.

'But my dear man,' said the old fisherman who told me the tale, 'ye could tell it wasn't no corpse. Why, the box was so heavy it took four strong men just to shift it on skids from the boat to the long cart! The axle of the cart – a two-inch iron bar – was bent by the load. Even the horse was never any good afterwards. His wind was broken.'

The ship's crew sailed off for their summer's fishing, saying they'd come back for the coffin and its salted corpse in the fall. But if they returned, it must have been on a dark and lonely night, to dig up the coffin and get it back to the ship somehow, without help. Most people believe that they never came back, and that the half-ton coffin still lies interred in the old graveyard. No local man would try to dig it up because of the dread of starting spirits.

On a small point at Renews there is an old battery even more ancient than the ones in Ferryland. Its cannon bear the Tudor Rose of the time of Elizabeth I, but its fort is in complete decay, and even the guns are half-buried in the turf.

Dozens of wrecks have piled ashore near this place, sometimes one on top of another. When the S.S. *Florizel* broke up here in 1916 with great loss of life, she stirred up the remains of an ancient wreck that has never been identified. The day after the *Florizel* went down the fishermen fetched up with their jiggers a big bronze plaque weighing 114 pounds. It is still at Renews, where I have seen it myself. Its crest is a lion with the head of a stag, and five feet of scroll-work spell out the words 'The Edwards Line'. There is no record at Lloyds of London of there ever having been a shipping company with that name, and there is not even a tradition of any wreck with which the big bronze plaque can be associated.

This strip of coastline is world-famous among bird enthusiasts. There are large colonies of seabirds on the off-shore islands, numerous migrants on the tidal flats, frequent strays from the tropics and from Europe, some of them belonging to species never seen elsewhere in North America.

Almost every spring, as early as the third week of April, such southern song birds as scarlet tanagers and indigo buntings begin appearing on the Southern Shore, which is the first land-fall possible to them if they miss Cape Cod while riding the south-westerly storm winds.

The tidal flats at Renews are covered, in late summer, with migrating shore birds. I have sometimes seen seventeen or eighteen species sharing the same acre of mud and sand. Mixed flocks of Hudsonian curlews and golden plovers arrive by the thousands in August and early September, and feed on the great crops of berries just inland from the shore. Ruddy turnstones root among the rocks. Sandpipers and ringed plovers and sander-lings swarm over the dark mud between the tides.

Just over the hill from Renews is Cappahayden. The ponds and rivers of this region are famous for their trout. The upper reaches of Chance Cove waters in particular yield some of the best brook trout fishing to be found anywhere. Fishermen equipped with topographic maps can reach these waters by walk-ing from the road, for the country is open and mostly treeless.

From Cappahayden you can walk for miles over grass-covered cliff-tops toward Chance Cove. There is also a trail through the woods to the Chance Cove barachois. It is most often reached, however, by a three-mile hike straight across barrens and swamp from the highroad. Chance Cove is favoured both by hunters and by fly-fishermen. It is a lonely spot without inhabitants since all its people moved in a body to the United States many years ago. They left behind their sheep, which ran wild and were slaugh-tered by gunners visiting Chance Cove for ducks or ptarmigan. Why the people left is a bit of a mystery. The tale is told along the shore that they were driven out by the ghosts of drowned seamen, for thousands of men lost their lives on this treacherous shore.

Near Chance Cove the remains of an iron ship are wedged into a cliff a hundred feet above the sea. The towering tempest that threw it up there must have been one of the worst storms in the history of the Atlantic Ocean. But it was not storm so much as fog and tide that doomed ships along this shore. A number of shipping routes converge near Cape Race, at a place where a strong but fickle current sets toward shore. Ships sailing by dead reckoning were often much nearer the breakers than their captains imagined. To add to everything else, this coast lies on the normal hurricane track of late summer and fall.

Every cove and headland has its story of sudden death: Long Beach, Mistaken Point, Clam Cove, Shoe Cove, The Drook. Beside them all lie the bones of wrecks, piled one atop the other.

In 1958 a big ship went ashore at Long Beach. An American warship ran aground north of the cape in 1942. In earlier times, when rescue work was haphazard and communications poor, the wrecks were often wholesale disasters. Five or six hundred lives were lost in the wreck of the *Harpooner* – no one knows the exact number, since only men were on the sailing list. Their wives and children by the hundreds went down uncounted and unnamed. The *Anglo-Saxon*, a ship of the Allan Line bound from Britain to Quebec with 446 passengers and crew, struck the rocks at Clam Cove on April 27, 1863, and 237 people were drowned. Many of them were buried on the spot. Their graves may still be seen on the bank of Clam Cove Brook.

The *Little Drake*, a square-rigged British man-o'-war carrying between 300 and 400 men was lost with all hands near St. Shotts. Corpses continued to wash up on the beach for days afterwards, the men of the settlement burying them in the sand without reporting the disaster. So far as the British Admiralty knew, the *Little Drake* vanished at sea without trace. Her anchor can still be seen at low tide, with a ring large enough for a man to crawl through with ease.

In the summer of 1901 there was many a glorious lost week-end in these parts, for on June 5 the *Assyrian* was wrecked near Cape Race with a full cargo of spirits. Crew and passengers were rescued without loss, and the cargo claimed as salvage. The same month another ship ran ashore near Cape Broyle with a cargo of champagne and other French wines, and cut crystal tableware packed in barrels. Not knowing the value of cut glass, the people threw it over the side, but for a while there was a brisk barter of champagne for whisky. There are still men on the shore who remember buying champagne for twenty cents a quart.

Beyond Cappahayden the country takes on the character of the great Barren Lands of the Canadian Arctic – not as cold, of course, nor so densely covered with flies in summer, but with the same landscape, and even similar kinds of wildlife. Cape Race can be reached by a fourteen-mile sideroad. Ten miles past the junction is the ancient town of Trepassey, inhabited by Basques and French even before the English settled this shore. Lord Baltimore appealed for help from England to expel the French from Trepassey in 1627. How long they had been there before that nobody knows. After Baltimore's brief stay they came back, and they were still there a hundred years later when the French colonies were incorporated into English Newfoundland. Trepassey was the easternmost outpost of French Canada, a way-station to the St. Lawrence and the beginning of a complex of settlement that stretched through Placentia and St. Pierre, along the south coast of Newfoundland, through Acadia, Cape Breton, and up-river to the heart of the North American continent.

The Basques left their names on the map of Newfoundland at this point, as they did at the other end of the south coast. Biscay Bay and Biscay Bay River are named for them. The latter is the best salmon stream on the Avalon Peninsula, and also carries good runs of sea trout.

From Trepassey the road runs for twenty-two miles across the Cape Pine Barrens to St. Mary's Bay. The barrens are one of the most popular birding regions in Newfoundland during the autumn ptarmigan shoot.

The character of the countryside changes completely on the St. Mary's Bay side of the peninsula. Here, in contrast to the rugged grandeurs of the Southern Shore, it is pastoral and sylvan, the park-like countryside extending past such admirable fishing streams as Little Harbour River to the estuary of the Salmonier. This is a popular river for small grilse fishing – so popular that you practically have to line up to get a chance to cast. The salmon are small, and the fishing not all that good, but the river has a reputation that refuses to die.

From Salmonier the Salmonier Line runs fifteen miles to the Trans-Canada Highway. Its chief attraction is the Deer Park, a forest and game reserve full of fishing lakes. North Harbour River, Rocky River, Colinet River, and Back River are all in this immediate region, and all have exceptional fishing for sea trout, brook trout, or ouananiche.

The entire loop of approximately two hundred miles can be completed in a day's drive, with a little time for sightseeing along the way, provided you start early and are willing to finish late. It is much pleasanter, however, to stop over at Trepassey, Salmonier, or Colinet. Anglers, of course, will wish to spend longer, exploring the really great fishing waters on this route. I have fished in almost every part of Newfoundland, but the largest brook trout I ever caught was taken from Loon Pond in the Deer Park on the Salmonier Line. The largest I have ever seen out of the water came from Back River. And the largest I have ever seen either in or out of the water was in a pond that drains into Chance Cove Brook, ninety miles south of St. John's on the Southern Shore.

17. South-Coast Fortress

Placentia, the old French capital of Newfoundland, lies in a classically beautiful setting on the east shore of Placentia Bay. Built on a tiny sea-level peninsula, it faces a crescent-shaped inlet and is flanked by two deep fjords that run inland for six miles. Behind it, and on either hand, rise the steep, wooded hills, crowned with the ruins of old forts that made it such a formidable stronghold three hundred years ago when it was the principal guardian of the sea route from Europe to the Great Lakes.

If you take the most direct route, by the Trans-Canada Highway and the Argentia cutoff, Placentia is an hour and a half by road from St. John's. The alternate, offering an interesting return trip by way of Routes 8, 6, and 3, takes about two-and-a-half hours.

The origin of the French colonies in Newfoundland, like the English, is lost among the sketchy records of the sixteenth century. The first church in the island – probably the first in Canada – was built at Placentia by the Portuguese early in the sixteenth century, rebuilt by the French in the seventeenth, and by the English in the eighteenth. A Basque priest was stationed in Newfoundland, probably at Placentia, in 1549. The town was then the centre of a Basque fishery employing 6,000 men. They continued to fish there under the French until they were expelled for insurrection during the colonial wars.

Placentia had been a major fishing station from around 1500. It became an official French colony and Newfoundland's strongest fortified town in 1662 under the governorship of DuMont, who landed troops, colonists, and eighteen guns for shore batteries. It was reinforced with more colonists, troops, and guns in 1663, when Gargot was named permanent governor. British naval reports of that period give a summer population of 15,000, mostly Basque and French fishermen who assembled there for the allotment of fishing stations by the governor.

The French brought real civilization to Newfoundland for the first time. Before that it had been under the haphazard rule of pirates and fishing admirals. Even before they occupied the town in force, as early as 1650, they had rebuilt the church. A school and a hospital quickly followed, and the Franciscan Order was established there by the Bishop of Quebec.

The French cleared land for farming, brought in such tradesmen as stone-masons and iron-workers, and offered generous subsidies to settlers, regardless of their nationality. As a result, most of the Irish and many of the English in Newfoundland moved to Placentia and accepted French citizenship.

They created a shipbuilding industry that continued for almost three centuries, for Placentia, besides all its other advantages, had forests of virgin timber at its back door, and access to them by water.

Under Frontenac the town was strongly fortified, with a great military establishment known as Fort Louis at sea-level, and redoubts on the surrounding hills. I visited the strongest of these, on Castle Hill, while archaeologists were excavating it in 1965. It had walls faced with cut stone eight feet thick on the outside and two feet thick on the inside, with earthen fill between. No ships then afloat had enough firepower to reduce such a fortress.

The colony at Placentia was an immediate success, and gave birth to many smaller colonies along Newfoundland's south coast. As least twelve of them were still in existence, some engaged in agriculture as well as the fishery, when Newfoundland passed under English rule fifty years later.

When William of Orange came to the throne of England he promptly denounced the treaty with France and declared war. One of the specific aims set forth in the declaration of war was the recapture of Newfoundland, then mainly in French hands.

Though the town of Placentia was strongly garrisoned, it took no part in the fighting for the first four years of the war, when action in Newfoundland was confined to raids and counter-raids by privateers. One Basque privateer sailing out of Placentia, John Svigaricipi, became a great French naval hero, capturing hundreds of merchant vessels and warships from the English. Among his prizes was the 100-gun English ship of the line,

Princess, for whose capture he was decorated by the King of France. But he was killed, apparently in the attempt to capture Ferryland by sea in 1694, and was buried at Placentia, where parts of a monument erected to his memory are still preserved along with other Basque headstones in the old Anglican church.

That same year the French completed their fortifications and in 1696 they launched their campaign to evict the English from Newfoundland. An abortive naval action against Ferryland and St. John's failed to capture either, but was followed, in November, by the victorious march of Pierre LeMoyne d'Iberville with his mixed force of French and Abenaki soldiers, overland from the French to the English capital. D'Iberville not only captured Ferryland and St. John's, but burnt every English settlement in Newfoundland with the sole exception of Bonavista. Two small islands in Conception Bay resisted capture, but the home settlements of the fishermen who took refuge there were destroyed. The Irish servants of the English planters were accepted as French colonists, and some of them enlisted in the French army, but the English settlers, except for those who hid out in the woods, were stripped of all their possessions and sent back to England penniless.

The following year the English sent 1,500 troops to recapture Newfoundland, but before they went into action the fighting was temporarily halted by the Treaty of Ryswick. Peace lasted only five years. Then followed a series of raids and counter-raids during which all the English settlements, and most of the French, were destroyed. Placentia was the only town in Newfoundland that escaped being put to the torch. When the war ended with the Treaty of Utrecht in 1713, Placentia was handed over, intact, to the English. The French were given their choice of moving out or accepting English citizenship. About seventy or eighty of them remained. The others moved to St. Pierre, back to France, or, in the case of those who felt themselves finally committed to the New World as colonists, to the small French settlements strung out along Newfoundland's south coast from Placentia Bay to Port-aux-Basques.

A Newfoundland fishing master, Captain Taverner, was commissioned by the English to police the south coast, and for a number of years he made voyages westward to Port-aux-Basques, administering the oath of allegiance to French settlers, and surveying and recording their fishing berths. His reports, preserved in the public records, leave room for doubt concerning his truthfulness, and tend to confirm the charge made by some of his contemporaries that he accepted bribes from the French in lieu of a change of citizenship.

Placentia remained in English hands ever afterwards. The old French forts were rebuilt, crudely but effectively, and a new one, Fort Frederick, was erected to strengthen the defences. The English stonework that can be seen in the ruins today was amateurish and clumsy compared to the sophisticated masonry of the artisans sent out under Louis XIV. But it served its purpose. Placentia was held against the French in 1762, during a later round of the colonial wars, even though the English capital of St. John's was lost for the third time to a French expeditionary force. English sovereignty in Newfoundland was finally confirmed by the Treaty of Paris in 1763, and, though the wars following the French Revolution brought brisk fighting to the island once more, Placentia itself was left in peace. The last shots between French and English in Newfoundland were exchanged in 1796. Placentia then became a peaceful and prosperous fishing settlement, its remaining French population gradually absorbed by English and Irish immigrants. Its shipbuilding industry flourished, reached a peak in the nineteenth century, when some of the island's most famous shipbuilders worked there, and then fell into decay as the demand for wooden ships declined. By the time of the Second World War shipbuilding at Placentia had all but ceased.

Then, on the eve of America's entry into the global conflict, Winston Churchill and Franklin Roosevelt reached an agreement giving the Americans a 99-year lease on any number of military bases that they might choose to build in Newfoundland. One of the sites that they selected was Argentia, a flat peninsula jutting into the bay just outside Placentia harbour. It became a major naval and air station, and is the only American base in the island of Newfoundland still in operation.

With the building of the Argentia base, the character of Placentia began to change rapidly. Boys who had run barefoot through its grassy streets put on steel safety boots and went to work on dozers and diesel shovels. Men who had handled nets and lines all their lives quit fishing to learn the construction and maintenance trades. Even farmers became sign-painters. The town that had been in turn a military fortress and a fishing community now became a dormitory for base workers, a suburb to a much greater fortress than Placentia had ever been.

On a warship anchored in the bay in 1941 Churchill and Roosevelt held the meeting at which they issued the Atlantic Charter, one of the major propaganda documents of the war, guaranteeing the Four Freedoms to all the peoples of the earth, once the Anglo-American victory over the Axis Powers was complete. During the Battle of the Atlantic Argentia was mainly a base for anti-submarine patrol. Later, during the Cold War, it was a base for the mid-Atlantic radar patrol conducted by heavily modified Super-Constellation aircraft. Today it remains in operation, a shadow of its former self, a base with little or no strategic significance.

In 1963 Placentia held a massive celebration of the 300th anniversary of the founding of the French colony. In 1965 the Historic Sites Branch of the Canadian government began to reconstruct Placentia's military history by excavating the old forts.

Digging into the ruins of Castle Hill, which rises, brooding, above The Gut, where the tides sweep river-like in and out of the twin fjords, they unearthed truckloads of artefacts – more than 3,000 rounds of grape-shot, numerous ceramic pieces, and ironware of seventeenth-century French manufacture. They also restored and reconstructed some of the stonework – enough to show the shape of the ancient artistry with which this fort was built in the days when New France was a power almost unchallenged in the lands beyond the Western Ocean.

The alternate return route (8, 6, and 3) touches in turn the shores of Placentia, St. Mary's, and Conception bays. It begins at Southeast Arm, runs up through pastoral countryside to Southeast River, and continues to St. Mary's Bay at Colinet. Nineteen miles from the junction in the town of Placentia you come to Cataracts Provincial Park, where two small brooks, both branches of North Harbour River, meet in a remarkable rock gorge with spectacular waterfalls. The Gorge is spanned by a highway bridge, and circled by trails, duckwalks, and flights of wooden steps for the convenience of visitors. Those so inclined can climb down to the bottom of the gorge and get themselves soaked with spray. Other parts of the small park include woodland and bogland with a good sample of the local flora, including a dozen species of wild orchids.

Southward from Placentia, Route 8 runs along the Cape Shore for twenty-nine miles to St. Bride's, then twelve miles across the peninsula to Branch in St. Mary's Bay, with side roads to Cape St. Mary's and Point Lance. A road now being built will connect Branch through North Harbour with Route 6, forming a loop drive around the south-western arm of the Avalon Peninsula, the fourth major loop in this part of Newfoundland, completing the peninsula's road system, which now includes approximately a thousand miles of highways.

Except for Branch, near the cape, and North Harbour, at the extreme northern end, the western shore of St. Mary's Bay is completely unoccupied – the longest stretch of unoccupied coast in the entire island. Perhaps for that reason it is an exceptionally good area for fishing and for small-game hunting. Most of the fishing- and hunting-grounds are reached by boat either from Branch or from one of the small harbours across the bay.

The shore on the Placentia side presents a complete contrast. It has an almost continuous chain of settlements – ten between Point Verde in the north and Point Lance in the south – all of them small, and all settled by people of West Country Irish descent.

There are many beautiful beaches along this shore, but no good harbours. Much of the country is grassland, given over to scrub cattle, a few goats, and a native race of hardy sheep.

The people here have the beautiful, lilting accents of Galway and County Clare. They are great talkers and spinners of yarns, often heavily spiced with the supernatural. Visitors from Ireland, tramping over the peat bogs and grasslands of this region, or sharing a glass of grog and swopping stories by a kitchen fire, are invariably reminded of home. You can even watch the sun go down in the infinite sea to the west, for the fifty-mile expanse of Placentia Bay reveals no hint of land on the other side.

18. The Bird Islands

The sea-bird sanctuary of Cape St. Mary's is forty miles by road from Placentia. It is the only bird sanctuary in Newfoundland that can be visited without a boat.

Few experiences in life can be more impressive than a visit to a large bird colony during the nesting season. The gannetry at Cape St. Mary's is such a colony. Besides the gannets, there are large colonies of other birds, notably murres and kittiwakes, that surround and invade the nesting-grounds of the Bird Island where the big black-white-and-yellow sea birds are top dogs.

The gannets are impressive because of their size, their colouring, and their social habits, the kittiwakes because of their courage, the murres because of their seemingly countless numbers and ability to withstand a fantastic degree of overcrowding. The whole complex community is impressive as an example of life in a state of furious ferment: primitive, savage, engaged in fierce struggle, and yet, withal, amazingly well organized. A visit to a colony of this sort is an experience that no one can ever forget.

Bird Island is not really an island at all, but a piece of the cliff at Cape St. Mary's split off at the top and still connected at the bottom, far below. It is said to be impossible to climb the rock without a rope or similar equipment, and it certainly looks as if it would be difficult, to say the least. Perched on the dome of this perpendicular rock, the birds are completely safe from four-footed predators, and in a position where visitors cannot actually walk among their nests, though you can approach within a few yards of them if you have nerve enough to perch on the edge of a perpendicular cliff.

Cape St. Mary's is practically unapproachable by sea. Before the road was built, supplies for the lighthouse were hoisted up the cliff on a winch-operated cable car, for there is no boat landing anywhere near that gives access to the flat tableland. It is flanked by Point Lance on one side and St. Bride's on the other. The area of the cape itself is exceedingly wild and barren, the cliffs breathtakingly steep and dangerous. A famous naturalist, working on bird colonies near the cape with proper climbing equipment, was killed when he fell from a cliff.

You can now drive to within about a quarter of a mile of the colony, the rest being an easy walk over moorland. One visitor who made the trip was a lady of eighty-four.

Gannets are not only among the most impressive of all birds, but are also comparatively rare. There are only six colonies in the New World, three of them in Newfoundland, at Cape St. Mary's, Funk Island, and Baccalieu. You can spend a long time watching a colony such as that at Cape St. Mary's, especially if you go in late June or early July when activity is at its peak and numerous things are going on at once. When I visited the colony in June, the birds were still laying and still building nests. They were squabbling over nesting material, including a square of fish net that they had picked up on some neighbouring beach, though most of their nesting material was seaweed. They were performing various greeting and bowing ceremonies, stealing pieces of each other's nests, gabbling away like a flock of geese, and constantly commuting between Bird Island and the sea.

The colony made a deep impression on three of the five senses, though the smell, even on the leeward side of the rock, was not nearly so bad as you might expect. No doubt it gets worse as the season advances and the collection of excrement, broken eggs, and rotting fish accumulates. So far as I could see when I visited it, there was one dead gannet on the top of the rock, and no evidence of broken eggs or attacks by predators. There is always some mortality, however, particularly among chicks, later in the summer. The birds do not have sense enough to remove the dead, but simply allow them to lie and rot *in situ*.

The murres, duck-sized black-and-white birds, looked tiny beside the gannets. They were certainly losing some of their eggs, for I picked up fresh shells along the cliff-top. The culprits, I judged, were ravens, a small flock of which wheeled back and forth through the cleft dividing Bird Island from the cliff face.

There were no gulls except for the kittiwakes, which nested

in very small groups on ledges so tiny that you would think them incapable of providing a roost for a pigeon. Sometimes there was only one bird on a splinter of rock, sometimes two, with their backs to the sea. Their position as cliff-hangers in spots too small even for the murres apparently protected them from the larger birds.

The murres were past counting. It is no use saying that I 'estimated' ten thousand in the water. I guessed that there might be that many, or twice that many, plus some thousands on the cliffs, and many others in the air. They nested on every suitable ledge from the top of Bird Island all the way down to the splash line. It was most instructive to watch the few murres that had invaded the gannet colony itself. They looked like midgets among the huge gannets, little black things perpetually in a pose of self-defence and defiance, veritable Israelis surrounded by Arabs. Each murre stood upright, its egg between its feet, bill pointed upward at the surrounding gannets, ready to sell its life dearly in defence of its square foot of territory. And even though there was keen competition for nesting space, the gannets apparently respected the belligerent little murres.

Among the thousands of murres there were a few razor-billed auks, 'tinkers' as Newfoundlanders call them, now quite rare in these waters.

Horned larks were nesting in small depressions in the turf all over the moorland above the cliffs. One was actually nesting in a hole that looked like an abandoned rat burrow, right on the edge of a sheer drop of some hundreds of feet. Why did the larks choose such places, so easily approached by man or other land animals, while the far more powerful gannets, murres, and kitti-wakes sought inaccessible ledges? The answer, undoubtedly, was that the larks were comparatively inconspicuous, coloured like the vegetation, while the black and white sea birds stood out boldly against the land.

The visitor to Cape St. Mary's should be as quiet and well-behaved as possible. A gannet colony is too rare a thing to allow it to be subjected to unnecessary disturbance. This one, so far, is open to the public. If it is respected, it may remain that way. If not, it may have to be closed off, like many other bird sanc-tuaries, and entrance forbidden to all except a few who go there under government permit.

You need a **permit** to land on most of the other bird islands around the Newfoundland coastline, though not to visit them by boat. The best-known colonies are at Funk Island, Witless Bay, and Baccalieu.

One of Newfoundland's specialties is petrels. They are rarely found in-shore, though they sometimes come in on a storm, and remain to fly over the land for a day or so. They are familiar to all seamen and fishermen, who call them 'Mother Carey's chickens'. These beautiful little birds fly like butterflies, bobbing and dipping and turning in the air. They always remind me of swallows, though they are a bit larger and their flight is more erratic.

Petrels are perhaps the least wild of all wild birds. They will alight quite readily on your outstretched hand, or on your head, and will allow you to pick them up from the ground or from the deck of a boat without a protest.

Some scores of thousands of petrels nest on small islands around Newfoundland. There are colonies of these and other sea birds at Witless Bay, twenty miles south of St. John's, where the sanctuary includes three islands, all close to shore. They may be visited by boat from Witless Bay, Mobile, or Tors Cove.

The Witless Bay Islands are world famous. Besides Leach's petrels, they have dovekies, black guillemots, puffins, razor-billed auks, common murres, thick-billed murres, common terns, arctic terns, kittiwakes, herring gulls, and greater black-backed gulls. Most, though not all of these birds nest there.

Even more remarkable, in some respects, is Funk Island, with millions of nesting sea birds in its crowded and turbulent colony of gannets and murres. One of the most impressive bird islands in the world, it lies thirty-nine miles north-east of New-foundland in a stormy area, and is completely harbourless; you have to land, if at all, by jumping from a boat to the rock. The boat must either stand by to take you off again, or return for you when the weather is 'civil'. For these reasons, Funk Island is likely to remain the privilege of very special visitors.

Baccalieu is a magnificent island, high and craggy, more than three and a half miles long, at the northern entrance to Concep-tion Bay. It is best visited by small boat from either Bay de Verde or Grates Cove, two fishing settlements on Baccalieu Tickle, 110 miles from St. John's. The island is two miles off-shore, and has a good landing.

Baccalieu has enormous bird colonies – gannets, gulls, kitti-wakes, both species of terns, both species of murres, guillemots, puffins, and razor-billed auks. There are about 30,000 adult kittiwakes, and, in late summer, perhaps an equal number of fledglings. Murres are so plentiful there that the fishermen call them 'Baccalieu birds', after the island. Leach's petrels nest in burrows in the turf, entering and leaving only at night. The population is fantastically high, the breeding colonies there and at Witless Bay totalling several million birds. Puffins, which also nest in burrows, are much less common than the petrels, but there are some thousands of them at Baccalieu.

The puffins are handsome and amusing birds with large, parrot-like beaks banded in bright red and yellow. Like the murres, they are tame and easy to approach during the nesting season, and make good subjects for photographers as they sit in the sun on the rocks.

Baccalieu is open to the public, and no permit is required to land there. Visitors to Funk Island or Witless Bay Islands must have permits if they wish to leave their boats. Applications for such permits should be made to the Minister of Mines, Agriculture, and Resources at St. John's.

19. The Marine Drive

There is a highway that Newfoundlanders call 'The Road Around the Bay'. Its name comes from a time when cars were a novelty, roads were few, and the trip around Conception Bay from St. John's to Carbonear was an all-day adventure.

There is a highway called 'The Marine Drive', which was built especially for the scenery along the Atlantic shore north of St. John's. It runs out to Cape St. Francis, connects with other shore roads, and joins the Road Around the Bay at Topsail. From there the road continues past Cape Baccalieu, doubles southward along the Trinity Bay shore, and meets the Trans-Canada Highway at the Whitbourne Crossing, fifty miles from St. John's, forming a complete loop of 280 miles.

Numerous short-cuts permit the motorist to choose almost any part of this loop. It is possible, for instance, to omit Cape St. Francis and about half the Bay de Verde Peninsula. If this is done, the amount of gravel road is reduced to thirty-two miles. Of the total loop of 280, a distance of ninety miles remained unpaved at the end of 1967.

Just north of St. John's on the Marine Drive (Route 22) you come to Logy Bay, a bold, cliff-ringed inlet with a modern marine laboratory in the shape of an enormous sea anemone perched on its rocks. A branch of Memorial University at St. John's, the marine lab is devoted to basic research into the life of the sea. It attracts leading scientists from various parts of the world, and makes an important contribution to man's knowledge of the oceans. It is not open to the public.

A sideroad near Logy Bay climbs up to the radar station at Red Cliff, an abandoned relic of the Cold War that sits over a spectacular sheer drop to the surf of the open Atlantic.

141

Beyond Red Cliff the road drops down through farmland to the little villages of Outer Cove and Middle Cove, and to the brooding cliffs and beaches that give the Marine Drive its special character. This portion of the route follows an old bridle path that was used in the eighteenth century and improved to carriage-road standards in the early years of the nineteenth.

Beyond Middle Cove the route number changes from 22 to 18 before joining the Torbay Road from St. John's, climbing a ridge, and dropping down a long, gentle slope to the large fishing village of Torbay.

It was here that Colonel William Amherst landed troops from Halifax and Louisbourg at dawn on September 13, 1762, to retake St. John's from the French for the last time. His force consisted of elements from three regiments – Highlanders, Scots, and German mercenaries.

They were opposed by French skirmishers as they landed. Three of Amherst's men were wounded, and three Frenchmen taken prisoner in the woods above Torbay. They marched six miles to Quidi Vidi, east of St. John's, and fought a short battle for possession of the village just before dark. Amherst then opened Quidi Vidi Gut, which the French had blocked with sunken shallops, and used it to land artillery and supplies. His troops remained at Quidi Vidi on the fourteenth, and launched their attack on Cuckold Head, above the Gut, before dawn on the fifteenth.

They took the hill by surprise, stealing past the sentries and gaining the summit before the French discovered them. They lost only five killed and nineteen wounded in this crucial battle, which placed them on a parity with the French, who still held Signal Hill, closer to St. John's.

That night the French garrison abandoned Signal Hill without a fight, and the French fleet sailed out of St. John's, being allowed to escape unchallenged through some incredible piece of stupidity on the part of the strong English naval force stationed outside. On the sixteenth the English forces occupied Signal Hill without opposition.

The French still held one fort in St. John's on the seventeenth, and exchanged some artillery fire with the English batteries on the hills. Amherst then sent a letter to the French commander, the Comte d'Haussonville, threatening to massacre every man in the French garrison unless the fort was surrendered to him intact. The French at first rejected this ultimatum, but later agreed to terms – that the officers should keep their arms and supplies, and that all the troops should be embarked for France. Seven hundred and nine Frenchmen surrendered. The English had lost a total of sixteen killed and thirty-eight wounded in this most economical campaign of the Seven Years' War.

Signal Hill, where the battle ended, is now a national historic park, with the Queen's Battery and a fine stone powder magazine completely restored. Other relics of various wars, including the Second World War, remain in ruins.

Inside the park there is also a monument to the Italian inventor Guglielmo Marconi, who, on December 11, 1901, flew a kite from this spot carrying an aerial attached to a radio receiver, and picked up the first wireless signal ever transmitted across an ocean, thus dramatically launching the era of international radio, which he continued to dominate for the next thirty years.

The village of Flat Rock, about four miles beyond Torbay, has an elaborate shrine, built in the rocks of a cliff beside the church by a modern parish priest. Open-air masses and other services are held there, and the shrine attracts large numbers of visitors. The village is remarkable for its rock formations, which shelve smoothly out into the sea like pavement.

This shore, both north and south of Flat Rock, is of interest to rock collectors. From some of the cliffs you can collect perfect crystals of iron pyrites in large·squares, like cubes of pure gold embedded in stone.

Beyond Flat Rock is the gloomy little inlet of Shoe Cove, with its satellite tracking station, and the large fishing community of Pouch Cove, where impressive surf piles up along the shore, and the fishing boats are winched out of the water on skids up a long, steep slipway. Pouch Cove also has picture-postcard fishing stages and flakes on stilts above the surf, once a common sight in Newfoundland, but now becoming a rarity.

From Pouch Cove a three-mile dirt road runs to the lighthouse at Cape St. Francis. The cape is a black, brooding, surf-spattered headland with off-shore shoals and white-ringed islands – an impressive place to visit on a fine day after a north-east gale. A deep-water passage inside the shoals and islands is often used by ships familiar with the coast. They then round the cape right under the perpendicular cliff, within hailing distance of the lighthouse perched high above them.

First settlement on the Conception Bay side of the cape is Bauline, a small and prosperous fishing community sitting in a little bowl between hills that rise almost to a thousand feet on both sides. The road tops a crest and makes a breath-taking plunge into Bauline's stage-set of a harbour. There is no harbour, really, just a stormy boat landing with a slipway behind a short piece of concrete breakwater more than half of which has already been demolished by storms.

Bauline is a wild, surf-battered cove, with a hardy and resourceful breed of men. Sometimes most of the male population must turn out to help a boat make a difficult landing.

One of the most successful of the fishermen, Roland LeGrow, who sold out a bus line some years ago to invest his money in cod traps and to return to the occupation of his forefathers, told me:

'There have been times, coming in to that slipway, when I wouldn't have given two cents for my life. . . . And yet, I love the sea, you know. I wouldn't exchange this life for any other. Still, each man has to make his own decision. I've made mine. A lot of the youngsters have gone away from here, of course, to jobs in the city or in Labrador. Some of them come back to fish for a few weeks in the spring – just for lobsters and salmon, you know. I'm glad my own sons grew up here. It's a place where we all work together. A boy in Bauline is everybody's child – but you can't expect them to understand what they're leaving, I suppose.'

We were 'chewing the fat' in Mr. LeGrow's net loft, where nets and traps were knitted and repaired amid the strong, heady perfumes of paint and tar and oakum. Net lofts are great places to meet and talk with fishermen. There is a long tradition of sitting in net lofts on winter days, while a fire burns in the store below, giving its heat to the loft, and swapping yarns like ladies at a sewing bee while you work at the twine.

On a hill above Bauline stands the huge black barking kettle. There are still a few copper ones in Newfoundland. This one is made of iron, and looks like something out of a witches' scene in *Macbeth*. In spring they fill it with a tarry mixture (it used to be bark from the forests), light a fire underneath, and, while the aromatic smoke and steam drift down over the village, whole trap crews cure their nets, steeping them section by section in the hot liquid to ward off attacks by airborne fungi, bacteria, and marine organisms.

Portugal Cove, twelve miles south of Bauline, is the largest fishing settlement on the south shore of Conception Bay, and the terminal for the Bell Island ferry. One of the oldest English settlements on the shore, it was attacked and burned by the French on December 2, 1696.

Here in 1873 a twelve-year-old boy named Thomas Picco produced the first acceptable evidence that the giant squid, or kraken, was a reality and not a fable in a class with the sea serpent, as scientists had previously insisted.

On October 26 he was at the tiller of a small boat with two men named Theophilus Picco and Daniel Squires, when they saw what they thought was part of a wreck, approached it, and prodded it with an oar. The kraken, apparently asleep on the surface, woke up, lifted its enormous beak out of the water, and wrapped two of its sucker-clad arms around the boat, which immediately began to sink.

The boy dropped the tiller, grabbed a small axe, and chopped at the arms until he had cut them through. The monstrous squid then disappeared in a sea of black 'ink', which these creatures use for defence, and no doubt grew new arms to replace the ones it had lost. The men took the two arms ashore and fed the larger one to their dogs, but the Reverend Moses Harvey of St. John's, an amateur scientist and historian, secured nineteen feet of the smaller arm and an account of the incident from the boy. It was the first partial specimen of a kraken ever reported to science, and, as it happened, an exceptionally large one. Harvey later collected a smaller, but complete, specimen of the giant squid.

Newfoundland seems to be the principal area of this monster's range, though there are old reports of it (once regarded as fables) from many other parts of the world. A number of complete specimens have been recovered recently from Newfoundland waters. Dr. Frederick Aldrich of the marine laboratory at Logy Bay is the world authority on this species.

Seven miles up the bay from Portugal Cove lies the tiny island known as Little Belle Isle. It is now covered with grass and is sometimes used for sheep pasture, but it used to be covered with brush and stunted trees until it was burned during a German attack in the Second World War.

Here an English planter named John Earle, who with his family was the only inhabitant of Little Belle Isle, held out single-handed against the French in 1696. Earle reasoned correctly that after the capture of St. John's on December 1 and 2 the French would rest for a week or two, giving him time to fortify his island.

There is only one landing-spot on Little Belle Isle – a beach with a small pond on the southern side. Otherwise, it is surrounded by cliffs. Earle raised earthen embankments above the beach, and made wooden cut-outs to resemble men crouching behind them. He had a collection of muskets, which he loaded and propped on the embankments beside his wooden soldiers, and a single small cannon (probably salvaged from a ship), which he placed in position to command the beach.

It was more than a month and a half before the French made a move. On January 19, 1697, they put out from Portugal Cove in longboats. John Earle waited until the first boat was well within range and then sank it with a single expert shot from his cannon. The second boat hastily retreated. He then ran from one wooden soldier to another, firing off his muskets as rapidly as possible. The French, apparently believing that the island was strongly defended by a determined party of fishermen, left it alone, and proceeded along the shore of the bay on foot to Harbour Main. Earle's courage and ingenuity saved his plantation, the only one in Conception Bay that was not put to the torch in the winter of 1696-7.

As you drive from Portugal Cove to St. Phillips, and on to Topsail, the entire bay seems to be dominated by the frowning bulk of Bell Island – the 'Iron Isle' as Newfoundlanders called it for generations. This cliff-encircled chunk of rock, six miles long and two miles wide, had for half a century the biggest iron mine in the British Commonwealth, and for a while in the world. There are believed to be three billion tons of ore in the beds under Conception Bay. Seven miles of undersea tunnels were built to mine it. At its peak the population of the island reached 13,000 and its production 3,000,000 tons a year.

Iron was discovered there accidentally in the nineteenth century, when a prospector examined heavy rocks that were being used as ballast by fishermen. They began shipping ore in 1895. It was mined at first with picks, shovels, and wheelbarrows, then with power drills and hand cars in open pits, and finally in great underground drifts with automatic machinery.

At the time of the Second World War it was important enough to be attacked twice by German submarines. They sank two ore ships of 10,000 tons each on September 5, 1942. It was during this attack that Little Belle Isle was burnt. They returned on the night of November 2, sank two more ships, and blew up the pier, striking it dead centre and hurling pieces of it to the top of the Island, 200 feet above. The loaded ore boats sank like stones with great loss of life. Canadian shore batteries replied to the attack, but their shooting was so bad that the shells landed in cabbage and potato gardens near St. Phillips, three or four miles from their targets. There is an apocryphal story that the U-boat commander later sent a postcard to a girl on Bell Island whom he had taken to a dance the night before the attack.

After the war the mining operation was mechanized, using highly sophisticated machinery, including the longest slope conveyor in the world. Then, without warning, in June 1965, the mines closed. Eighty million tons had been extracted. But Bell Island ore is not adaptable to modern smelters, and it seems unlikely that the enormous ore deposit under the bay will ever be worked again. The island, still with 7,000 people, is now mainly a welfare colony. But, when spring tides flood parts of the old workings, the bay even yet is stained red with iron rust for miles around.

Beyond the southern headland of Portugal Cove is the small inlet of Beachy Cove, a great beauty spot and a favourite place for hardy swimmers. In addition to a small beach set between cliffs, and a fine waterfall, Beachy Cove has a handsome rock formation known as The Lion's Head, bearing a striking likeness to a heraldic lion rampant. Early in this century Beachy Cove became a favourite summer resort for St. Johnsmen. Recently, as roads were improved and kept open all year, city people began moving there permanently. My own house is on Witch Hazel Ridge, above Beachy Cove.

St. Phillips, a fishing and farming settlement three miles beyond Beachy Cove, has a safe small-boat haven in a pond behind a high beach, with a dredged channel leading to the sea. Since the cliff-edged shore of Conception Bay South has not a single natural harbour anywhere along its entire length, St. Phillips is popular with pleasure-boat owners as well as fishermen.

Topsail, Chamberlains, and Manuels, three small towns forming a continuous built-up area along the shore, are all essentially suburbs of St. John's, within ten to fifteen miles of the capital by Route 3. Topsail was a summer resort for wealthy St. Johnsmen by the first half of the nineteenth century. With its neighbouring towns, it has continued in this role ever since. Manuels has a barachois with access to the sea for very small boats only, and only at high tide. There is good swimming, camping, and sea-trout fishing at Manuels.

There is also a Cambrian fossil-bed lying on both sides of Manuels River at the point where it empties into the barachois. Millions of trilobite fossils are buried there, in rock so soft that you can literally dig them out with your fingers, though a small rock pick or chisel is a help. They are free for the taking.

The Manuels trilobites are mostly small, bug-like animals, when found intact in the rocks, but you can recover pieces of much larger ones that ran to a foot or more in length before they were broken. I dug out a tail section of a trilobite there in 1967. A palaeontologist later sketched out a reconstruction of the complete animal. It was fourteen inches long, and looked like an enormous wood-louse with the head of a cockroach. The Manuels trilobites lived on the muddy floor of a shallow sea approximately 520,000,000 years ago.

You can also dig fossils at Bell Island, Brigus, and Branch. The bed at Branch yields very large specimens in almost perfect condition, enabling students to study such details as eye structure and angle of vision in animals that have been extinct for half a billion years.

A mile beyond Manuels River lie the large salt-water lakes of Long Pond, recently converted into a very safe double harbour by dredging. The inner harbour, headquarters of the Royal Newfoundland Yacht Club, has been connected by a seven-foot dredged channel to an outer harbour with a deep-water pier. Talc, a soft green stone that you can carve with a knife, is mined in the hills near here and shipped from Long Pond to be ground into powder for industrial lubricant.

The bold, Gibraltar-shaped island three miles offshore from Long Pond is Kelly's, once a pirate careenage, now a picnic spot for boat-owners. Kelly's has a handsome little beach, a pond in which you can swim, a park-like mixture of field and forest, and stories of buried treasure. Though many a hole has been dug there, it is by no means certain that anyone ever recovered anything, though four men from St. John's did dig up a chest of gold and other valuables at near-by Little Belle Isle in 1860.

But at Kelligrews, just west of Long Pond, the fishermen tell of a pair of American treasure-hunters who arrived there a few years ago, hired a boat from a fisherman, took several cases of equipment to Kelly's Island, camped there for a week, then returned the boat, paid off its owner, and shipped everything out by train. Everyone thought that this was just another unsuccessful treasure-hunt. But when the fisherman hauled up his boat for the winter and drained out the bilges, he found, according to the story, two gold coins encrusted with dirt. They dated from the sixteenth century.

Much better documented stories of treasure come from other parts of Conception Bay, especially from Cupids and Baccalieu.

Most of the twelve miles from Long Pond to Holyrood is farming country. There are beaches, but no harbours. Holyrood has a small harbour at the mouth of a brook, and a junior sailing club with instructors and racing snipes. Its two deep arms, both open to the sea, are sheltered enough to provide dockage for a fish plant and an oil refinery. The Golden Eagle refinery imports crude oil from the Caribbean, and produces a complete range of petroleum products which it sells throughout Newfoundland and parts of eastern Canada.

A rubber factory that started at Holyrood in 1952 was less fortunate. After a few years of producing leaky rubber boots on worn-out machinery imported from Europe, it closed down, made a bonfire out of its surplus rubber goods, and the Newfoundland government picked up the bill for the loss. The former rubber plant, with its saw-toothed glass roof right beside the road in Holyrood, is used today as a shed.

This was one example of a factory brought to Newfoundland by the government during the 'industrial development' period of the early 1950s. Ten other factories of various sorts were built in Conception Bay. Hardwood and wallboard, boot and shoe, and knitwear plants are still operating. Besides the rubber plant, those that failed include machinery, battery, leather goods, and chocolate plants, two textile mills, a glove factory, and a tannery. Since the plants had been financed almost exclusively by the government, the public loss was great. Twelve million dollars had to be written off on account of the Conception Bay plants, and an almost equal amount was lost on other industrial and mining schemes of the same period.

20. Traders and Seal-hunters

At Holyrood there is a complete change in the character of the Conception Bay shore. The harbourless cliff-faces of the south side of the bay are replaced by a continuous series of deep inlets, ten of them altogether between Holyrood and Carbonear, with excellent anchorage and good harbours. This was the mercantile and seafaring region of Conception Bay North, the home of the foreign-going fleets that made Newfoundland one of the world's great trading nations in the nineteenth century, with almost a thousand sail of ships plying in and out of her ports.

Colliers, Brigus, Cupids, Spaniard's Bay – the harbours succeed one another in an endless panorama of ever-changing maritime scenes with little white towns set between the hills and the landwash. Pastures and hayfields and vegetable gardens climb up the slopes toward the forests, but the houses face the sea, for fish and seals and foreign trade gave all these towns their birth.

Brigus, fifteen miles beyond Holyrood, is like a small west-country English port, with tree-shaded streets, picket fences, fine homes, and a waterfront formerly so crowded that one merchant blasted a roadway right through a huge rock to give him access to the only remaining spot where a wharf could be built.

The famous American artist Rockwell Kent lived and worked at Brigus between bouts of small-boat voyaging, and produced some of his finest pictures there. The local people looked on him with deep suspicion, and he retaliated by emphasizing his eccentricities. He was finally hounded out of Newfoundland in war-time as an undesirable alien and a suspected German spy. Nobody stopped to wonder, apparently, what a German spy could be doing in the quiet little village of Brigus. The Premier has since publicly apologized on behalf of all Newfoundlanders for the way Kent was treated – but he fared no better in his home country than he had in Newfoundland: he was treated as a Cold War prisoner, and was refused visas and travel permits on the grounds that he was a Russian sympathizer.

Captain Bob Bartlett, the arctic explorer, was born and reared at Brigus. He skippered one of his father's ships to the Labrador summer fishery while still a teen-ager, and went on to become one of the foremost ice navigators of all time. He began sailing with Robert Peary in 1898, and was captain of Peary's ships on all the latter's polar expeditions.

In 1908, on the S.S. *Roosevelt*, Bartlett actually cleared from Sydney, Nova Scotia, 'for the North Pole', the only time such a clearance was ever recorded. He sailed the *Roosevelt* to within 452 miles of the Pole, then accompanied Peary on his famous 'dash' over the ice by dog team to a point which he estimated to be 87 degrees and 48 minutes north latitude, the 'farthest north' then reached by man. On Peary's orders, Bartlett then returned to the ship, while Peary, with his Negro servant and four Eskimos, continued the journey on which he later claimed to have reached the North Pole.

In 1917 Bartlett sailed to Etah in north Greenland and rescued Donald MacMillan's Crocker Land Expedition (the one that proved the last of Peary's 'discoveries', Crocker Land, to be nothing but a figment of the imagination). Bartlett continued making arctic voyages into the 1930s, receiving a long list of honours from the United States and other governments, and from geographical societies around the world.

In an old home belonging to his sisters at Brigus one room is devoted to a Bob Bartlett museum, containing pictures, maps, citations, relics of his voyages, and his collection of medals and awards.

Cupids, a harbour just across a narrow neck of land from Brigus, was the site of the John Guy plantation of 1610. There is no tradition of pirate activity at Cupids, except for complaints by the early governors of the colony that pirates were constantly enticing their men away from their lawful occasions to join the crews of their ships. Perhaps some of the colonists returned, enriched by piracy, to their homes in Cupids. Anyway, however it got there, Mrs. LeGrow, a resident of the town, dug up from her garden in Cupids in 1810 a box of English and Spanish gold coins.

Guy's plantation was a mixed farming, fishing, and milling operation, and was probably the first organized attempt at commerical farming in Newfoundland, though there must have been at least some gardening by the fishermen, since Guy's manager, Mason, refers to the local people using carts to haul fish from the beaches for fertilizer on their ground. Guy's farmers had success with 'sommer and winter corne . . . wheate, rye, barlie, oats and pease'.

Only three or four miles from the farms cleared by Guy's colonists is the largest farm in modern Newfoundland – Russwood Ranch, owned by Premier J. R. Smallwood and members of his family. It has over 500 acres under cultivation, and some 5,000 acres of rough pasture. Pigs, mink, cattle, sheep, poultry, and pheasants have all been raised there on a more or less massive scale. The Premier himself lives on the ranch, and commutes to his office in St. John's by car.

Across the water from Cupids is the long, narrow finger of the Port de Grave Peninsula, one of the oldest and most successful fishing areas in Newfoundland. At Port de Grave the fishermen will tell you that their forefathers were living there long before Guy and his colonists arrived. The way they tell it, it sounds as though it happened only yesterday, instead of 360 years ago:

'Yes, b'y, he come sailin' in here jest after the ice went off the coast that spring – early in June, I 'low, though I can't tell ye the exact day. Three ships he had, an' a crew of around forty, countin' the women. Looking fer a place to start a colony, he were, but o' course all the best fishin' rooms along this shore was already bespoke. . . .

'But one o' the skippers here thought o' this little harbour jest around the pint there to the south – 'twarn't really suitable fer fishin' ye understand – an' he called one o' he's hands an' says, "B'y, go up the bay with these fellers an' show 'em that little harbour where the brook flows in from Long Pond," and so he went, and that's how Cupids got started.'

If you follow the local road along the Port de Grave Peninsula to its end, you will come to the fascinating little village of Hibbs's Hole.* Here the tiny harbour is protected by a sea-wall connecting a chain of rocky islets to form a snug haven just about

*Variously rendered as Hibb's Hole and Hibbs' Cove on maps and road signs, but 'Hibbs's Hole' is the original name, and is pronounced as three syllables.

the right size for an outdoor performance of *The Pirates of Penzance.*

Hibbs's Hole is a good place for fish, and the people there fish with might and main. If you drop in any time during late summer you will see them on the small wharves, heading and cleaning and splitting the fish as they come ashore from the boats. Barrels of rotting cod livers lie open to sun and air on either hand. They bubble and ferment, and the oil gradually separates from the livers, the solids mostly sinking to the bottom. The perfume of rancid oil and rotting fish that rises from the barrels is all but overpowering, and many a visitor, looking at this first stage in the manufacture of Vitamins A and D, has sworn off tonics for life. Here the women, as well as the men, work at the fish, cleaning, splitting, and salting as the wives of fishermen did in every Newfoundland outport for hundreds of years. Some of them even go out to the nets in the trap boats with their husbands, a thing very few Newfoundland women have ever done.

An American artist, George Noseworthy, and his wife adopted Hibbs's Hole in 1966 and got permission to use the old schoolhouse as a studio. Not long after, a fisherman dropped in and asked George, 'Would ye like to have an old cannon ball to stick on yer shelf?' It was the start of the Hibbs's Hole Fishermen's Museum, the only thing of its kind in Newfoundland. Owned by the fishermen, and furnished with hundreds of items that they dug out of their attics and net lofts, it has the finest collection of home-made gear, tools, and colonial artefacts ever put together in the island, and gives a far more complete picture of colonial life than does the Newfoundland Museum at St. John's.

Approximately ten miles from the Port de Grave crossing you enter the town of Harbour Grace, once the capital of Conception Bay, and Newfoundland's 'second city'.

Named for Havre de Grace in France, it was visited in 1520 by the founder of that great port, Jean Ango of Dieppe, the French admiral of the high seas under Francis I. Like Queen Elizabeth and Francis Drake at a later date, Francis I and Jean Ango had an arrangement by which the latter fitted out fleets at his own expense, sailed under royal protection, and shared the loot with the king. He brought a strong fleet to Newfoundland, sacked all the non-French ships and fishing premises in the eastern part of the island, then sailed to Brazil, up through the chain of the Antilles, collecting ransom as he went, and back to Newfoundland before sailing home to France laden with plunder. His raids continued for over twenty years. Besides the port of Havre de Grace, later called Le Havre, he built a great castle in Normandy which is still preserved.

Harbour Grace was dominated by a succession of pirates, including Easton and Mainwarring, until a branch of the Cupids colony was formed there some time after 1614. Robert Haymen, governor of the colony, there wrote the first book of English poetry ever produced in the New World, and a second book, addressed to the King of England, setting out principles for colonizing North America.

In 1630 the English rebuilt Easton's old fort, where the Roman Catholic Cathedral now stands, commanding the harbour entrance and the bar. But in 1696 it was attacked by the French and totally destroyed, its fourteen fishing plantations burnt. It was rebuilt, but destroyed by the French again in 1705. By 1778 the population had increased to 5,768, and by the mid nineteenth century to over 7,000.

It was then a mercantile, fishing, and sealing port.

Harbour Grace, with its sister ports of Carbonear, Brigus, and Bay Roberts, had built up a large fleet and a large trade by the middle of the century. In the 1850s more than 15,000 men in 400 ships sailed 'to the ice' each spring and brought home an average of more than half a million seals a year.

The seal hunt was a cruel, barbarous, risky trade, in which men lived like savages, wallowed in blood and filth, risked their lives constantly, and sacrificed their ships as a matter of course. More than a thousand Newfoundlanders died hunting seals – some 300 on foot or in small boats, and some 750 in ships. But a ship had less chance than a man, who could usually walk away on the ice and hope for rescue. No one ever tried to count the sailing ships that perished among the ice pans. But of the first fifty steamers that went to the hunt between 1863 and 1900, no less than forty-one were lost at sea.

The merchants, of course, made money out of it all, and even the sealers occasionally made money. On one voyage before the end of the last century they received $303 each, at a time when $300 must have seemed to a Newfoundland fisherman an almost incalculable fortune. And there were exceptions to the long story of disaster among the floes. Captain Henry Thomey sailed out of Harbour Grace to the seal hunt in the same square-rigged ship for thirty years in succession, and later commanded two other ships at the icefields, finally retiring without ever having lost a ship or a man.

As the steamers took over, the hunt in sailing vessels ended. But there was an expanding ship fishery along Labrador, similar to the fishery that had been carried on by English ships in Newfoundland for more than three hundred years. As Newfoundland had been England's colony, so Labrador was now Newfoundland's. The schooners went north in early summer, and returned in autumn to their Newfoundland ports with loads of heavy-salted fish. At the peak of this trade, more than five hundred ships sailed north each spring, while another fifty or sixty, mostly very large vessels, sailed to the banks off the south coast. Both these great fisheries lasted until Newfoundland joined Canada in 1949. During the 1950s they died. Today not a single ship sails to the banks, and not more than a dozen to Labrador. A fleet of deep-sea trawlers has taken their place.

The trading fleet vanished with the fishing ships. The tradition of wooden shipbuilding that we took over from the French in 1713, and that created the great mercantile firms that flourished in St. John's, Brigus, Harbour Grace, and Carbonear, was nearly useless in the age of steam. The sons of men who had built windjammers were confined to building trap skiffs and jack boats. It was not until the 1960s that Newfoundland began building her first steel ships, trying, in some measure, to regain the maritime greatness that she had known in the nineteenth century.

The population of Harbour Grace declined with its fleets and its trade. In 1880 it was still over 7,000. By 1900 it had dropped to 5,000, by 1940 to 2,000. The emigration to the paper-manufacturing towns, to St. John's, and above all to the United States, had taken on the aspect of a flight of refugees. The depression, and then the war, halted the movement. Confederation reversed it. Today, as part of a general population explosion, the Conception Bay towns are growing once more.

Harbour Grace was swept by fire in 1832 and again in 1858. There were violent riots in 1860, as Protestants and Catholics fought over the elections to the newly established responsible government. They fought again in 1883, when the Orange

Society insisted on parading through the Irish section of the town on the day after Christmas, and precipitated a gun battle in which four people were killed and a number of others wounded.

That same year, in a spectacular earth tremor that was heard and felt for many miles around, the craggy island just off the harbour-mouth split in two, leaving the lighthouse, with the lightkeeper and his family, perched on the edge of the abyss. After his night of terror he refused to return to the island, and the lighthouse was replaced with an automatic beacon.

Harbour Grace still has many relics of its mercantile past, of its shipbuilding and whaling days, of the great families that grew rich on its trade. Today it packs fish and manufactures footwear, and is a dormitory town for construction workers. You may still see some of the brutal little whaling ships, blunt and ugly, rusting at their moorings in the harbour, and, under the shadow of the cathedral, a hideous little stone dungeon of a jail, relic of the march of civilization in the nineteenth century.

The first airstrip built in Newfoundland was at Harbour Grace, and it became the departure point for many pioneering flights across the Atlantic. Most of those that did not start from Harbour Grace started from St. John's, though there was no airstrip at the capital and fliers had to use pasture land for airfields.

Hawker and Grieve made the first try at a non-stop flight across the ocean on May 18, 1919, in a twin-engined Sopwith. They came down in the Atlantic with engine trouble, 1,100 miles east of Newfoundland, ditching their plane beside a freighter which rescued them.

On the same day Raynham and Morgan started from St. John's, but crashed on take-off.

On June 14, 1919, Alcock and Brown made the first successful flight in a converted Vickers-Vimy bomber from St. John's to Clifden, Ireland. They had good luck and strong tail-winds which helped them complete the crossing in 16 hours and 12 minutes, a record that stood for twelve years.

Amelia Earhart, Kingsford Smith, and many other famous fliers made use of the Harbour Grace airstrip in pioneer Atlantic and round-the-world flights.

Newfoundland continued to be important in Atlantic flying up to and including the time of the Second World War, when the Atlantic Shuttle Service was established at Gander, with planes taking off in relays every two minutes at the height of the war. Air museums at Gander and Harbour Grace commemorate this pioneering work and tell the story of the development of the airplane as the principal means of international travel.

Carbonear, separated from Harbour Grace by Saddle Hill, has a somewhat less violent past and a more stable population than its neighbour. There are about 5,000 people there today, only a few hundred more than in the middle of the last century. Even in the worst years of the emigration, its population never fell below 3,300.

Carbonear Island, at the harbour-mouth, was fortified in 1679, and successfully beat off two French attacks in 1697 and 1705. But the town was burned each time, twenty-two plantations going up in flames in 1697. The French reported that Carbonear then had the best-built houses in Newfoundland, and that some of its merchants were worth more than a hundred thousand pounds sterling (three or four million dollars in today's funds).

It was garrisoned, and a fishermen's militia to assist in its defence was formed in 1745. Old guns from this period can still be seen on Harbour Rock Hill in the centre of the town. The regular troops did not do nearly so well as the fishermen who had fortified the island in the preceding century, however. Both town and island were captured by the French in 1762.

Carbonear produced a great breed of shipbuilders, sailors, and fishermen. Captain Hugh Horwood, my great-grandfather, sailing out of Carbonear to the seal hunt in 1869 in the brig *Isobel*, got caught and crushed in the ice off Cape St. Francis. As the ship sank, he and his crew got over the side with all their gear, and, with their sea bags on their backs, landed at Shoe Cove near the cape. They then walked twenty miles overland to St. John's, another twenty miles from St. John's to Long Pond, twelve miles across the ice of Conception Bay to Brigus, and finally twenty-five miles overland from Brigus to Carbonear, a total march of about eighty miles over snow and sea-ice, carrying all their gear and supplies with them. They all got home in good spirits and good health, though they had 'lost their voyage', as the saying went.

Michael Kearney, the most famous Newfoundland ship-builder, worked in Carbonear. His masterpiece, the brig *Thomas Ridley*, was launched there in 1852 at the dockyard owned by John Rorke and Sons. She was 106 feet long and 170 tons. My grandfather, Captain John Horwood, made his first foreign voyage in her at the age of eighteen in 1875. Kearney had another ship on the stocks for the Rorke firm when he died. She was finished and launched by Richard Horwood in 1862, and named the *Shamrock*. She was the last square-rigged vessel built in Carbonear.

The timber of Conception Bay was almost all used – much of it wasted – in the nineteenth century. As the tree-line crept back farther and farther from the settlements, and as real timber trees, which may have taken almost a century to grow, became scarcer, the shipbuilders moved elsewhere – to Bonavista Bay, Notre Dame Bay, and the heavily timbered inlets of the south coast. My grandfather built and launched a schooner – the *Lord Kitchener* – at Carbonear in the early years of the twentieth century, but by the time of the First World War shipbuilding at Harbour Grace and Carbonear was virtually finished.

Nevertheless, one of the principal industries of Carbonear today is a large woodworking factory, where the great-grandsons of the nineteenth-century shipbuilders turn imported timber into mouldings and doors and window sashes. Their brothers and cousins work all across Canada as carpenters, carrying on a tradition of woodworking skill that goes back in their families into the eighteenth century.

Beyond Carbonear, the Conception Bay shore changes its character once more. The deep inlets give place to little coves and broad sand beaches. When I was a boy learning to swim from the Carbonear rocks, we regarded the town, with its satellites of Freshwater and Victoria ('the village'), as the end of civilization. Beyond lay the North Shore, inhabited by folk whom we regarded with the tolerant amusement that Americans have for hillbillies. They were the Snopeses of Conception Bay, without the tradition of the old families, the planters, the shipbuilders, and the merchant seaman. And in the twentieth century, as you might expect, they have come into their own. They have succeeded in trade, business, and politics, if not in the arts and professions.

You can approach the North Shore through Crocker's Cove, Freshwater, Clowns Cove, and Blow-Me-Down. But the road to Blow-Me-Down is narrow, winding, cliff-hugging, and gravelled; you may well prefer to follow the pavement through the inland town of Victoria to Salmon Cove.

Salmon Cove is a beauty spot and a holiday resort. At Salmon Cove Sands there is swimming and sea-trout fishing. The sands form great dunes, a wide, flat beach, and underlie the surrounding meadows. They were not laid down by the sea, but are a deposit of inland sand brought to the shore by winds funnelling down the valley from the direction of Victoria.

The beach at Northern Bay, fifteen miles beyond Salmon Cove, is larger, and, in recent years, more popular. Here there is a provincial camping park near a long crescent of sand beach fully open to the surf from the north and east. Sea bathing here requires great hardihood, however, since the water is pure, undiluted Labrador Current, rarely reaching 50 degrees F. even on the hottest summer days. At the end of the beach there is a small, deep pool of fresh water where a brook falls over a ledge. A plunge into this pool, after a venture into the near-freezing surf, feels like a plunge into a hot bath. The little pool varies greatly with the vagaries of the sands, shifted from season to season by storms. It often has a school of salmon confined in such a small space that you can see them quite easily at close quarters while swimming under water.

Bay de Verde, near the tip of the peninsula, is a large fishing settlement in one of those crannies in the cliffs that must be approached by means of a breath-taking descent from the hills above. The artificial harbour was created by blasting down a hill of solid rock and dumping it into the sea to form a break-water. Even so, the violence of the storms that sweep around Cape Baccalieu plays havoc with harbour, wharves, and fishing boats. Bay de Verde is an old settlement, which had fourteen houses and ninety men when the French captured it in 1697.

From Baccalieu Island, just off Bay de Verde, comes a story of pirate treasure recovered from the sea by fishermen in the nineteenth century. According to the historian H. F. Shortis, the treasure consisted of two kegs filled with Spanish-American gold. It was dredged up from a small cove on the shore of Baccalieu by the use of grappling hooks. The fishermen who found the treasure divided it among themselves and tried to keep it quiet, but word leaked out, and the Newfoundland government sent a magistrate to claim the 'Queen's portion'. Only a small part of the reported treasure was ever found by the authorities, however. Some of the fishermen took their money and emigrated from Newfoundland, but one who lived out his life at Grates Cove left a leather shot bag filled with gold coins to his son.

Grates Cove is just north of Bay de Verde. It is one of those places where some of the trap crews have to hoist their fish out of the boats on cables running a hundred feet and more to the top of the cliff.

Grates Cove has a well-known rock with some old carvings on it on a cliff face well above high water. Some of those who formerly examined it, including a curator of the Newfoundland Museum, professed to be able to read the names, 'IO CABOTO', 'SANCIUS', and 'SAINMALIA' quite plainly. It was, of course, attributed to the first Cabot voyage, 'Io Caboto' being an Italian form of John Cabot, who had gone to England from Venice. For my own part, I am unable to read anything on the rock. It certainly had some kind of inscription at one time, but I doubt that anything can be deduced from it today.

At Old Perlican, eight miles south of Grates Cove, you are in Trinity Bay, and at the beginning of a chain of twenty-five settlements that march evenly along the shore from Grates Point to Dildo Arm. In general, they have a rustic atmosphere that contrasts sharply with the old mercantile towns across the peninsula in Conception Bay.

Old Perlican was a farming as well as a fishing settlement when d'Iberville captured it on January 3, 1697. He reported thirty head of cattle, flocks of sheep, and herds of pigs, and 130 men, besides women and children.

Heart's Content, about half way along the Trinity Bay shore, was fortified by the local people in 1697, but surrendered without resistance on January 8, when the French offered them quarter. D'Iberville then used the town as his base for operations in both Trinity and Conception bays until he left to return to Placentia in March.

Abbé Baudoin, the chaplain with the French army, recorded in his diary of the expedition the arrival at Heart's Content of an Irish youngster who had escaped from the English on Carbonear Island, swum across the tickle to Crocker's Cove, and then walked to Heart's Content to join the French forces. The Irish, said Baudoin, were treated by the English as slaves, and deserted to the French at every opportunity. This particular young man arrived at Heart's Content 'badly frostbitten', as might be expected of anyone who had swum across even a narrow strip of Newfoundland seawater in the winter and then walked the twelve miles across the Heart's Content barrens.

My grandmother made the same trip on foot — properly clothed and in midsummer – to see the world's largest ship, the *Great Eastern,* land the first successful Atlantic cable at Heart's Content on July 27, 1866. It joined a cable across Newfoundland to Cape Breton, providing the first telegraph link between the Old World and the New. A second link was completed through Heart's Content two months later, when the *Great Eastern* fished up and spliced a cable that had been broken and lost in mid ocean the year before. The two cables could transmit a total of about twelve to fifteen words a minute, and revolutionized international communication.

Heart's Content then became the major relay station of the Anglo-American Telegraph Company, with a staff of fifty operators and maintenance men. Cables at first cost $5 a word, and were largely confined to the financial transactions of big companies, but by the end of the century rates were down to twenty cents a word, and Heart's Content was handling 3,000 messages a day.

Toward the middle of the twentieth century, however, modern technology made such relay stations as Heart's Content completely unnecessary. Cable operations there were first curtailed, then abandoned, and now the town has become once again the quiet fishing village that it was before Cyrus Field, the pioneer of the Atlantic cable, and the *Great Eastern* arrived there over a hundred years ago.

The road from Heart's Content continues for another thirty miles to the head of Trinity Bay through a group of quiet and picturesque fishing villages. Just beyond the whaling and mink-farming settlements of Dildo and Blaketown, near the head of the bay, it connects with the Trans-Canada Highway. This is the Whitbourne Crossing, fifty miles from St. John's, and the end of the Conception-Trinity loop. It is one of the major intersections of the Newfoundland road system, with trunk highways running to St. Mary's, Placentia, and Trinity bays, as well as to the Atlantic shore and central Newfoundland.

21. The Miracle of the Caplin

All along the east coast of Newfoundland, summer begins with the Caplin Scull. At Outer Cove and Middle Cove, at Torbay and Beachy Cove, at Northern Bay and Spillers Cove, as June begins to mellow toward July men slip down to cliffs and beaches every day at dawn to inspect the landwash and the green waters heaving restlessly beyond. Then one morning word runs like wildfire through the villages, 'The caplin are in!'

An explosion of activity follows, as everyone makes for the sloping ridges of sand and gravel, men with cast nets, some also with horses and carts or beach sleds, boys with bar nets and dip nets, women with buckets and washing tubs, even people from the city with saucepans and colanders. They all go to reap the incredible harvest of the caplin, small silver fish that pour ashore in billions for a week, so plentiful that you can often catch them with shovels, or load a truck in half an hour with the help of a simple cast net.

The oceans off Newfoundland are one of the world's richest feeding grounds for fish. Here, where the Gulf Stream meets the Labrador Current, there is a terrific growth of animal and vegetable plankton. Feeding on these riches, thousands of millions of the most prolific food fish reach maturity every year — none more numerous than the seven-inch caplin (pronounced *cay*-plin), dark green and silver and iridescent, and shaped like slender torpedoes.

As the water warms, and sunlight filters down through the shallow sea, chemical changes in their bodies set off powerful instincts that drive the caplin relentlessly toward shore — toward fulfilment of their life cycle, toward death and renewal. For many will never reach the spawning beaches, and most of those that do will never return to sea. Only a few will ever again reach the indigo depths from which they now rise toward the shallow, sun-washed in-shore waters. In vast numbers they stream past the headlands, past Cape St. Francis and Cape Bonavista and Cape Baccalieu, into the bays, and on toward the sand and shingle beaches, compressed ever more and more into dense schools that darken the water, obscure the bottom, and can even slow a power boat that plunges through the living mass of small bodies.

This is the Caplin Scull, the annual miracle that renews the Newfoundland fisheries and makes them the most productive in the world.

For as the caplin crowd toward shore, everything else in the sea follows along behind: big sharks and small flatfish, mighty whales and foot-long squid in vast shoals — a regular nature parade. The whales come dancing over the water, tossing their heads and shaking their tails as if in play. The squid come pulsing through the shallows, moving backwards by jet propulsion. Both feed upon the caplin until they are glutted. Millions of little fish are scooped into the following jaws, some singly, some in bucketfuls. But they close their ranks, moving in tight formations, and continue without deviation toward shore.

Most important of the many creatures following the caplin are the enormous masses of cod. This fish, which was the basis of the Newfoundland economy for half a millennium, is drawn toward shore by the caplin, and so arrives at the trap berths where it can be taken by the millions in the traps and the cod seines. Landings of cod in Newfoundland run into the hundreds of millions of pounds annually. They are most plentiful while the Caplin Scull is on, though many remain throughout the summer, feeding on other small fish that come to shore in their turn. A few part-time fishermen who put briefly to sea when the caplin arrive are spoken of contemptuously by the full-timers as 'fishing only in the Caplin Scull'.

But when the caplin first arrive even the hardened cod-fisherman is likely to neglect his net loft in favour of a few hours on the beach, working amid the explosive violence that he finds there. The caplin blacken the water of the coves, often in a solid mass from headland to headland. They crowd the beaches, and, if the surf is at all heavy, are rolled up on the shore in great waves, stranded, and left to die by the retreating tide. These windrows of caplin are sometimes three feet deep and a quarter of a mile long.

The cast net is a circular mesh, seven or eight feet in diameter when fully spread, edged with leaden balls and fitted with drawstrings that close it like a purse. I have often landed more caplin than I could carry with a single throw of the net, and I once filled a jeep and a motorboat in less than an hour at Beachy Cove. Bar nets will catch even more. Taken out by a boat to enclose a section of the swarming caplin, the bar net is then drawn toward shore, or 'dried up' like a cod trap, until the fish can be dipped out of it with brailers. Ten tons or so are often taken in a single haul, and a large bar net can take a hundred tons or more.

Though most Newfoundlanders love to eat caplin, either fresh, corned, or smoked, only a very small part of the total catch goes directly for food. Some millions of the little fish are used to catch larger fish on baited trawl-lines, and are frozen by the public bait depots to be sold back to the fishermen in fall and winter when bait fish are scarce. Some are put into pits and covered with sod or topsoil to rot down to compost, and are mixed with rotted peat or straw for fertilizer. Thousands upon thousands of tons of caplin are spread directly on hayfields, dug into potato gardens, or buried around the roots of rhubarb and cabbage plants, where they quickly turn to raw fish manure. The Newfoundland soil, in most east-coast outports, is not very fertile, but such fertility as it can boast is largely due to fishermen spreading caplin upon it for the past three or four hundred years.

A beach party with a caplin fry – a thousand or so of the little fish, fresh out of the sea, cooked until they crackle, and washed down with generous draughts of Demerara rum – is a real Newfoundland event. In these circumstances, the odour of sizzling fish mixing with the wood smoke, and salt air to quicken the appetite, some people have been known to eat a hundred caplin at a sitting.

Many outport families put away a barrel of corned caplin – lightly salted and sun dried – for the winter, and some make an extra barrel for their dogs. These cured fish need only two or three minutes cooking in a frying pan or a hot oven. They are smoked not only in smoke houses or smokers improvised out of barrels or puncheons, but even in the tops of chimneys, with green spruce boughs in the stove to produce plenty of aromatic smoke. But the best smoking mixture includes blackberry bushes, peat, and wood chips.

The sex life of the caplin, which starts this whole chain of activity, is a weird and wonderful thing. To begin with, nature plays a mean trick by keeping the sexes segregated. Swarms of lonely bachelors packed densely together arrive at the spawning beaches and mill about in utter confusion, wondering where all the ladies are. At a few beaches, the females may never show up at all, to the great delight of the caplin catchers, who regard the larger, meatier male fish as the only one fit to grace a plate. Even at beaches where the girls put in a belated appearance, their consorts usually arrive several days ahead of them, and die by the millions without the solace of a female fin.

But when the sexes do manage to keep an assignation, there is frolic such as few fish enjoy. The caplin are quite unlike their larger cousins, those puritans of the animal kingdom who mate only by correspondence, without bodily contact. They not only enjoy physical courtship – they mate in *threes* rather than in pairs. The males have special little hooks on their fins designed for the sole purpose of seizing females. They have ridges along their sides for holding her firmly in place. Two of them capture a single female, and conduct her, struggling, to the beach. There, between high and low tide, in water an inch or so deep, they line her up between them, and she deposits her golden spawn while they emit clouds of fertilizing milt. When breeding is at its peak, the water becomes cloudy with milt and the foreshore spongy with spawn. The tiny eggs surround and encrust each pebble or grain of gravel, so that the whole beach becomes springy, like a carpet, as you walk along the shore.

The Caplin Scull is not just a phenomenon of nature, but also a period of the year, and even a special kind of weather – 'mausy' weather, with high humidity, frequent fogs or drizzles, easterly winds; Caplin Scull weather has so long been associated with full cod traps that some fishermen are willing to swear that easterly winds and light rains bring the fish to the land.

The furious activity of the Caplin Scull lasts from about the middle of June to the middle of July, for the caplin strike in at slightly different times on different beaches. For those few weeks all the fish plants work overtime, taking boatloads of fish from the in-shore fishermen, sometimes round, but usually 'gutted-head-on', fresh from the knives, and often cleaned on board the boats as they come in from the trap berths. You can always tell a boat on which they are cleaning the fish as they come to shore by the flock of gulls that follows it, rising and dipping, feasting on the offal that is thrown over the stern.

The fish are filleted, frozen, and packaged, some frozen into large blocks to be made into fish sticks. The fishermen themselves work an eighteen-hour day, but even working around the clock the plants are often unable to handle the glut. They then turn away whole boatloads of fish, which must be split and put into salt, or occasionally dumped back into the ocean, for the Caplin Scull is a season of great plenty, even, occasionally, of excess. It is not unusual for a small open trap skiff, powered by a single-cylinder gasoline engine, to land 30,000 pounds of fish daily while the caplin are in.

Those who have time for sport can find plenty of it on the caplin beaches or in the waters just off shore. Among the fish that follow the caplin right to the rocks are perch and sole, both of which are very easily taken with baited trout hooks or light spinning rods. Casting from shore between the shoals of caplin, an angler can easily land in an hour more sole than he can carry. The fishing is fast, and you never can tell what you may hook around the edges of a swarm of caplin.

Those who like to get down where they can meet the fish eye to eye have also learned that the Caplin Scull is a happy hunting-ground. Skin-divers and spear-fishermen, chasing the fish that chase the caplin, find them so plentiful that they soon become choosy, and take only the largest specimens. It is reasonably safe sport, too, for no dangerous fish are known to frequent Newfoundland waters regularly. The only large, common sharks are the enormous Greenland basking sharks, plankton eaters that never attack swimmers. The scuba-diver's greatest hazards are the chances that he will be beaned by the lead balls of a cast net or hooked by some small boy who is fishing for perch from a headland rock with a trout pole.

Then, one morning, there is silence along the beaches. Three weeks after the miracle of the Caplin Scull begins, it is over, though there may still be caplin for a week or so in other coves to the north or south. Without the myriads of tumbling fish that one had come to expect, the surf, breaking on the foreshore, looks strangely empty. The sand or gravel is coloured with the golden spawn. But that, too, will vanish within a few days. It will hatch into uncountable numbers of minute larval caplin, enough from any one beach to populate the sea. That is why, no matter how many adults are killed during the Caplin Scull, there are always plenty of youngsters to take their place. Any one individual of the tiny caplin that swarm seaward from the spawning beaches has but a very slight chance of reaching adulthood, for the larvae float about defencelessly in the plankton layer, feeding on microscopic creatures, and being fed upon by all the numerous larger plankton eaters. The chances against survival are probably thousands to one, but that slim chance is enough to produce the vast black swarms of caplin that will litter the beaches in succeeding years. Newfoundlanders have landed caplin by the billion each year for centuries past without seeming to affect their numbers in any way. Even more than the annual adventure of the seal hunt, the rhythm of life in Newfoundland is timed by the Caplin Scull.

The surviving adults move back toward deep water, and in recent years men have been pursuing them there with drift nets, trying to extend the season when caplin may be taken in bulk, since they are a valuable fish for meal plants producing the ingredients for cattle and poultry feeds, and – experimentally – for high-protein meal that may some day help feed the hungry millions of humanity in the depressed areas of the world. So far, these drift-netting experiments are inconclusive.

The caplin that have escaped the fish, the whales, the squids, the kingfishers, the puffins, the gulls, and above all the humans, swim slowly, in beautiful formations, their small snouts in line and tails flicking in unison, toward the open sea. There they sink slowly through the layers of sunlight toward the waters of midnight blue from which they came to begin the cycle of another year. They will feed in the upper layers of the sea, and seek safety in the colder and darker depths. In their own secret places of the mighty Atlantic, where the mixing of the cold and warm currents bring masses of the minute creatures on which they feed, and mineral salts to feed their food, they will browse and grow fat, and the spawn within them will ripen toward next year's Caplin Scull, toward another dramatic episode of death and renewal.

The beaches that the caplin leave behind are at first littered with the debris of their living and of their dying. But the sea has a wonderful way of cleansing its shores. First come the gulls and terns in great, wheeling flocks, squabbling and calling, inviting others to share the feast, then, when they arrive, trying to drive them off. There is nothing less consistent than a gull. They quickly devour most of the dead caplin. The tiny rock crabs and the sand spiders creep out at night to dispose of the scraps. Bit by bit, all the carnage is absorbed, once again, into the fabric of life.

And then, one day, a spring tide comes in, following the track of the full moon, creeping higher than any caplin could reach, beyond the line of the surf, washing the sand, the pebbles, the water-worn boulders, then retreating, past the line of the kelp, along the off-shore shallows. When dawn breaks again the beach lies clean and empty and scoured, as though the Caplin Scull had never been.

22. Bright and Bitter Burin

The boot-shaped Burin Peninsula, 106 miles long, dips down through the Atlantic toward the Gulf Stream from the south coast of Newfoundland. Flanked by the great bays of Fortune and Placentia, ringed by islands and deeply slashed by inlets, it is almost on the doorstep of the Grand Bank, the vast off-shore fish nursery that attracts trawler fleets from around the world, provides the Burin Peninsula with its current affluence, and makes it a 'growth centre', draining population from the bays and islands all around.

The Burin Peninsula enjoys many unique features. It has some of the biggest fish plants and some of the worst roads in the province. It has the best soccer team in the Atlantic provinces, the largest shipyard, the most deadly mine, and the cleverest rum-runners in Newfoundland. Its chief towns – Marystown, Burin, St. Lawrence, Grand Bank, and Fortune – all have strong individual characters that set them apart from all other towns in the island. They are well off the main route, too. It is 100 miles from the Trans-Canada Highway to Marystown, 125 to St. Lawrence, and about 140 to Grand Bank and Fortune.

If you face west from Fortune on a fine day you can see the peaks of L'Anglade, the wild French island twenty-five miles away on your port bow. It is part of the tiny colony of St. Pierre and Miquelon, the last remaining scrap of the empire of New France, and the only European colony in North America today. The peaks float just above the horizon, like volcanic cones on southern seas, while, seemingly farther off, the Bill of Miquelon rises far ahead, and abandoned Brunette broods on the starboard beam. The ship-like shape of Sagona Island is a darker stain against the cloud-blue land of the Hermitage Peninsula to the north, and a sailor with world-girdling eyes can see on rare occasions the loom of distant mountains beyond Bay d'Espoir.

The men who watch the sea along this shore know all these places well. They were born at Sagona and Belleoram, at Great Jarvis and Point Rosie. Some of them left the big island of Brunette a few years before it was turned into a game reserve and stocked with buffalo. Others sailed into Miquelon Bay for cargoes of rum or white lightning to be landed at Lories or Lamaline or Point-au-Gaul.

All of them fished on the stormy grounds of Fortune Bay, and many on the dangerous banks to the south. Their fathers fished in cross-handed dories. Their grandfathers chased whales in oar-powered longboats. They are the men of the south coast, whose ancestors were expelled from Placentia when the English took it from the French, hired as servants in the Channel Islands when the great Newman Company went out to trade in fish and oil, or landed here as planters and sharemen in the great days of the shore fishery and the transatlantic fish trade.

They and their fathers were always on intimate terms with death and the violence of nature, for these were the men who manned the banking schooners, sailing and rowing into winter gales, baiting trawls in snowstorms, chopping foot-thick ice from decks and bulwarks, watching their dory-mates go under, clutching helplessly at trawl lines, or waiting in the eternal fog for dories that would never return. It was a hard, cruel, dangerous life, with limitless scope for resourcefulness and heroism, a life of small material rewards, filled with struggle and fierce pride and the bitter joy of hard accomplishment.

It is a strange life they lead now, sitting on winter evenings before the ghostly screens of television sets in oil-warmed drawing rooms while their sons struggle manfully with the mysteries of the binomial theorem, and their baffled wives try to learn the secrets of washer-dryer cycles. It is a long step from the outhouse at Turnip Cove to the tiled bathroom in the modern subdivision with its thirty-year mortgage. Many thousands of Newfoundlanders have made the step in our own time.

And some thousands of these displaced people have come to the Burin Peninsula, or moved from its villages into its towns. They have built there a strange, almost contradictory collection of settlements.

On the peninsula today you will find the clean, scrubbed,

stately look of Puritan, New-Englandish Grand Bank; the fishy smell of Fortune, crowded about its tiny artificial harbour; Marystown awakened suddenly from its rural sleep to the spitting of red-hot rivets, licking its social wounds, angry at the invading English who came to show Newfoundlanders how to build steel ships; the bitter, brooding agony of St. Lawrence, where a whole generation of men have been crucified for profit, sent into underground pits rotten with radiation, condemned to die of lung cancer with the probable complication of insanity from brain tumours before death; the collection of pocket-edition villages that add up to bright but discontented Burin.

Strung between these towns, and spread along both sides of the peninsula, are tiny outports of incredible beauty, snuggled into almost miraculous harbours: Beau Bois, Jean de Baie, Harbour Mille, Bay L'Argent. And among them are the thin, arthritic fingers of the roads, probing between the hills.

The leap was such a long one that most of those who made it cannot really explain what it meant to them. Only the younger ones seem sure of themselves, seem to know what it means to move from the middle of the nineteenth century to the middle of the twentieth in a single year.

'The older people just aren't with it,' a rather long-haired teen-ager from the fringes of Grand Bank confessed. 'They're still living up at Grand Beach or over at Mose Ambrose or some such place – in their minds, anyway. They don't know what hit 'em.'

'Electric lights, yes,' his mother agreed hesitantly. 'We had them for the first time when we came here. But it isn't the *lights* that make the difference, you know . . . it's the other things . . . it's . . . well, everything is changed, you know . . . everything. . . .'

The houses, of course, seem almost miraculous – houses that run themselves with buttons and thermostats, for people who graduated from woodpiles and scrubbing boards. And there are supermarkets to replace the storehouse and the barrel of salt beef.

'But it's not houses, either, really,' the woman continued. 'It's other things.'

'Like cars,' her son chipped in. 'You don't live in a house nowadays. A house is a place you sleep. You live in a car.'

'Yeah,' his friend agreed. 'So what do we need? We need a road. Not a cart track, man, a road.'

The thin, arthritic fingers have served their time. The generation now growing up is going to have straight blacktop built to sixty-miles-per-hour standards, or know the reason why.

Travel they take for granted. Some of the men and women who moved into Grand Bank and Fortune from the outlying fishing settlements had never gone anywhere in their lives except as far as St. John's on a coastal boat. The teen-agers regard Montreal as next door. In the summer of 1967 they were coming and going in droves:

'You been up to Expo? Everyone's been. Kids. Grandfathers. *Thousands* of people. Newfies, I mean. I bet more people got off this rock for the first time this summer than in the last ten years.'

All of a sudden, everyone's going places. Car crazy. There are enough cars in Newfoundland to put the whole population of Newfoundland and Labrador on wheels all at once, and take the whole population of Prince Edward Island along in the back seats. It creates problems, of course. Towns that were laid out for three or four dozen buggies have their hands full finding space for a thousand motor cars. Some of them have had to sacrifice sidewalks in order to get a double motor lane between the houses.

A man working at landing fish on the Grand Bank pier grinned out of his oilskins (he was handling sloppy saltbulk with pickle dripping all over the place) and said, 'I'm just dumb, I guess. I've been doing this for almost thirty years. But this stuff is still the basis of everything we got. Everything here sort of sits on top of the fish, you know – mostly fresh, now, of course. . . .'

'There's not a fish being made here today,' an idler on the pier observed. 'The beach is all growed over. I mind when schooner loads was spread to dry all summer long, and women in their bonnets making it. . . .'

'Yes, they call us a growth centre,' another man agreed, 'and there's all kinds of work here now. I don't know if it can last, after the federal and municipal jobs are finished – the town council is just completing the paving of *all* the streets, you know, and the government is completely rebuilding the waterfront. That's taking a lot of men. . . .'

But in spite of the prosperity, the full employment, the almost frantic expansion (Grand Bank and Fortune will soon merge into a single town along the three-mile road that separates them, and are already discussing a municipal merger), there is an air of serenity at Grand Bank that nothing has altered, a sort of Sunday-morning atmosphere that broods over the narrow, clean streets between the stately old houses.

'We didn't always have this Sunday-morning look, though,' a retired merchant confessed, 'not when we had nineteen bankers sailing out of this harbour. Why, we had a beach – just our own firm – where you could spread 2,500 quintals of fish. The bankers would discharge in salt bulk, you know, and the women would spread it and make it. . . .'

Newfoundland fish is still measured in quintals – 112 pounds dry weight; 2,500 quintals would be about half a million pounds after it is split and salted but not dried.

'All the bank fish was made by the women – every cod's tail – and a hundred women might share $1,000 between them. It was a wonder that kind of thing lasted as long as it did. All that had to happen was the women to refuse to go on the beach day after day for that back-breaking work, and the bank fishery would have come to an end, right there. . . .

'But it's over now, of course. Today you've got to stand in line in Grand Bank to buy a salt fish when a bit of it arrives at the store.'

Some dry fish is still produced, as well as fresh fillets, in an artificial drying plant. But the plants don't produce the kind of fish that a Newfoundlander would eat, as a rule. Dryer fish may be fine for export, but 'eating fish' ought to be sun-cured. One man described it as 'Slop – cullage, ye know – about all we get is what's left over after the choice fish has been picked out.'

Then he looked out at the umbrella of wheeling gulls that rose and dipped above the breakwater.

'We loved 'em when we was boys,' he mused. 'To eat, I mean, o' course. But just look how tame they are now. Nobody eats gulls any more. It is even against the law.'

The docks at Fortune produced a busier breed of men. Activity there was almost frantic, the entire docking area being redesigned and rebuilt so that even the dockside philosophers were at work. A few people found time to talk, though.

'We're a lot more independent than we used to be,' one man said. 'You feel free here. My poor old father was never out of debt in his life, God rest his soul. Maybe you'd say I'm in debt, too, what with paying for a house on a mortgage, but somehow it feels different. I *own* a piece of that house, and it makes me feel proud, and it's a good house, too, and I don't have to worry about not being able to meet the payments, or about not having enough food for the winter, the way folks used to have to worry, where we came from.'

A family that moves to an approved growth centre such as this can get substantial government help. There is a basic $1,000 grant, plus $200 for each member of the family up to a maximum of $3,200. There is another grant of $1,000 for the purchase of land in an approved settlement, or up to $3,000 for purchase of a serviced building lot in a housing development such as the one at Fortune. A family of five can qualify for a total of $5,000, a family of ten for $6,000. The balance can be financed by mortgage. The result of all this is that thousands of families have moved from the tiny headland settlements and from off-shore islands to the larger towns.

Author Farley Mowat, who spent six years at Burgeo on Newfoundland's south coast, calls it a 'sadistic scheme' to force outport people to abandon their homes and their way of life 'in order to be fitted into the brave new world'. They must, he says, 'move as rootless migrants to the unlovely and unwished-for industrial centres, there to lose themselves in the faceless jungles of mass-man'.

The picture is not that simple. For one thing, there are more outport Newfoundlanders today than there ever were before. The growth centres have not even managed to keep up with the population explosion. More than a hundred little settlements have been written off, it is true. But almost a thousand remain. A hundred more could go without making any noticeable difference to the character of the province.

Some of those who have moved have no sympathy with the view that they are being degraded into a faceless jungle.

'Mr. Mowat never had to live in Muddy Hole or Lally Cove,' one of the migrants at Fortune observed. 'Only place he's lived is in Burgeo — a modern town with a big fish plant. He never had to go down on the rocks in leaky old sea-boots and pick kelp and mussels for something to eat.'

'Did you?'

'Yes, I did, when I was a youngster, and times were hard. We're not going back to that kind of life, even with welfare and baby bonuses and things to help out.'

There are, all the same, many people who refuse to be centralized, and thousands of others who are bitter and frustrated because they moved, when they should not have, to places where they can get no work, and now are far worse off than they were before. There are even strong movements, here and there, opposing government pressures toward centralization. Toslow has been written off. But Allan's Island has not been, and probably will not be.

The people in the growth centres are in some respects a new breed. There is a new feel to these people. It is not just their confidence in the future, their new sense of security, but the shift in their social attitudes too. A lady who has lived all her life in Fortune Bay and has seen the whole pattern of social change from the early 1900s, summed it up like this:

'People used to be more dependent on each other, in a way – closer, more neighbourly – you *depended* on your near neighbours; you couldn't have managed at all without them; people helped each other just as a matter of course. Today everyone seems to be independent – thinks he is, anyway. . . .

'But in fact, I suppose, people are even more dependent today than they ever were. They just depend on people who are farther away. They depend on the government, or on somebody from St. John's who knows how to keep a freezing plant in repair. Instead of depending on ourselves and our neighbours, we depend on people we never see at all. I'm not saying it's a bad thing, mind you – but you can see how it makes people different, makes them think they're standing alone, when they aren't, really.

'If some kind of disaster cut us off today from the rest of the world we'd all be dead in ten weeks. I remember the time when we could have been cut off for ten years, and we would have had a hard time, but we would have survived. We'd have made out, you see, as our people did for hundreds of years. We couldn't do it any more, though. . . .'

It is a strong and vigorous area, the Burin Peninsula. There is none of the feeling of quiet resignation, of waiting patiently for death, that permeates some parts of the south coast. Even without government help, it would still be one of the strongest growth centres in the province. Its problems – primitive roads, shortage of power, factional rivalry – are being solved. And the people have a sense of buoyancy, almost of bounce, that might be hard to match in most parts of Canada.

From Grand Banks and Fortune there is a daily passenger service in summer to St. Pierre and Miquelon. Though the town of St. Pierre is only twelve miles from the tip of the Burin boot, the boat trip from Fortune is thirty miles, and takes two and a half hours. St. Pierre consists of just one town, with about 5,000 people, and there is a small settlement of Basque fishermen on the much larger island of Miquelon. The town is very compact, and you can see it all on foot very easily.

St. Pierre is the only completely European town in the New World. It is as thoroughly French as anything in France, and much more French than anything in Quebec. Artists love its compact harbour, its public square, and its European architecture. The food at St. Pierre is excellent, the liquor is good and very cheap, and you can get French wines of every quality at prices that Canadians can scarcely believe. European perfumes, jewellery, watches, and fine textiles are also sold there tax-free.

You have to go through customs going to and coming from St. Pierre, but you do not need a passport or a visa. Visitors who go to the island from Newfoundland will find the French officials most obliging.

You can visit Miquelon from St. Pierre either by chartered boat or on tours arranged by the tourist office. The two large islands of Miquelon and L'Anglade, joined by a narrow ridge of sand dunes seven miles long, have many fascinating natural features. The dunes themselves are a remarkable formation, and they contain bones of numerous wrecks from ships that tried to sail between the two islands, never suspecting that they were connected by a sand-bar. The Big Barachois, a large salt-water lake at the northern end of the dunes, has thousands of seals that you can see at close quarters, and large flocks of water-fowl. The only settlement, consisting of about five hundred fishermen, is at Miquelon Bay on the northern tip of Miquelon Island. This is the place from which the modern-day rum-runners pick up their booze.

There are two loop drives on the Burin Peninsula. Starting from either Burin or Marystown, you can drive across the Peninsula to Fortune Bay, through Grand Bank and St. Lawrence and on around the toe of the boot to Placentia Bay, returning to St. Lawrence. There is not much variety on the lower part of the peninsula, and much of this ninety-nine-mile drive is along a bleak and barren shore. But on a day after a gale on the off-shore banks, the surf that comes rolling shoreward at High Beach, Allan's Island, or Point-au-Gaul can be truly spectacular. At Golden Sands, near Salt Pond, there is a fine swimming beach and a very comfortable resort. This loop is along parts of Routes 12, 11, and 14.

The other loop is much shorter. It runs around the shore of a peninsula that is almost a large island, connecting the town of Burin with Mortier, Port-au-Bras, Burin Bay Arm, Creston, Little Bay, and Beau Bois. Of the twenty-six miles, eleven are paved. The settlements on this small loop are among the most beautiful and photogenic in Canada. Out of Burin you take either Route 12 or Route 14, depending on whether you wish to drive clockwise or counter-clockwise around the loop.

Some of the side-roads on the Burin Peninsula also lead to settlements that nobody should miss. An attractive area near the head of Fortune Bay is reached by way of the Bay L'Argent cut-off, sixty-four miles from the Trans-Canada Highway. Crossing a low range of mountains, the road drops, after five miles, into a crescent-shaped valley, then branches, the left fork taking you to Jacques Fontaine and St. Bernard's. Bay L'Argent is a compact, prosperous-looking village in a setting of bold cliffs and long, slender arms of the sea. The silver-coloured rocks of the cliffs leave no room for doubt about the origin of the name.

The right branch of the road skirts a bold mountain and a sand beach and barachois to enter Little Bay East, then curves around a lovely arrangement of cliff and beach and sea to Little Harbour East and Harbour Mille. At Harbour Mille you should climb the hill that overlooks the settlement, and take your camera with you.

Boat Harbour, Parker's Cove, and Baine Harbour, all close together on the Placentia Bay side, and reached by short stretches of local road, are small villages with fine harbours. Rushoon, their next-door neighbour, has a deep inlet with steep land close-to. I once took a canoe out the bay from Rushoon to the squid jiggin' ground, and paddled around the surprised trap boat fishermen, who were there in a group, waiting for the squid. They regarded me with some wonder, and what I suspected was solemn concern for my sanity. But they soon came to the obvious conclusion:

'What part of the Mainland be ye from, sir?' one of them asked.

Jean de Baie, just north of Marystown, has a tempting beach, but its water is as cold as charity. Two minutes per dip was my limit, and after each plunge I was too cold to shiver. The sand, however, was invitingly hot, and flanked by cool, abandoned fields.

The people of Jean de Baie talked with interest and intelligence about their work in the fishery, and about the history of the settlement, which goes back, like so many others along this shore, to the days of the French fishing rooms, apportioned by the governor at Placentia.

Before I left Jean de Baie, children whom I had never seen before brought me flowers, including fragrant briar roses, that their ancestors had brought with them from Europe generations before, and that almost ran wild in hundreds of fishing settlements around the coast, festooning old fences with banks of red and white blossoms in August. It was a naïve, friendly gesture that brought me great pleasure, one more small strand tying me to these people of whom I am a part, for ever.

23. Voyage into the Past

Canadian National operates in Newfoundland a fleet of motor ships carrying passengers, mails, and freight to all parts of the coast. They link towns and villages and islands that no road can ever reach. Each day of the year they sail into earlier centuries, visiting people who have never seen an automobile or heard the whistle of a train, people who, except for the rare visits of aircraft on mercy flights with hospital patients, still live in the Canada of Queen Victoria's time.

Some of the trips by the coastal ships are longer than Atlantic crossings, taking you north to regions where, in midsummer, there is no night, and where floating islands of ice like white castles and cathedrals pass by in endless procession. Others last just two or three days – the 'bay runs' on which the ships poke about among mazes of islands visiting tiny fishing villages. And there are trips of medium length covering a few hundred miles of coastline in one or both directions.

The main run along the south coast from St. John's to Port-aux-Basques is perhaps the most interesting of the medium-length trips, since most of the ports of call cannot be reached by road.

The run begins at St. John's or at Argentia, but you can join the ship equally well at various points on the Burin Peninsula – at Grand Bank, for example, or at Terrenceville, near the head of Fortune Bay. From Terrenceville westward there are some 230 miles of virtually roadless coastline, until you reach Rose Blanche near Port-aux-Basques.

It is a spectacular shore, with long stretches of thousand-foot cliffs, and some places where the hills reach almost twice that height. Fjords with perpendicular walls falling straight into the sea cut through the cliff face to the river-bottoms, which are often far inland. The ship sails in and out of these fjords, docking in tiny harbours, or sometimes anchoring off shore at places too small for a ship to enter, loading and unloading freight in motorboats when she cannot tie up to a wharf.

Stops in the various ports of call are of unpredictable length. On one trip the ship may tie up all day at St. Alban's while she takes on a deck cargo of lumber. On the next she may stop only long enough to drop a couple of packages for the local store and exchange the news of the coastline. Since the navigation is tricky, and the captain must be on the bridge most of the time, the ship may occasionally tie up in harbour while he gets a couple of hours' sleep. But these men are expert sailors with a perfect safety record. Canadian National has never lost a passenger, either afloat or ashore, in Newfoundland.

The coastal voyages are informal and unpredictable, but they give passengers a unique holiday in a maritime setting that is never monotonous since one is never out of sight of land and never more than an hour or two away from the next harbour. The food on the boats is rather better than in most Newfoundland hotels and restaurants, though there is less variety than you expect ashore. The salt breeze gives passengers such appetites that they regularly eat four meals a day, the supper at 10 p.m. being just as popular as the other three.

Besides the changing coastal scene and the succession of fishing villages, the voyages give you a good sample of the life of the sea. There are always seals and whales, often hundreds of them, to be seen on any coastal voyage. I have seen as many as three separate schools of whales, all blowing at once, from the deck of a coastal boat. Sometimes dolphins follow the ships, or ride the bow wave, and there are always huge flocks of seabirds, including fulmars, shearwaters, jaegers, and other oceanic species that are rarely seen near shore.

One of the specialties of the south coast voyage is the eagles. Fortune Bay and Bay d'Espoir have the greatest concentration of bald eagles in Canada – perhaps in North America. There are also a few golden eagles, rare in Eastern Canada. The birds are present all year around, but tend to concentrate at certain seasons. I have seen twelve eagles at Burgeo in the winter, and forty-three on a single circuit of Bay d'Espoir in late summer.

Though they sometimes collect at towns such as Burgeo to

feed on fish scraps when other food is scarce, these magnificent, lonely birds usually live in high and desolate places, far from the homes of men. You will see them not while your ship is tied up at the pier, but while you sail between the cliffs of the narrow fjords. At Little Passage, after you leave Gaultois, you may see an eagle perched on every cliff top, or flying parallel with the ship and pulling ahead on slow, powerful wing-beats.

The eagle cannot live with Industrial Man for a next-door neighbour. Conservationists are worried about its ultimate survival in North America, for it has disappeared from most of its former haunts. Its reproduction is slow, and in some places has been stopped altogether where the eagles are eating fish contaminated by insect poisons. But Newfoundland's south coast will offer natural sanctuary to eagles for many years to come. Not only is it free from poisons and industrial waste, but the human population, except in selected areas, is decreasing. Many small coves and harbours have been deserted entirely, and long stretches of splendid eagle habitat are now completely uninhabited by man.

Leaving Fortune Bay on the westward run, you anchor at Pass Island in a narrow tickle between a rocky point and a rocky island where the surge heaves mightily and the tides are strong. Here freight and passengers must be transferred to small motorboats that are level with the bulwarks one moment and twenty feet below the next. But the small-boat seamen of Pass Island are experts, never known to drop either a package or a passenger over the side.

This place was formerly called Isle d'Esprit, and there is, indeed, something rather spirit-like or ghostly about the area. Off on the starboard bow as you round the cape is the main entrance to Bay d'Espoir, and it, too, was once called the Bay of Spirits. Visiting it by small boat, you soon learn the reason why. Just inside the entrance is Goblin Head, and beyond that the Three Goblins – Great Goblin, Middle Goblin, and Little Goblin – all well-named, too, for if any place on earth looks haunted, it is the region of the three goblins. I once spent the night in Middle Goblin Bay, a round bowl ringed by steep hills of black spruce, white rocks on shore and bottom, a strong undertow gurgling about the anchor chains, and as spooky an atmosphere as I have ever felt in my life.

The name of the bay has an interesting history. The French

called it Baie des Esprits. English settlers, who displaced the French and the Jerseymen in the nineteenth century, corrupted this to Bay Despair. Finally, Newfoundland officials, disliking the associations of this name, and knowing that it was corrupted from a French original, decided to restore it. But instead of Baie des Esprits they made it Bay d'Espoir, Bay of Hope, no doubt for the best patriotic reasons, and because hope and despair are opposites. It is still pronounced 'Bay Despair', however.

From Pass Island you sail up a narrowing bay to Hermitage, a prosperous fishing settlement founded by the French at an unknown date. Captain Taverner found them cultivating rye there when he visited the coast to enforce the terms of the Treaty of Utrecht. Just across the run, you enter Gaultois, a modern fish-plant town that formerly had a whale factory on the flat island in the centre of its harbour. The whales of Hermitage Bay were pursued, first by Basques, then by Acadians who came all the way from Nova Scotia each summer for the hunt, then by Jerseymen who came out from the Channel Islands for the Newman Company (owners of Gaultois in the early nineteenth century), and lastly by English settlers in small whaling ships. The Jerseymen used no ships in their hunt, but pursued and harpooned the huge creatures in hand-powered boats.

There are traces of the earlier Jersey settlement all along this coast, especially in Bay d'Espoir, which you enter by way of Little Passage (you'd swear you were sailing up a river) between Long Island and Hermitage Head. Patrick's Harbour, Barachois de Cerf, Raymond's Point, and other small harbours, now deserted, have old forges where iron was once worked for whaling and shipbuilding, roads with carefully-laid stone embankments, and quantities of old brick now buried under a few inches of turf but still showing, when excavated, the trademarks of firms in the Channel Islands.

Bay d'Espoir is ideal cruising water for small boats: almost a hundred miles of protected waterways, landlocked, deep, well provided with harbours, free of almost all hazards. I know of only two places in the bay where you can manage to hit a sunken rock, and both are within a few yards of shore. In most places you can run straight into a cliff without touching bottom. Indeed, one of the Canadian National coastal ships actually did this, denting her nose, but never so much as scratching her keel.

Farley Mowat and I spent a month cruising about Bay d'Espoir in his 30-foot schooner, *The Happy Adventure*. She had started life as a jack boat – a small fishing vessel – at Fermeuse near Cape Race. Farley put in larger masts and re-rigged her for cruising, with jib, jumbo, foresail, and mainsail. She never would sail very close to the wind, but she was a joy to handle when running free.

Schooner sailing is almost a lost art in southern Newfoundland, though it has been revived at the yacht club in Conception Bay. No one on the coast could give us much useful advice, though in fact we scarcely needed it as we felt our way, one man at the tiller and the other working the sails, which were stained brown as mahogany from soaking in a bark pot and sometimes streaked white with salt as we headed into the flying spume off the open parts of the shore. We were very cautious sailors. Only on the open coast was our seamanship ever put to the test, and then not severely.

One day as we drove up Hermitage Bay with a stiff breeze pushing us along at nine knots, and everything drawing, the wind began to increase while the waves grew higher, and Farley suggested that we shorten sail. I opposed the idea, hoping to see what she would do when pushed to the limit. The ride was beginning to feel exciting. Unfortunately, the limit was soon reached. The increasing wind bent the spars like fishing rods – twelve degrees at least, Farley said, though I'm convinced myself that they weren't bending more than ten – the rigging was groaning under the press of sail, and it was obvious that something – maybe the mainmast – was soon going to snap under the strain. There was nothing for it but to head into the wind and take in sail.

The job of doing this fell to my lot (as I well deserved), while Farley remained in perfect comfort and vast responsibility in the bone-dry cockpit. The nastiest part was standing out on the bobstay, handling the headsails, following the old rule of one hand for myself and one for the ship, as the bowsprit dipped deep into every green comber, plunging me at intervals into the near-freezing water of the Atlantic, then lifting me again to the tender embrace of the September gale. But there was some compensation in the thought that I was doing what my ancestors had done so well for hundreds of years, and that I was, perhaps, the only Newfoundlander handling sails at sea that day.

Later, as we lay at anchor with our kerosene lights aglow, discussing the passage over a glass of St. Pierre rum, it seemed well worth the hard work and the wetting.

Our voyage was a journey into a land now rarely seen except in the history books. We had no fancy modern gear (no radar or echo-sounder or two-way radio), but sounded our way into uncharted bays and coves with a lead line, as the Basque fishermen had done on this same coast five centuries before us. We entered a wilderness without human inhabitants, where the air was filled with eagles and the waters were filled with whales. We waded naked in the shallows of landlocked bays to collect shellfish for food, as the Beothuck Indians did in the days even before the Basques. We feasted on clams and huge snails and scallops, and ate pink ocean perch pulled from the deep trenches of the central bay.

We visited such fishing settlements as Richard's Harbour, Pushthrough, Piccaire, and Hermitage Cove, besides numerous harbours once populous but now uninhabited — places such as the Goblins, Patrick's Harbour, and Barachois de Cerf. Everywhere we went we attracted great interest among people who had never expected to see a small schooner under sail any more. We must have looked rather like music-hall pirates — bronzed, weather-beaten, barefoot, with red beards blowing in the breeze and the banner of the Basque nation (a gift from the fishermen of Miquelon) fluttering at our masthead. This banner, with the intertwined crosses of the Basque provinces, had not been flown officially since the Basques last revolted against their Spanish conquerors and joined forces in the Carlist rebellion that was defeated in 1876. One Newfoundland coastal skipper, who had searched through his flag book in vain, came on board to ask us what on earth our banner was supposed to mean.

We spent a month examining uninhabited harbours where successive layers of turf cover the Basques of 400 years ago, the Jerseymen of 200 years ago, and the settlers of the last century, some of whom walked right across Newfoundland from Bay of Exploits and made their homes in Bay d'Espoir. The places where most of them chose to live are the only ones still inhabited — the small cluster of lumbering settlements at the very head of the bay, from St. Alban's on the west around to Conne River on the east, the region that now supplies most of Newfoundland's electric power.

Half way up Bay d'Espoir a high, wooded rock known as Rich's Island sits in the middle of a veritable Piccadilly Circus of waterways. Here no fewer than six navigable runs converge, and the first sailors to venture into these spectacular reaches must have had an interesting time exploring dead ends before finding their way to the great river-bottoms and wooded valleys where they went for ships' spars and keels and timbers.

Southward from Rich's Island is the main bay leading to Pushthrough. South-west rise the smoky blue cliffs of Lampoides Passage. Eastward, the narrow and dangerous Little River Run opens into the uncharted bay known as Lobster Cove. Arran Arm and the passage toward the head of the bay open to the north-east and north. Finally, to the north-west, there is a narrow opening between the mountains. This leads past schools of mackerel, loons that dive at your approach, and seals that sit on the rocks to watch you go by, into Roti Bay – a bowl-shaped depression surrounded by an arctic-like landscape where thin green turf is cut by white ribbons of quartzite laid bare by arrow-straight streams that have washed away the few inches of soil to expose the bedrock below.

Though Roti Bay looks barren and windswept compared with the deeply wooded hills of its neighbouring coves and inlets, it is a place where you can eat like a gourmet while living off the land – or, to be more accurate, off the sea bottom.

We entered Roti Bay at evening, and sounded our way with the lead line to anchorage at a pleasant little cove bearing the unlovely name of Clay Hole.

The still night came swiftly as we anchored, and the still morning followed it, with a low tide exposing the weeds of great mussel beds and a long, curving sickle of shoreline showing every evidence of abundant life and growth. We took the little tender and rowed ashore, driving off a big, bewhiskered seal that was happily feeding on the mussel bed.

The morning was clear and warm, with nacreous pink and pearl in the sky, the water so still and pure that we could see bottom in three fathoms and watch the starfish slowly crawling among the weeds. As the water shoaled off to about two fathoms, there were the large, palmate shells of scallops, dressed in white and brown, and with the rich tinge of purple that the artisans of Tyre learned to extract 3,000 years ago, to make the most costly and famous cloth in history – the Tyrian purple that they traded to the kings of the earth from Britain in the west to fabled courts of farthest Asia.

In a cove just outside Clay Hole we found a bed of small white clams. Beyond low-water mark huge sea snails, peri-winkles, or 'wrinkles' as some Newfoundlanders call them, crawled over the rocks. Some of them were monsters of their kind, fully three inches in diameter. In the water beyond the mussel bed we found another species of clam – big fellows weighing perhaps a quarter of a pound each, looking almost like oysters.

We spent the morning wading in the shallows, loading the little boat with white clams and brown clams, blue mussels and periwinkles – more than we could eat in several days, but, fortu-nately, you can keep shellfish almost indefinitely in buckets of salt water, so we requisitioned every bucket and boiler on board, and filled them full of delicacies for which, in a metro-politan restaurant, we would have had to pay maybe ten dollars a pound.

That evening we made a big clam chowder with thyme and dried mushrooms and a little finely-chopped kelp for flavouring. Farley later insisted that this was the most delicious meal he had ever eaten, but my own vote went to the periwinkles, which we boiled in sea water, then dipped in a sauce made with but-ter, garlic, and St. Pierre rum. The white clams we ate with a sauce that included milk and white wine. The blue mussels we cooked in a chowder with canned vegetables and dried herbs.

That night we set out two wattle traps, baited with scraps of fish, in about two fathoms of water, and in the morning when we took them up we had two large crabs. We wondered, as we sat down to our cabin table that morning, how many other people in Newfoundland were making a breakfast of fresh crab meat and mayonnaise.

We visited each of the other runs in turn. Our trip up Little River Run was the trickiest and the most interesting. We knew that it was dangerous to a vessel under sail, so we stowed our canvas and went up with the flood tide under power.

Early in the last century the Little River Run was used by the Jerseymen working for the Newman Company at Gaultois, who went there to cut timber. They made the passage under sail, having no auxiliary power. And at least one of them came to grief one dark night trying to sail a forty-tonner out of Little River Run on the ebb tide with a head wind. His wife was at the tiller, his small children below, and not another soul aboard. As he ran forward to back the headsails for a short tack in the contrary wind, he tripped in a loose rope and went over the side, where he was quickly sucked down by the current. This left the vessel in the sole charge of the woman, who managed, somehow, to clear the mouth of the passage, bring the ship's head to the wind, lower the sails, and drop anchor. Next morning, with the tide running out of the passage once more, she took the dory and rowed against the current all the way to Lobster Cove, where some of the Jerseymen were working at logging. So she managed to save herself and her children. Of such stuff were the wives of the pioneers.

The trip up Little River Run under auxiliary power was easy enough. It was a brilliant day, and we could see the long finger of the mid-channel reef at the entrance. We watched the tide running like a river, actually gurgling past the rocks and tugging at our bows. The run narrowed at some places until it looked as if we could jump ashore. Then, suddenly, it opened into the broad, level expanse of Lobster Cove – a sheet of salt water that looked exactly like a large fresh-water lake.

Here, again, we were due for a surprise. The Admiralty chart showed Lobster Cove only in dotted outline, with no depth soundings. But right in the middle of it, the chart showed a large, oval island, perhaps a hundred acres or so in extent. This island simply wasn't there. We sailed across Lobster Cove taking soundings as we went. In the place where the chart showed the island we found six fathoms of water. We later sounded our way around the bay, finding everywhere a smooth sand or mud bottom with depths of three fathoms or more. There had never been any island in Lobster Cove since men began to sail the ocean. Little River empties into the eastern end of Lobster Cove, forming a shallow harbour protected by sandy points. It is a domain such as pioneers dream about: well watered, well wooded, supplied with fish and game, and not a living soul within many miles.

One of the most interesting places in Bay d'Espoir is the Indian settlement at Conne River. The people are part Micmac, part white, many of the Indian men having married white women from St. Alban's across the bay, but they still have an Indian tradition, and some of them still read and write the Micmac language.

We found among the oldest of these people stories concerning the Beothuck Indians – traditions handed down by their grandparents and great-grandparents for a century and a half. Some of them also knew the unwritten history of their own people, and of the double migration, direct from Nova Scotia and overland from Hall's Bay in northern Newfoundland, that had brought them to Bay d'Espoir 150 and 200 years ago.

Of all the places that I visited in Bay d'Espoir, Conne River is the one that I wish most to visit again – not only for the traditions that may still survive among the people there, but also for their individual charm and sincerity and friendliness – qualities all too often lost in the headlong forward rush of North American civilization.

Leaving Bay d'Espoir, the coastal ship calls at Pushthrough (where you can push a boat through the back passage out of the harbour though it is too narrow to navigate under power), and McCallum, where on fine autumn days you may still see acres of split codfish drying in the sun.

Richard's Harbour, the next port of call, is a tiny settlement ringed by cliffs. To leave it any way except by boat through the dog-leg channel, you have to scale the rocks, hand over hand, for hundreds of feet. François, sixteen miles farther west, is an even greater oddity, practically built on a cliff-face in a cup-shaped harbour. They say that to walk anywhere in François you need one leg longer than the other. At Cape La Hune the cliffs rise to a 1,400-foot peak. Strangest of all is the run into Grey River, where the ship heads straight for what looks like a sheer, solid cliff until she seems to be on the point of collision. But just as everyone is convinced that the captain, having lost his mind, is going to take her down with all hands, the merest crack opens up, the ship slips through a slit in the rocks, and a narrow bay stretches ahead.

Ramea and Burgeo, two island settlements west of Grey River, are among the most important fish producers on the south coast. From their modern filleting and freezing plants they ship direct to Boston. Something of the Boston influence, too, can be seen in the Burgeo supermarket, which imports much of its food direct from the United States by fish carrier.

Burgeo is in a most picturesque setting among a mass of islands. 'Virgeo' would probably be a better spelling, for the Virgeo Isles were named originally for the Eleven Thousand Virgins. Any sceptic who wonders where eleven thousand virgins might be found is reminded that they were recruited by a group of mad churchmen in the Middle Ages to go on a crusade to the Holy Land in the belief that God would automatically deliver Jerusalem into their sinless hands. They were, of course, kidnapped en route and sold into Moslem harems, where virgins commanded a good price. There are those who regard the entire episode of the Eleven Thousand Virgins as a swindle arranged by white slave dealers, but, be that as it may, the Burgeo Islands were named in their honour.

From Rencontre Island in the Burgeo group come artefacts of the Boreal Archaic culture, made by a people who inhabited eastern Canada before the first Indian arrived.

West of Burgeo, the ports of call become fewer. There are only Grand Bruit, La Poile, and Rose Blanche before you reach Port-aux-Basques, where the voyage ends, and you can get connections for North Sydney, or, by road and rail, for St. John's. Other connections within reasonable distance of Port-aux-Basques are at the west-coast airports of Stephenville and Deer Lake. It is also possible, in summer, to fly by scheduled float plane from Burgeo to Gander, and from Gander back to St. John's.

On the western part of the south coast, between Burgeo and Port-aux-Basques, you will see the native water dogs, the ancestors of the Labrador Retrievers, one of the two pure-bred dogs that have originated in Canada, the other being the related Newfoundland dog. The water dogs are black, sleek-coated, web-footed animals, and look exactly like Labrador Retrievers except that they are more robust and broader in the chest.

These dogs are all born with a love for swimming that shows itself just as they grow out of puppyhood. They will dive from a wharf or a rock to catch fish without ever being trained to do so. Some, indeed, will dive habitually for their own food, and prefer to catch fish for themselves rather than to be fed at home. They are born retrievers, and will dive instinctively from low cliffs into white surf to retrieve ducks shot by their masters. At

La Poile there is even a dog that comes down regularly to meet the coastal ship and to beg passengers to throw things overboard so that he can show off his retrieving skill.

The other native Canadian breed, the Newfoundland, originated on the east coast, at or near St. John's. It is a huge, sweet-tempered animal, also with a natural affinity for water, and also with webbed feet, developed by natural selection over many generations. The Newfoundland is bigger, much more heavily furred, and with a larger, kinder-looking head than the water dogs. It is the greatest of all life-savers.

The most famous rescue by a Newfoundland dog took place at Isle-aux-Morts, eight miles from Port-aux-Basques. Here the passenger ship *Despatch*, out of Liverpool bound for Quebec City with 163 people on board, went ashore on a submerged reef one dark night in the last century. She started to break up in the surf, and round after round of rockets was fired in the hope that fishermen somewhere near by might see them and come to the rescue.

The only man within sight of the distress signals was a fisherman named George Harvey. He put out from his cove in a small boat manned by himself, his seventeen-year-old daughter, his twelve-year-old son, and his water dog, Watch. The boat could not approach within a cable-length of the wreck because of the surf, and seemed itself to be on the edge of disaster.

But the dog, at a command from his master, plunged over the side and fought his way, inch by inch, through the yeasty white water to the ship. Someone in the crew quickly bent a line to a belaying pin and threw it to the dog. He turned around and fought his way back to the boat. The Harveys then took the line ashore, used it to haul a rope, and subsequently to rig a breeches-buoy on which every person from the *Despatch* rode safely above the breakers to the land.

George Harvey and his children received the gold medal of the Royal Humane Society, a reward of a hundred gold sovereigns, and a letter from the King commending their bravery.

But such rescues were common. This particular dog even duplicated his feat six years later when the *Rankin*, a cargo ship from Glasgow, ran ashore in almost the same place. Again he swam to the ship, took a line ashore, and saved the twenty-five crewmen with no loss of life. On numerous occasions Newfoundlands, as well as the water dogs, swam through impossible-looking surf either to or from a ship carrying a life-line. Someone has estimated that the Newfoundland saved more than a thousand human lives in the nineteenth century. The dogs are among the most intelligent and tractable of animals, but are too big to be popular as pets in our time. There is still a healthy breed of them in Newfoundland, however, and a few thousand registered owners all over the world. The Newfoundland has also been used to produce other races of web-footed dogs by cross-breeding, for no other dog ever evolved a webbed foot. All the web-footed retrievers on earth are descended from the two Canadian races.

Both the Newfoundlands and the Labrador Retrievers had a purely mongrel ancestry. They developed by the intermarriage of all sorts of ships' dogs brought to the island by European fishermen from the fifteenth century onwards. It was four hundred years before kennel owners started to standardize the type. They are outstanding examples of the benefits of cross-breeding and of the survival of the fittest over a long period.

Newfoundlanders themselves originated in the same way.

24. The Coast of Labrador

I am writing this in the shadow of pencil-thin black spruces, with the roaring cascade of a river sounding in my ears and four Indian children playing inside my tent. Across a small, steep valley where the river grumbles downward over pink and grey glacial boulders to meet a sheltered arm of the sea, there is a bold, craggy hill with slick black rocks that rise straight upward toward a sky of intense and gem-like blue. In a wide, smooth draw of the mountain, topped by turf and berry bushes, there is a snowfield, spread out like the wings of a monstrous butterfly. From the snowfield a stream leaps outward to fall like a frayed skein of silver thread far down to the rocks below.

Above the mountain an osprey is soaring on lightly-bent wings, surveying, with his hawk-like vision, the shallow and fish-sheltering water below, where a canoe with three men paddling carefully comes poking among the immense rocks that were dropped upon the floor of the inlet when the last glacial ice-sheet retreated from this part of the world six thousand years ago.

'Osprey,' I remark to the Nascaupi Indian beside me, and, as he looks dubious, I add by way of explanation, 'Fish hawk'.

'Yes,' he agrees, nodding with pleased eyes. 'Fish hawk. Dive from high up. Catch fish.'

This is Davis Inlet, Labrador, almost a thousand miles by coastal boat from St. John's. The man is Ben Riche, and the boys playing in my tent are his sons and nephews. The Riches are important people in these parts. Ben's father, old Joe Riche, has been the Nascaupi chieftain almost as long as people can remember. Ben himself is the ablest man in the tribe – the best hunter, the best woodsman, an experienced traveller and leader.

It was he, a few years ago, who led a party of Indians on the five-hundred-mile hike from Davis Inlet to North West River and back again, the first time it had ever been done in summer, which, of course, is the most difficult time to travel overland in the north.

Ben is pleased that I remember his great trek, and that I admire his ability to live like his ancestors. For he set out to face 250 miles of wilderness with a crowd of women and children to feed, almost wholly without supplies, with only a net and a few hooks and a gun. And he not only got them all through, but they were well and healthy, if a bit ragged, when they finished their trek. There probably isn't a white man alive who could have done it, even alone, much less with a crowd of dependent camp-followers.

Not that Indian children are so dependent, either. The four children playing in my tent – none over twelve years old – are in some ways even more child-like than white boys of the same age. They tumble and tousle one another, and when I join in their horseplay they are as pleased as puppies getting petted. Yet two of those boys have already gone trapping on the Labrador Plateau in the winter, and one of them equalled his father's catch of fur, so his father, Ben's brother, informs me. In spite of their appealing childishness, they are able to face the woods like real Indians, and, in spite of their relative poverty, they obviously get more pleasure out of life than do the gadget-ridden city children of my acquaintance. Some of Ben Riche's children were born in a tent in midwinter a hundred miles from the nearest house, with Ben acting as midwife.

It is now early summer in northern Labrador, the last week of June, and in spite of the snowfield across the valley, and a shaded snowbank in the trees behind our tents (very useful as a refrigerator for bottled or canned food that the dogs cannot steal), the afternoon temperature climbs up to around eighty, and the sun gives us a deep coat of tan. The water, a shallow and sheltered part of the inlet, even gets warm enough for swimming.

For some reason that I have never understood, the northern sun achieves a greater intensity than the sun in more temperate regions. A technician working with a camera crew at Davis Inlet tells me that the light intensity there is 10,000 Kelvins, and though I do not know what this means I am obviously supposed to be impressed. Another outsider who boasts that he tans at an unheard-of rate and doesn't know what it is like to suffer sunburn, nevertheless turns bright red and looks, at least, as if he has discovered what sunburn is all about.

We do not have the midnight sun at Davis Inlet, but we have something even better – a sunset that begins at half past ten and goes on all night, merging into a beautiful dawn before three a.m. At solar midnight – one o'clock summer time – it is light enough to read comfortably outdoors, and you can see the position of the sun as an intense patch of light rising above the red and purple horizon. You cannot see the north star because the sky is still blue, but you can tell the exact position of celestial north by the position of the sun. The sea, meanwhile, becomes a sort of pea-green that must be seen to be believed. There is absolutely no night, but in summer you might describe northern Labrador as the land of the pea-green twilight.

There are a few blackflies and mosquitoes, though there will not be enough of them to bother anybody very much until some time in July. In any case, the flies in Labrador are not nearly so plentiful as they were fifteen or twenty years ago. Nobody is able to explain this fact. Something – perhaps some new factor in the ecology introduced by modern man – has cut the blackfly and mosquito population down to perhaps a tenth of what it was in the 1940s or 1950s.

Camping in Labrador is not very different from wilderness camping in Newfoundland. True, I have the nest of white-crowned sparrows within fifty.yards of my tent door – a lovely little domed nest roofed with blackberry twigs and holding five violet-spotted eggs, something I would hardly find in the Island. And two red squirrels chatter and sing from tree-top to tree-top. But though the scenery is a little more grand and the nights a little more spectacular, I might almost be camped at the foot of the Long Range instead of the Merrifield Mountain.

Labrador camping trips are easy to arrange. You simply go north to any chosen point on the coastal ship, and disembark. You can get the same ship on its return a few days later, or the sister ship about a week later, since two of them are on the run, one going north while the other goes south. Or, if you do not wish to stop over, you can make the return voyage either from Goose Bay (to which you can fly) or from St. John's. The round trip from St. John's takes about two weeks. But if **you want** deck cabins you may have to make reservations a year or more in advance. For stateroom accommodation you need to reserve three or four months in advance. The round trip from St. John's to Nain, approximately 1,300 miles each way, is the most popular summer voyage in eastern Canada, and the demand for accommodation exceeds the supply. The distance varies somewhat, since the ship calls at some ports in only one direction, and will also go out of her regular route to pick up freight for northern points. Stop-overs depend on connections at each point. At Davis Inlet, for example, stop-overs will be for two days, twelve days, or a month. At Nain, the northern limit of the voyage, the ships arrive approximately once a week.

Except in the deck cabins, which are hard to get, accommodation on the ships is uncomfortable. The four-berth staterooms are crowded, overheated, and under-ventilated. The crew-members have to work beyond their capacity. The stewards sometimes literally work around the clock trying to make the passengers comfortable, and if they sometimes forget what you've ordered for dinner it is just because they are dizzy from lack of sleep. The captains and their officers manage the tricky navigation along one of the world's most dangerous coastlines with admirable precision. But they can do nothing about the inadequate basic appointments. There are, for instance, only four showers to serve 113 passengers. That's the way the ships were built. You have to eat in two, or sometimes three, shifts. The lounges and music room can accommodate only a minority of the passengers at any one time.

But, in spite of the inadequate facilities, you can get an enormous amount of pleasure out of the voyage along the Labrador coast, especially if you are a hardened old campaigner like me, who has been down to Labrador nine times. I make a point of doing everything possible for myself, almost never summoning a steward. I nip into the galley and make my own coffee. I take showers at four o'clock in the morning. I sleep at all sorts of odd hours when not all of the other three inmates are using the over-used atmosphere in the stateroom. One of the peculiarities of a sea voyage seems to be that you can fall asleep instantly, any time you lie down. I spend most of my time on deck – and that, of course, is the place to enjoy a voyage.

The specialty of the Labrador trip is the icebergs, and, occasionally, early in the season, ice-fields. The bergs, calved from the glaciers on the west coast of Greenland, may spend years drifting about in the Arctic before the Labrador Current catches them and starts them moving southward to their death in the Gulf Stream. An endless parade of them passes along the coast of Labrador throughout the summer. Some are white, some have intrinsic shades of blue and green, all are coloured by reflections and prismatic effects. Sometimes the captains of the Labrador ships will alter course slightly and pass close to icebergs to give passengers a chance to take photographs.

There are also whales and seals and thousands of sea-birds, and the Labrador specialty, the marine mirages. In this amazing effect of the summer light along the Labrador coast, entire islands will appear above the horizon, or inverted in the sky. Others will sit on thin blue stalks like mushrooms growing out of the sea. I have never known anyone to photograph one of the mirages successfully, though I see no reason why it couldn't be done with sensitive film and a very long lens.

You may run into bad luck, and get some fog or rain or wind. But this is not the rule along Labrador, and especially northern Labrador, in the summer. As you go north along the Atlantic coast the weather gets finer, the rainfall less and less. Northern Labrador gets more sunshine than any other part of the Canadian Atlantic shore.

Temperatures on the open sea remain low, rarely getting above the sixties, but at the heads of the deep bays to which the ship penetrates – at Port Hope Simpson, for instance, or at Goose Bay or North West River – the temperatures are often in the eighties and sometimes in the nineties. The only problem at North West River in summer is drought. If there were enough rainfall, it could be an important agricultural community. Even with the lack of rain, the Grenfell Mission there manages to raise field crops enough to supply its hospital and boarding school, and some of the local flower gardens are very handsome indeed.

The trip up Hamilton Inlet and Lake Melville to Goose Bay is one of the highlights of the Labrador voyage. Goose Bay is 150 miles from Indian Harbour on the open coast, at the inner end of a salt-water lake that stretches almost to the centre of Labrador. The largest coastal town, Happy Valley, lies right beside it. The loveliest village in Labrador, North West River, built by trappers two and three generations ago, is thirty miles from Goose Bay and connected by road. The Hudson's Bay Company, the Grenfell Mission, the Oblate Fathers (serving the Indians), and the Newfoundland government all have stations at North West River. It is the only place in Labrador that has large numbers of all three races – Indian, Eskimo, and white. They manage to get along with very little friction.

The predominantly Eskimo settlements do not begin until you reach Hopedale. Nain, the farthest north of the permanent settlements, is almost entirely Eskimo. Some people go north of Nain to Nutak, Hebron, Saglec Bay, and Nachvak Fjord for seal-hunting and fishing. This part of Labrador, beginning at the Kiglapait Mountains, is the most spectacular and cruel-looking country in eastern North America. The Kiglapaits are 3,000 feet high, sheer rock, rising straight out of the sea. Farther north, the mountains get even higher – 5,550 feet at Nachvak Fjord, with sheer drops of more than 4,000 feet from cliff edge to ocean. I have never felt so insignificant as when sailing along the foot of the northern Labrador cliffs in a small boat. These mountains are fittingly named for the great and terrible spirit worshipped and feared by the pagan Eskimos – Torngat, the god of the storm and the wild.

Few visitors ever see this part of the country. Scheduled passenger service ends at Nain. Beyond that lie three hundred miles of coastline that can be visited only by chartered boat, or on the occasional schooner or freight boat that will agree to take passengers.

It is possible to buy some excellent articles – handiwork, art objects, and Indian goods – on the Labrador voyage. During stops at St. Anthony, Cartwright, and North West River, you may be able to purchase clothing, woven goods, carvings, and other items made under supervision of the Grenfell Missions. At Davis Inlet you can buy from the Oblate priests, and sometimes also from the government store, absolutely genuine Indian work, made by traditional methods and to traditional patterns without any outside pressures or influences whatsoever. Besides beautiful deerskin moccasins, the Davis Inlet Indians make good deerskin drums with goose-quill rattles, the best bears-paw snowshoes that you can buy anywhere, and some items of deerskin clothing, embroidered with traditional designs. There is not much good Eskimo work for sale anywhere on Labrador, but you can sometimes buy fine sealskin boots with duckskin tops at Nain. The children there will also sell you beautiful samples of Labradorite, a semi-precious variety of iridiscent feldspar that is made into jewellery in Newfoundland.

The coast of Labrador has changed very little in my lifetime. Cities are rising in the interior, far to the west, but the coast is not greatly different from the coast first visited by Dr. Grenfell in 1892. It is still one of the truly unspoiled, truly great, truly primitive places of the earth. Though you can now reach the main centres of Labrador by plane in a few hours, I still prefer to visit it by coastal ship, doing nothing whatsoever except lounging on deck while the ship threads her way among the thousands of islands and up the long fjords that slice through the purple land toward the interior. I have done it several times in the past, and I can still think of no more delightful way to spend a couple of weeks.

25. The Last Tent-dwellers

Along the shores of Labrador's greatest waterway lives the southern band of the Nascaupi Indians, or the Montagnais-Nascaupi as some anthropologists call them. There never was much difference between Montagnais and Nascaupi, a very slight dialect variation, much less than you would note between Boston and New York, for example. They have precisely the same cultural heritage, the same stories, the same beliefs, the same hunting methods, and since white men arrived in Labrador they have been constantly intermarrying. Whatever difference might once have existed between the two bands had disappeared at least a hundred years ago.

Their highway is the Lake Melville system of inland water, navigable by ships for two hundred miles from Holton on the coast to the mouth of the Nascaupi River, which stretches toward the base of Hudson Bay. Some fifty thousand square miles are drained by the great rivers which meet in this tidewater lake, some of it still prime trapping and hunting country.

The Indian summer is a regular season in this virgin land, for it is one of the few places in North America where the forests have not been cut or cleared. All the numerous logging and timbering operations started in Labrador over the past century or so have failed, and left the forests intact. Here trout is a staple food, and caribou meat, rather than bread, is the staff of life.

The finest of hunters, and skilled in a variety of beautiful arts, the Nascaupi are among the last peoples in North America to retain their primitive way of life. Many of them still live in tents all year around, though those at North West River now have wooden houses, and even the Davis Inlet band has gone so far as to build wooden foundations for their canvas tents. They can cut timbers by hand out of the forests and fashion them into the ribs and planks of excellent canoes. They make the strongest, lightest snowshoes found anywhere. They can work caribou hide into thick cloth for clothing or into hard, thin parchment for drum heads.

At one time the wanderings of this people took them the length and breadth of the Labrador Peninsula, five hundred miles inland to Ungava Bay, a thousand miles north and south, from the Gulf of St. Lawrence to Hudson Strait. There are still some Indians living who can draw rough maps of the entire peninsula from personal knowledge and observation.

The southern band, which has gone considerably further in the process of 'turning white' than has the band at Davis Inlet, is centred at North West River, where they have a church and a school, access to a hospital, and two stores at which to trade.

There was no Christian mission to the Labrador Indians until 1930, and no resident priest in Labrador until 1952, except for a priest at Pinware in the Strait of Belle Isle, which no Indian ever visited. When the Oblate Fathers arrived in 1952 the Nascaupi were a vanishing race, fading rapidly from the face of the earth. Disease and starvation were taking an annual toll from a people whose numbers had once gone into the thousands, but by then had shrunk to less than three hundred souls. The Labrador Indians had never lived on a reservation, never signed a treaty. No provision was made for them in the terms of union between Newfoundland and Canada, and the federal government refused to accept any responsibility for them. In a report that I prepared for the provincial government in 1950 I predicted that they would all be dead in about ten years.

A branch of the great Algonkian family of tribes, they had refused to have anything more than a trading relationship with the whites. Their hunting grounds had been restricted more and more as white trappers took over parts of the great watershed where they hunted, all the way back to the height of land, 200 or 300 miles to the west. Their numbers shrank with their hunting grounds. They died from introduced diseases – things like measles, which every white child recovered from, but which killed Indians, who knew nothing about treatment, as though it were the Black Death. Their health grew steadily worse as they came to rely more and more on store supplies of flour and lard and sugar and tea without any knowledge of nutrition. When Father Pirson arrived at North West River in 1952 there were 161 Indians there, 120 at Davis Inlet, and their future looked hopeless.

It is to the everlasting credit of the Oblates that they rescued the Labrador Indians from extinction, set them on the path to recovery, and tried to smooth their transition to the white man's world. Since the arrival of the missionaries, the Indians' numbers have almost doubled. The priests have started schools where the Indian children get instruction, first in their own language and later in English. As a result, English is beginning to be a working language among the Nascaupi for the first time, and one of the greatest barriers separating them from the whites is being broken down. They are also encouraged to make the fullest possible use of the health services offered by the Grenfell Mission, and as a result of this their gravest health problems have been solved. In the tribe today there is a great excess of children and young people, and only a few elders, from the time when death seemed about to triumph over the entire race.

These young Indians sense, in an obscure way, that the visitor from the outside represents their own future. Their ambition is to live like white people – not like white people in cities, for they have no conception of what cities are like, but like the white people that they see in the attractive frontier settlement of North West River. The girls want to have a house of their own with a store-bought broom and a crib for the baby instead of a hammock. The boys want to drive trucks or bulldozers. For a long time these people held themselves deliberately aloof from Europeans. Now, at last, they have faced the necessity of 'turning white'. They have lost their centuries-long battle to remain Indians, and are accepting defeat with the best grace that they can. The best of them are now trying to make a compromise, to work with and for the white people at the kinds of jobs where they excel – as foresters, prospectors, guides, and in other outdoor occupations. The government, which, on occasion, hires every available man to fight forest fires, says that they are the best fire-fighters they have ever had on the pay-roll, and has put a few of them on the permanent staff of the forestry division.

The Labrador of the Indian is on the way out. For though the coast remains largely unchanged, the interior forests do not.

Great airports, mining towns, railroads, the world's largest power development, have all been built or are well under way on the Labrador Plateau, the Indian's former hunting ground. A highway is being built right across the middle of it. White sportsmen have everywhere taken over the fishing, and, in western Labrador, the hunting as well. Bush planes and helicopters visit every lake and river. Almost 20,000 white people have gone to live on the Labrador Plateau within the last ten years.

So they look to a future among white men, not in the forests of their ancestors. Mrs. Anna Hammond, principal of the Indian school at North West River, who has taught Indians for many years, says that the children love to read Westerns about cowboys and Indians. They invariably identify themselves with the cowboys, she says, never with the Indians.

The Eskimos made their decision for the white man's way of life a lot earlier than the Indians. At Nain today just about everybody speaks English, and the children even quarrel in English. They have gone in heavily for machines and gadgets of all kinds. Some of them have telephones in their houses. Most of them know the intricacies of internal-combustion engines, and indeed there seems to be a great mechanical aptitude, a surprising thing in a stone-age people, which the Eskimos were until recently.

They have a knack for getting along with white people. Eskimos are naturally happy, naturally cheerful, incurable optimists and extroverts. Everywhere that the races have been allowed to mingle in a natural way, by their own choice, they have gotten along extremely well, and there has been a good deal of intermarriage, often producing markedly superior children.

It was not all brotherly love in the old days, however. When the first Moravian missionaries arrived on the coast of Labrador to minister to the Eskimos in 1764, they found Eskimos and French (displaced Acadians) living in reasonable harmony, and intermarrying to some extent. Some of the Eskimos could speak French well enough for the missionaries to communicate with them in that language. But between the Eskimos and the English, or English-speaking Newfoundlanders who went north for fishing or whaling, there was implacable hatred and warfare. The Eskimos, who had purchased guns from the French settlers, were not by any means as helpless as the Beothuck Indians in Newfoundland, and seemed to be able to hold their own against the whites. Nevertheless, they were being driven gradually from their sealing and whaling grounds, and in time would have been exterminated, like the Beothucks, if the Moravians had not arrived, taken the Eskimos' part, and stopped the slaughter.

The Acadian French of southern Labrador, augmented by a few Newfoundland settlers and traders, and intermarried with the most southerly bands of the Eskimos, formed the basis for the third racial group in Labrador – the Livyers. Livyers are white or near-white natives of the coast. The word is said to have originated from 'live here', and might in that sense include all residents. But in the days of the great Labrador fishery there were three broad classes of fishermen: the schoonermen, who went north from Newfoundland and fished from ships, the stationers, who went north from Newfoundland and fished from the shore, and the Livyers, who also fished from the shore but lived in Labrador all year around, usually moving out to temporary homes on headlands or islands in the summer, and back to more comfortable quarters in the forests or the heads of the bays in winter – the white migrants of the barren shore.

The Livyers, at first French-Eskimo, were gradually mixed with settlers of other races. English, Scots, Welsh, and a few Scandinavians all settled in Labrador and married Livyers. Soon there were no Eskimos left south of Hamilton Inlet. They had all been absorbed into the Livyer population. Most of the Livyers today are black-haired and a little darker than most Europeans, perhaps approaching the colour of Spaniards, who, like the Livyers, had the benefit of a racial transfusion some generations back. But many Livyers with blond hair, fair skin, and blue eyes keep cropping up, too. The racial mixture that produced this sturdy breed is by no means homogeneous.

At one place in Labrador modern Eskimo-white relations have been less than harmonious. That is at Makkovik, a northern settlement about half way between Goose Bay and Nain.

Makkovik was originally an Eskimo village. Later it became a Moravian mission station, with a migrant Eskimo population that moved back and forth with the hunting, but always came into the village for religious festivals. Eventually, however, the Eskimos moved away for better hunting, or disappeared by intermarriage. They were replaced by Livyers, mainly of Scandinavian origin with names such as Andersen, and whatever Eskimo blood these people had they were ready to deny with heat.

When the government decided to close down the northern post at Hebron, they resettled most of the Hebron Eskimos at Makkovik in houses that they built for them, not intermingled with the houses of the Livyers, but in a sort of subdivision, off to one side. A second Eskimo subdivision was created on the other side of the Livyers, for another band of Eskimos from Okak Bay who had formerly traded at the government post of Nutak, which had also been closed.

The Livyers didn't like the Eskimos' living habits, and the Eskimos didn't like the Livyers snobbishness. Differing views on the sharing of food and of hunting gear contributed to further friction. Soon the Livyers were calling in the R.C.M.P. and demanding that the Eskimos be punished for various petty offences against the white man's law. No fewer than seventy Eskimos were carted off to jail from the small settlement in a single year. And that, at the moment, is where matters stand. There has been nothing similar in other parts of Labrador, where integration and intermarriage have proceeded without government assistance.

The outlook for all three races on the coast is quite uncertain. It remains a primitive, frontier country without great economic prospects. The Americans arrived during the Second World War and put up their first small weather stations. They flocked north during the Cold War and built a chain of radar installations stretching from St. Anthony to Saglec Bay. They employed some of the people, especially at Cartwright, which began to take on a distinctly American flavour. Juke boxes and pinball machines and fish and chips and Coke arrived on the coast of Labrador. The Canadian government, anxious to make at least a gesture toward defending the North American continent from Russian conquest, organized the Eskimos into a nominal militia, and armed them with government-issue rifles to repel a Russian amphibious landing, should one be attempted. From time to time they issued ammunition, too, as the first issues were used up in target practice (the targets usually being seals, of course).

But now it is all over. The Cold War thawed. The military

fortification of Labrador came to be recognized for the expensive foolishness that it had, in fact, always been. The radar stations closed. The Americans departed. Their disc-shaped antennae still stand as monuments to an era of hysterical nonsense, but the Americanization of the coast, which seemed for a time to be inevitable, is quickly being forgotten. After the brief upsurge of the Chewing Gum Era, the coast of Labrador is going back to the Livyers and the seals.

It may well be that the coast has no future in the twentieth century, and will gradually be deserted, as the northern settlements of Ramah, Hebron, Okak, and Nutak already have been. The same cannot be said for the Labrador interior, where the twentieth century has descended like a thunderbolt from heaven.

26. The Wave of the Future

Labrador City is the only Newfoundland town completely indistinguishable from mainland Canada. It could be built in any part of the Northwest Territories, in Nouveau Québec, or even in Alaska, without any notable difference in its character or its appearance. Perhaps it is a symbol of Newfoundland's future, for it is the only large community that has appeared in the province since Newfoundland entered Confederation.

Western Labrador's only claim to distinction is a series of world records: the biggest integrated iron-ore complex, the largest hydro-electric plant, the most powerful machines of their type on earth – things of that sort. Twenty million tons of the earth's crust is processed there each year.

The town itself (Labrador City and Wabush, under separate municipal governments, are really a single community) is a place of sharp contrasts. Plastic and chrome and tile, concrete and synthetic stone and asphalt keep company with bears and porcupines. An automated railway that runs itself without a human soul on board must watch with its electric eyes for caribou at the crossings.

Flying over the Labrador Plateau, you get the feeling of infinity. The land is flat, endless, and monotonous, a tangle of lakes and rivers and muskeg and patches of forest that seem to extend for ever in all directions. You wonder how mere humans ever had the courage to face it, to come to terms with it, to make their homes there. But men will do just about anything for money. And western Labrador, forbidding as it looks, is immensely profitable.

For the Labrador Trough (a mineralized depression plunging four hundred miles southward from Hudson Bay) has one

of the world's greatest iron ranges, and seems fated to become
one of the major industrial centres of Canada. Mining, milling,
and shipping of iron ore, hydro-electric production, transport,
and related services have already attracted 50,000 people to this
region shared by Newfoundland and Quebec. The population
will probably double by 1980.

Though travel in and out of western Labrador is mostly by
air, with numerous daily flights from St. John's, Deer Lake,
Moncton, Sept Iles, and Montreal, there are also passenger
trains on the fourteen-hour run between Labrador City and the
Gulf of St. Lawrence. These trains are patronized mainly by
sightseers, for, unlike the plateau where the mines are situated,
the valleys of the Wacouno and the Ashuanipi, through which
the north-south line runs, have spectacular scenery. The rail
line is, of course, mainly used for ore shipments. Trains hauling
125 cars each, and measuring almost a mile, arrive at Sept Iles
ten times a day.

There is not much tourist accommodation in western Labrador. The Sir Wilfred Grenfell Inn at Labrador City is comfortable, and has a good dining-room and bar, but is always
crowded, and requires reservations a long time in advance. You
can visit Churchill Falls only as the guest of Brinco, the company developing the power, for there is no public accommodation at all.

Life in this wilderness has many oddities: thousands of motor
cars, for instance, all shipped in by rail, and all confined to
about thirty miles of local roads, the longest drive being to a
provincial park on a lake near Labrador City. There are many
boats and private planes, for money flows freely, all the jobs
are highly skilled and highly paid, and there is no unemployment. Sailing and fishing are the major sports, for wilderness
lakes stretch eastward in a connected chain for thirty-five miles
from the mines. Tourist outfitters at Labrador City will fly
fishermen to lodges on one of the interior lakes for as little as
$50 return.

But apart from wilderness sports and the occasional visits of
wild animals, there is little feeling of the frontier at Labrador
City. The houses and public buildings are all permanent and
well constructed. The schools are the best, physically and aca-
demically, in Newfoundland. There are restaurants, movies,
bowling alleys, a public library, a recreation centre, and two

social clubs running imported floor shows, all of them exceptionally well equipped.

Labrador City is Newfoundland's first bilingual community. French and English are used about equally, have about equal status, and a very high proportion of the people are fluent in both languages; and there is a high degree of mutual respect and integration between the two cultures.

The climate is cold, except for brief periods in the summer when it is usually wet. Since it is almost 2,000 feet above sea-level, the Labrador Plateau is seven degrees colder than would be normal for its latitude. Winters are cold and dry, summers cloudy and cool. A weather station at Sandgirt Lake, between Labrador City and Churchill Falls, registered the record low for the province – 55 below zero. Nevertheless, the winters are pleasant. A foot or so of powder snow falls early and stays on the ground. There is rarely any wind. Cloudless days follow one another in a long succession, and skiing (and even winter sun-bathing on the enclosed deck of the ski-lodge) is very popular.

The ore that keeps Labrador City running lies all around, literally in mountains. The largest chunk is three and a half square miles in area and nobody knows how deep. Proven reserves will last more than a century at present rates of extraction.

The mining and milling are practically automatic processes, done by giant machines and computers that run themselves except for watching and maintenance. The operators are housed in control rooms that look like the flight decks of space ships, full of buttons, switches, and banks of winking coloured lights. There is no mining in the old sense, just machines of monstrous size and power tearing down the mountains and reducing them to food for the blast furnaces of Canada and the United States.

The power for this industrial monster comes from the Churchill River, already producing a quarter of a million horse-power, and destined to produce between six and ten million when its development is complete. Most of the power will be used by Quebec, but a large fraction of it will be used in Labrador for further industrial development.

The Churchill Falls power station, now being built, is under a thousand feet of rock in the heart of a mountain, and drains tens of thousands of square miles of lakes through stainless steel tunnels to turn its ten generators. More than twice as powerful as any previously built in the western world, it will produce six million horsepower at 474,000 volts.

The Churchill gives an impression of almost supernatural power. As you stand on the alpine meadow, drenched with spray, beside the main falls, the ground trembles under your feet and a plume of spray rises into the heavens. For three miles above the falls the river roars and rages with frightening ferocity, heaping into a great ridge as it rushes between its narrowing banks in the half-mile-long, steep chute leading to the lip. The vertical drop from lip to plunge pool is only 245 feet, but when the cataracts above are added, the total drop is 1,040 feet.

The entire river is being diverted, and a new lake half as long as Lake Ontario created behind earthen dams to feed the power station. The designers of the plant, a thousand feet underground at the end of this lake, say that it will be out of the reach of frost or any other kind of weather damage or human attack, and would survive even a direct hit with a hydrogen bomb. They expect it to outlast the Great Pyramid.

The combined effect of the mining and power developments is to move Labrador directly from the stone age to the age of the atom. Almost within living memory its Eskimos and Indians were literally stone-age men, depending mainly on hand-made tools fashioned out of the materials that lay around them. Even the white men who had gone north lived primitive lives not far removed from those of the sixteenth-century whalers who explored its coasts and first taught its people the use of iron.

Suddenly it is a land of automation, with railways, airports, a highway being built across its heart, the beginnings of three cities, and the likelihood that, before the end of this century, its population will surpass that of some Canadian provinces. It is a frightening revolution, but perhaps, also, one of great promise. It is in places such as Labrador City and Churchill Falls that Industrial Man is being tested, and that he will prove or disprove the ultimate worth of his technology.

27. "... to Toslow we'll go"

We'll rant and we'll roar like true Newfoundlanders:
We'll rant and we'll roar on deck and below,
Until we see bottom inside the two sunkers,
When straight through the channel to Toslow we'll go.
— folk song by H. W. LE MESSURIER

If you take a boat at Famish Gut and sail among the tickles of Placentia Bay, following the track of the French refugees who fled westward before the conquering English two and a half centuries ago, you will come to domes of purple rock that rise stark out of black water with rings of white foam at their feet. Beyond lie great islands laced with rivers, Red Island and Merasheen, Sound Island and Bar Haven, Kings Island and Isle Valen.

There are long runs of calm water shining in the sun, sandy islands, rocky islands, islands green with turf, islands where the lone seal lies basking in the sun, islands black and white with birds that scream at your approach, and rise and wheel and mew in plaintive voices, and settle, grumbling, upon their rocks once more. Here are long echoes of human footsteps in places named by the fancy of an earlier time: Haystack, Harbour Buffett, Great Brule, Tacks Beach, and Rose-au-Rue.

On all these islands men have lived and died, known the sharp, pangful joys of childhood, the agony of love, the struggles and defeats and slow tarnishing of the years, the rest of old age, and the peace which is sure enough at its end.

Most of them lie empty now — not empty of life, but of men only, for life goes forward in a great tide, irresistible, filling all the chinks and crevices of the earth, reaching out to claim its waste places, bringing them slowly into its domain. And those that men desert soon bear great crops of fireweed or bracken, or harvest of silver-headed thistles for the buntings and the finches and the winter stores of small brown voles deep-buried under moss.

On most of these islands you may still see traces of men in the turf: the sunken squares of root-cellars, hearthstones made black by the wood fires of generations, potato fields that are now mere furrows under acres of wild pasture, leaving the land combed and tamed, and a little gentler than it used to be in the time before the coming of man.

And beyond the islands lies the farther shore, speaking with the music of surf on sunken rocks – St. Leonard's and St. Kyrens and Paradise Sound, Petit Forte and Marticot and Little Bona.

If you cross the narrow run from Merasheen and pass into the island-studded waters to the west, you will come to a narrow passage leading to a sheltered bay. St. Anne's is on the starboard, Great Paradise on the port, the cliff-hemmed cleft of Presque lies dead ahead. And here between the breakers, where the rocks and mussel beds absorb the surf, is a clear green channel leading to a little harbour.

Enter it, for this is a place of legend and of history, of beauty and of symbol. The fishermen of New France came to this small cove in the years when the Sun King sat upon his throne, and his sceptre spanned the oceans of the world. They came to gather fish from the shallow banks off shore, and they chose this little harbour for its safety. But they named it for its beauty. They called it La Tasse de l'Argent, the Cup of Silver.

As generations passed, and the French language was first submerged, then lost, the name of the small village was lost as well. It was corrupted more and more by people who no longer knew what it meant, until 'Tasse de l'Argent' became 'Toslow John'. But no one knew who Toslow John might have been: his deeds and his fame survived not even in legend. So at length they dropped the 'John', and the village became simply 'Toslow'.

Though scarcely more than a hamlet, with only a handful of fishing families sheltering among its hills, it became under that name the symbol of all the little outports around the thousands of miles of the Newfoundland coastline, and its tricky approaches became symbolic of coastal navigation everywhere. Every Newfoundlander who could sing a note, and most of those who could not, sang about Toslow. The great majority of the singers had never seen Toslow, nor had they any idea of where it was, but that did not matter, for Toslow existed in the land of the imagination; like the Islands of the Blessed, it was everyone's ancestral village, where his fathers had laboured and hoped and loved and passed in the end under its sod or its waves.

If you go to the village of Toslow today, you will see no nets spread along its green banks, no fish whitening its silver rocks, no children angling for tom cods along its brown stage-heads. For its people moved in a body, a few years ago, to another, larger island, up in the inner reaches of Placentia Bay. Their boats, their gear, their houses, even their stores and net lofts, went with them.

Perhaps it is best that way. No dusty road with cars or trucks will ever bring twentieth-century Canada into Toslow. It will be Newfoundland for all time to come. It is safe in the years that were. It will remain for ever inviolate, the village that gave us birth, that shaped us, that made us what we are, this happy breed of men that came, somehow, out of the fire and ice of the past, and stood upon this iron-black land, and looked fearlessly upon the sea and the surrounding hills, and called a little cove a cup of silver.

Appendix I

Canoeing in Newfoundland

Notre Dame Bay, biting deep into central Newfoundland, was used by both Indians and pioneers as the natural route into the wilderness. Since all but one of the largest rivers on the island flow north-eastward, most of the canoe routes to the interior begin either here or in Bonavista Bay, just to the east.

A big power development at Bay d'Espoir on the south coast now makes use of most of the waters from the inland plateau, and this development with its dams, canals, and artificial lakes, has opened up a practical canoe route right across Newfoundland from north to south.

The route is long and circuitous, running south-west by the old canoe trails of the Beothuck Indians, then almost due east across country that was scarcely passable before the power development, and finally south through a series of interconnected lakes to Bay d'Espoir.

The distance is approximately two hundred survey-miles, but more like three hundred water-miles. It should be attempted only by thoroughly experienced wilderness canoeists, or with a local guide familiar with canoe travel in the interior. There are many shorter canoe trips that are safe for the inexperienced.

The cross-country canoe route begins at Norris Arm on the Trans-Canada Highway, ten miles west of Notre Dame Junction and the Road to the Isles. From here it is fifty miles by river to Badger, the last settlement on the route, and jumping-off point for the interior. The lower Exploits River by which you travel to Badger is the largest in the island, and is quite an easy river for canoeing, even when going up-stream. There are two waterfalls and a power dam, but no long stretches of rapids. Sometimes you have to portage past log booms, but the river flows gently, meandering in places, through beautiful country well supplied with wildlife. You will certainly see moose and many waterfowl, even on this first fifty miles of the river. You pass two large towns, Bishop's Falls and Grand Falls, on the route.

From Badger it is thirty-five miles by the upper Exploits to Red Indian Lake. There are falls and, finally, a dam to be negotiated, before you get into the lake itself. There are alternate routes from the Red Indian Lake dam to Victoria Lake (the beginning of the big central water system), and since the patterns of water flow are being changed very rapidly by power developments now taking place, it is best to inquire on the spot about the desirability of either.

If you follow either shore of Red Indian Lake, you come, at last, to Lloyds River and Lloyds Lake. There is a portage route from the eastern end of Lloyds into one of the northern arms of Victoria. It is also possible to portage straight across the Annieopsquotch Mountains from the central part of one lake to the central part of the other, since the mountains consist of bare rock interspersed with peat bog, and are neither wooded nor very high. This portage is five miles long.

A more interesting route – a very attractive one indeed, before the power development – went by way of Victoria River, which enters Red Indian Lake four miles west of the dam. This river flows through some of the loveliest and wildest country in the island, with every bird and wild animal found in the Newfoundland interior, except only for the rare arctic hare that is now confined to some sections of the Long Range Mountains.

It is approximately forty miles by river from Red Indian Lake to the Victoria Lake Dam, on which construction began in 1968. Some of this forty miles is very rough going, with rapids and falls that have to be portaged, but there are also very long gentle stretches flowing through valleys of true wilderness grandeur.

The new dam, raising the level of Victoria Lake more than a hundred feet and more than doubling its area, will rob the upper Victoria River of most of its water. It may be necessary, therefore, to inquire about water-levels before undertaking this part of the trip by this route. There is a road by-pass that can be used as a last resort.

From Victoria Lake the new Victoria Diversion Canal leads into the interconnected lake system of the central Newfoundland plateau. This plateau, covering almost a third of the island, is so flat that all its major lakes and rivers are very nearly on the same level, and it is possible to travel by canoe from almost any part of it to almost any other part with no more than a half-mile portage across barren ground.

This, however, is the place where a guide becomes practically essential. On this great, flat stretch of land the waterways are so complex, the false leads into dead ends so numerous, that almost anyone unfamiliar with the terrain is likely to get lost. I have been over some parts of this route myself, but never over the whole of it, and not since the extensive flooding of the power development. It is fascinating but dangerous country. It includes the home ground of the major caribou herds in Newfoundland, and anyone crossing it will see caribou by the hundreds if not by the thousands.

The topographic maps of the area were made before the great Bay d'Espoir power development. Consequently they do not, at present, give even a vaguely correct picture of the water systems, which have been radically changed by the dams and the canals. Maps can be obtained from the Newfoundland and Labrador Power Commission at St. John's.

The Victoria Diversion Canal leads into Burnt Pond, and then through another canal into Granite Lake. The route from Victoria is almost due east for sixty miles through Granite and Meelpaeg Lakes (the latter now covering 170 square miles), and the Meelpaeg Canal to Great Burnt Lake, then south through a natural drainage system into Round Pond, Little Burnt Pond, and Long Pond, another thirty-six miles to the point overlooking the Bay d'Espoir power station. The portages from Victoria to Bay d'Espoir consist only of by-passing dams and penstocks.

The upper reaches of Bay d'Espoir itself are also ideal for canoe travel.

Best water conditions for river travel in Newfoundland are found in spring, while the rivers are high, but best weather conditions are from mid June to mid October. By June, unfortunately, most of the smaller rivers are so low that even a canoe will only float for short stretches before grounding on rocks or gravel. The typical Newfoundland stream is swift but shallow, and is often littered with boulders and stones left over from the ice age. There are a few exceptions, to be noted presently.

Lakes are quite another matter, of course, and Newfoundland canoe routes make liberal use of the many beautiful and often interconnected lakes in a province one-third of whose surface is water. But even lake travel has its special problems. Small lakes are calm enough for canoe travel in almost any wind conditions, but large lakes may sometimes be impassable to canoes for several days at a stretch, in which case you must be prepared to stay in camp, windbound.

A canoe trip that traverses some of the best trout waters, includes two salmon rivers, and can be made in mid summer without special problems, since it lies through a long chain of small lakes with only short stretches of river or brook, begins at Gambo and swings through a wide arc to Indian Bay. The only long portage is across the watershed from the Gambo to the Indian Bay drainage system. It is two miles, but it lies along an old logging road, so it is smooth going. The route is through Traverse Brook to Gull Pond, and from the Gull Pond run-in by road to Wing Pond, then by the lakes of the Indian Bay River to Indian Bay itself – a total distance of about forty miles. It should be planned as a two-day or three-day trip, depending on how much, if any, fishing is planned.

There are no restrictions against visitors to Newfoundland using canoe routes and wilderness trails, even without local guides. Sometimes, in periods of fire crisis, the forests outside the national parks are closed to all travel, but this is quite unusual. Except for the area of the Bay d'Espoir power development, inch-to-the-mile topographic maps, sold by both federal and provincial governments at very small cost, are available for the whole province, and show every feature of the ground, down to little streams a foot or so wide.

A more ambitious canoe trip, also starting at Gambo, takes you all the way to Gander Bay, with even less physical strain than the trip to Indian Bay – again with plentiful fishing en route. It follows the same course to Gull Pond, but takes the southerly instead of the northerly portage into Benton Lake. Seven miles of paddling then takes you to Benton, where you can get a truck to take canoe and gear to Gander Lake. If you wish to be a purist, you could follow Benton Brook for two miles to the same destination, but it would be very tough going.

Once into Gander Lake you have a great stretch of perfect canoe water – twenty-seven miles to Glenwood from Benton Brook, thirty miles by river from Glenwood to Gander Bay. There are two rapids on the upper three miles of the Lower Gander River, but both of them are passable under all water conditions, and neither is considered in the least dangerous by experienced canoeists. The last twenty-seven miles of the route are perfectly smooth, and a great pleasure to travel. The total distance is approximately eighty-five miles, and it is perhaps the easiest route of this length in eastern Newfoundland.

Both the lower and upper Terra Nova rivers provide good canoe water. The first falls is seven miles above Glovertown. Above that, it is eight miles to Big Falls, with more than twenty miles of lake and river lying above. Up to Big Falls, it is a salmon river. Above, the fishing is mainly for trout and landlocked salmon.

Indian or pre-Indian relics, some of very ancient date, are often found along the Terra Nova. There are also deposits of Beothuck Indian artefacts at Alexander Bay, where the Terra Nova enters the sea. One of the artefacts that I examined, taken from the river where it washed out of a sand bank, was a very large, ancient hand axe (*coup de poing*) of chipped stone, a purely palaeolithic instrument of the Boreal Archaic period.

It is said to be possible to travel by canoe from the settlement of Terra Nova, by way of Lake St. John, Eastern Meelpaeg, Jubilee Lake, and Hungry Grove Pond into the waters of Long Harbour, Fortune Bay. But I wouldn't try it myself, even in spring, let alone mid summer. The proper plan on the upper Terra Nova is to follow the river and its lakes so long as the going isn't too rough, then to retrace your route to the railway, the highway, or the sea. I should estimate about forty miles of canoeable water in mid summer in this region.

From Badger, on the Exploits, it is possible not only to take the route to Red Indian Lake and on to the deep interior, but also to follow a second excellent route by way of Badger Brook (really a fine river, despite its name) into the chain of lakes that formed the old Badger Drive of the pioneer loggers.

This chain of lakes and rivers leads northward approximately thirty miles to the big lakes above Badger Bay. Catamaran Brook Provincial Park, with excellent camping grounds, lies along the route. There is good fishing at some points. Possibly the biggest landlocked salmon in Newfoundland come out of the lakes of the Badger Drive. In summer they lie deep and must be taken by trolling.

The interconnected chain of Grand Lake, Sandy Lake, and Birchy Lake offers a flat stretch of water ninety miles long – a lot of it rather big water for small boats. From Howley, where Sandy Lake and Grand Lake meet, there is, however, a very interesting run through Sandy Lake and along Birchy Lake, with a short portage into Sheffield Lake.

Most of this route is protected, and the part that lies through the open waters of Sandy Lake has numerous bays where you can take shelter if it is needed. Birchy Lake is long and river-like. From the round pond at its end a portage trail a mile and a half in length, and very easy going, takes you into Sheffield Lake.

This large lake, though in fact triangular, looks square. It is surrounded by heavy forest, and gives the impression of being in remote wilderness, even though the Trans-Canada Highway is really barely out of sight. Strange and impressive-looking hills – Mount Sheffield, Mount Sykes, Mount Seymour – rise near by, while off to the south are the bare rock spires of the Topsails – The Main, The Mizzen, and The Gaff. Sheffield is the end of the canoe route, but it is not difficult to walk from there to the Topsails, following the brook that empties into Sheffield's southern corner until you reach the barrens. The ground is rough, and the Topsails themselves are in a bleak, Arctic-like stretch of wilderness. But it is really exceptional trout country, and the haunt of many wild animals. I have seen caribou, moose, lynx, and black bears, as well as small game, in the region between Birchy Lake and the Topsails.

The Upper Humber, just west of this system, also offers good canoeing, even when the river is low. It also has annoying stretches of rock ledges, rapids, falls, and log drives. But, in spite of it all, the Upper Humber is well worth the trouble, and once you make it to Alder Pond (which can be reached by private road as well as by public river) you have before you a truly magnificent set of headwaters where the fishing is unsurpassed. If you find time to spare from the salmon, you can also get splendid brook trout here. The largest one ever caught in Newfoundland came from the Upper Humber beyond Alder Pond.

Some years ago I pioneered a very pleasant little canoe route that follows an almost circular path beginning and ending in Terra Nova National Park, Bonavista Bay – a trip that can be made safely by almost anyone, and very easy going for most of the way.

In those days it began with a half-mile portage from the Trans-Canada Highway across peat bogs, but now you can begin at Sandy Pond, where there is a swimming beach reached by a motor road.

From the head of the pond there is a steady, canoeable brook running down from Dunphy's Pond (in Newfoundland almost all lakes, no matter how large, are called 'ponds'). For the last quarter of a mile you have to portage up the brook into Dunphy's Pond – a beautiful, island-studded lake, four miles long.

From Dunphy's Pond there is a short but steep (and mercifully down-hill) portage through open woodland into Pitts Pond, an even larger lake, a little over five miles long. Pitts Pond connects with Terra Nova Lake at the town of Terra Nova, a good place to break your trip before starting down the Terra Nova River to the sea.

The river route from Terra Nova to salt water at Glovertown is less than twenty miles. There are three short portages, around falls and impassable rapids. Otherwise the river is an easy run, and it offers good salmon fishing at least occasionally.

At Glovertown you come out on such a quiet, protected arm of the sea that it looks like just another lake. It is perfectly safe to paddle out the bay and around the headland (which is still protected by capes and islands from open water) into the adjoining arm, and so to Traytown. From there you paddle under the highway bridge into the inner reaches of Sweet Bay, and up the fjord-like arm past beautiful hill and cliff country to the narrows and the beach at its end.

At this point you are back within a few hundred yards of the highroad from which you started, and there is a well-cut trail up to the road. From there you may have to hitch a ride back to the Sandy Pond road from which you began your trip, but otherwise you will have closed the circle by canoe. This run can be completed in a leisurely way, with time for fishing along the route, in two or three days.

Appendix II

Trout, tuna, and other fish

As you drive into St. John's from the west, either by the Trans-Canada Highway or by Route 3, the large body of water that you see off to the left is Conception Bay. The city itself lies on the open Atlantic, separated from the fifty-mile inlet of the bay by a low, forested ridge averaging eight miles in width. The bay has always been at the city's back door, its playground, its bread box, and its sphere of influence.

Most of the bluefin tuna landed by sportsmen on the Atlantic coast each summer come from Conception Bay, and the great majority of them from a narrow strip of water less than fifteen miles long on its eastern shore.

World record tuna came from here in 1956, 1957, 1958, and 1961. They ran from 765 to 871 pounds each. Even bigger ones have been killed by harpooning. Bluefins are among the world's largest and strongest game fish. They put up terrific battles, sometimes lasting five or six hours, and often defeat the efforts of the best anglers. Of 743 tuna hooked in Conception Bay in 1964, only 316 were landed.

Conception Bay anglers boat 250 to 600 bluefins each summer, mostly between mid July and mid September, though a few are taken as late as early October. The fish average over 500 pounds each, but very few reach 700.

The record for one day's fishing is held by Mrs. Dorothea Dean, who boated five tuna with a total weight of nearly 3,000 pounds in a single day in 1964. That same year, Sam Charap of New York boated twenty-four during the month of September.

Conception Bay has the world's largest average run of tuna, except possibly for other Newfoundland bays, farther north, where regular sport fishing has not yet been established. Blue-fins of all sizes migrate northward from the West Indies each spring, but the smaller and younger fish drop off along the route, some spending their summers on the coast of New England, some off Nova Scotia, some along the south coast of Newfoundland. Only the oldest and heaviest ones continue around Cape Race, up the east coast, and past Cape St. Francis into Conception Bay or beyond. It seems that these huge fish return to the tropics in late autumn by way of Western Europe, the Azores, and the mid Atlantic, reaching the Caribbean in the winter, but knowledge of their life cycle is still incomplete.

Approximately thirty tuna boats are offered for charter in Conception Bay. Based at St. Phillips, Long Pond, and Holy-rood – ten, twenty, and thirty miles from St. John's – they charge $85 a day for a maximum of five anglers, and provide crew, tackle, and all necessary equipment for nine-hour trips beginning at 8 a.m. Since the demand at the height of the season always exceeds the supply, boats should be booked well in advance. Licences and guides are not required for any form of salt-water fishing in Newfoundland. Captains and crews of the tuna boats are experts in their trade, and know how to use their boats to the angler's best advantage, not only finding the fish, but manoeuvring so as to help the angler play it with the greatest chance of success. Fish caught are weighed, measured, and photographed for entry in international fishing contests.

Most tuna anglers stay in St. John's and commute the short distance to the boats. But there are also motel accommodations in or near the small ports out of which the boats operate.

There are, of course, many other kinds of fish besides tuna in Conception Bay. They provide one of the most important commercial fisheries in the province. They also provide sport for pier-head fishermen who are content with prizes smaller than the bluefin tuna.

Recently I went down to the wharf at St. Phillips with a heavy spoon-spinner and came home with five large flatfish, which I made into fillets of sole, pan-fried with potato chips. I also caught some dozens of other fish that I didn't want, and returned them to the water.

Sole are among the best of food fishes, and the most desirable that you can catch from a pier-head. Mackerel are sometimes taken from piers, too, by spinning on the surface. They are strong, sporty fish, and excellent eating. You can also fish for mackerel with light spinning gear from small boats. Since you can see these fish on the surface, often with dorsal fins breaking water, you always fish for them visually, never blindly, never casting over an empty stretch of sea.

It is sometimes possible to catch salmon from a pier-head, and there are some spots, such as the Gut at Placentia, where you can do it quite regularly. But checking the regulations is essential: stretches of salt water near the estuaries of rivers are often zoned as 'river' for fishing purposes, and subject to all the regulations imposed on river fishing.

The things you catch from piers are usually more modest than salmon, though often just as large. A lumpfish that I weighed on a pier-head in Conception Bay a few years ago went over thirty pounds. Sea-cats run to three or four feet in length. These are not to be confused with the cat-fish that Huck Finn caught in the turgid waters of the Mississippi. Sea-cats are quite a different animal. Unlike the lumpfish, which gives up almost instantly, the sea-cat puts up a fair fight for its life, though it stays and fights on the bottom, like an eel or a flatfish.

Occasionally you can catch codfish from a pier, though as a rule you must go off shore as far as the nearest headlands. They take spinners very readily, and, indeed, the 'Norwegian jigger' used by the commercial fishermen is actually a sort of large spinner operated on a hand line.

The humble conners are the most plentiful of all fish around Newfoundland piers, and rare indeed is the outport boy who doesn't catch them on baited hooks and shop string. They are members of one of the most famous families of food fishes, the perches, but run to small sizes, rarely more than ten or twelve inches long, even in deep water. The armoured skin and spiked fins make them difficult things to clean and prepare for the pan, but they are well worth it. Their flesh is very like that of fresh-water trout.

Of all the varieties of sport fishing available at St. John's, trouting remains by far the most popular. On May 24, the fisherman's holiday, the city is practically empty of men. 'Going trouting' on that day is not just a sport, it is a ritual, a religion. Anyone who doesn't do it is regarded as a little bit odd. But trouting for one species or another remains good throughout June and July.

Aside from ounaniche, or landlocked salmon, Newfoundland's only native trout generally distributed all over the island is the speckled brook trout (known locally, for some incomprehensible reason, as a 'mud trout', perhaps because it never lives in mud). This fish remains the most popular with anglers, even though it has to compete with imported rainbows and sportier European browns. Brook trout are by far the commonest fish in Newfoundland's fresh waters.

There are many good trout lakes within a hundred miles of St. John's. I should recommend as first choice, however, three areas close together near the Southern Shore Road.

First, Chance Cove Barrens. Every pond here has thousands of trout, a few of them growing to respectable sizes of one to five pounds. To reach the Chance Cove Barrens it is not necessary to beat your way through the woods. There is only low vegetation, and most of the ground is fairly dry. You can walk to the best fishing waters in an hour or so.

Chance Cove Brook, the eastern boundary of this great fishing ground, crosses Route 5 at a point seventy-three miles south of St. John's. (The distance is growing a little less, year by year, as the road is straightened and improved.) Except for sea trout at the estuary, the down-stream part of the brook is worthless. Good fishing begins about two miles up-stream from the bridge. Since the banks are wooded and rough, it is best not to follow the brook but to make a short detour to the south and west across peat bog and barrens, rejoining the brook where it empties out of the up-stream ponds.

The chain of lakes and ponds emptying into Chance Cove Brook offers excellent fishing. There are also big trout in some of the isolated ponds that have no surface drainage. Many of them are connected underground through a layer of glacial till that offers wide-water channels, and some of those less than a hundred feet across will have a big trout or two. A friend of mine caught a two-and-a-half-pounder in a pool so small that he described it as a mud hole.

Folklore says that there are 365 ponds drained by Chance Cove Brook. All of them lie within eight miles of the road, many of them within three, and all have good populations of speckled brook trout.

Second, Rocky Pond Waters. These are on the other side of the road, beginning a mile west of Chance Cove Bridge. The chain of small lakes and brooks stretches due south for six miles to Frenchman's Cove. A canoe or other light boat is a great advantage here, since there are fairly large lakes in the chain, but it has to be carried short distances between ponds, since the brooks are too shallow to float anything larger than a chip.

Rocky Pond touches the road at two points. From the other end you cross the watershed (just a few yards) into the chain of lakes and ponds draining into Frenchman's Cove. The fishing is at its best two or three miles from the road, but even in Rocky Pond itself large trout are occasionally taken.

Third, Biscay Bay Barrens. Four miles west of the Rocky Pond bridges there are two large lakes, the second having an island in its centre. This is Browsey Island Pond. On the opposite side of the road from the pond a large tract of open country, rocky ground interspersed with peat bogs, lakes, and scrub spruce, stretches away to the north-west. Anyone hiking over this country must carry a compass and note its bearings as he goes. The land tends to be featureless, confusing. And, since you are very near the sea, fogs sometimes roll in with startling suddenness, making travel by landmarks impossible.

From the northern tip of Browsey Island Pond, a magnetic-compass bearing north-west by north takes you to a little gully that you skirt on the western side. From there, a bearing north by west takes you to a magnificent lake, just two miles from the road. Here there is a square mile of water and good fishing. The lake has one island, with ground on which you can pitch a tent comfortably. In this region of glacial scree and peat bog decent camping ground is very scarce.

A small lake drains directly into the northern end of the big one. Just beyond, over a low ridge, is a tiny pond. The ridge constitutes a watershed. From this point, the drainage is south-west instead of south-east, ultimately into Trepassey Bay instead of into the open Atlantic. If you follow down the brook from the little pond, or take a compass bearing north-west by west, you will come in somewhat less than a mile to a large lake, connecting, by a series of channels, to many other lakes. Tracts of bogland lie to the north-west, but the bogs are firm enough for walking. To the south and east the country is drier, and mostly barren.

This is a happy hunting ground for anglers, and can be reached by seven miles of walking (or walking and canoeing) from the road at Browsey Island Pond. The trouting here really resembles those stories of the secret pools known only to wilderness initiates.

Just to the north of the barrens lies an interesting little water system that is, if possible, even better than those so far described. You climb over a ridge, and there, stretching away before you, is a perfectly straight valley with a chain of narrow lakes along its floor.

This chain runs north-east for eight miles to the southern slopes of the Butter Pot, and is drained by Renews River. Here you are in the country of the Masterless Men, an area still as wild and seemingly as remote as it was two centuries ago when they hunted and fished there for a living.

The small lakes and ponds of this eight-mile chain are connected almost end to end. Some are separated by short stretches of brook, never more than two or three hundred yards long. All the portages are very easy and very short. The total fall of the water is only a hundred feet in eight miles. The trout fishing is absolutely superb.

To reach this country, you must travel overland approximately ten miles. A few people do it on foot. I have done it myself by pond-hopping with a canoe. There are a total of six portages, the longest about half a mile over barren ground. I am told that the Butter Pot can also be approached by bush vehicles from the north-east, but I have never been over the route, nor seen any map or plan of it.

There is really no such thing as accommodation anywhere in this area. Unless you have use of one of the private cabins near the road, the only practical thing to do is to take a trailer or a tent.

Newfoundland angling waters are not stocked. They carry nothing but wild fish. For this reason you must walk at least a mile or two from the main roads (or travel an equal distance by boat) to reach good trout waters, and perhaps two or three times that distance for really first-class fishing. Visitors sometimes complain that the angling in Newfoundland does not justify its advance billing. That is because they are fishing in the fished-out waters by the roadsides.

Any poll of Newfoundland anglers would produce a heavy vote in favour of the speckled brook trout. It is outclassed in almost every way by rainbows and browns, but for some irrational reason we simply love the brookie. I admit it's silly, but I feel that way about it myself.

I remember a big brook trout that I hooked some years ago just as dark was falling on a cold, misty evening in early spring. I thought at first that I might have snagged the bottom, then that I might have snagged a sunken log. It was only when a fin actually broke the surface a few yards from shore that I realized I had a beautiful native trout. Perhaps the near-freezing water added to its natural sluggishness, for, though it was in the pink of condition, it came ashore almost as tamely as a codfish.

But when I saw what I had on the bank, I immediately forgave it for any lack of sportiness, and my heart began to beat with excitement. Here was the ultimate prize that every trout fisherman hopes for every time he casts into an eddy where a brook falls into a lake. It lay on the granite pebbles in the failing light, a vision of utter beauty, pink-bellied, gleaming chrome green on the back, silver along the sides, red fins edged with the purest damask, head cast in the mould of a blunt rifle bullet. I touched it almost reverently. Non-sportsmen will call me a fool, for only a sportsman understands this feeling of love and respect toward the thing that he kills. The Indians understand it. And we who share the wilderness, share it with them.

I picked up my trout by the gill covers, carried it that way on the long hike back to the road, and over the half-mile of road to my car, hoping to meet another angler and to feast upon the green gleam of envy in his eyes. Naturally, I didn't meet a soul.

Around the turn of the century, when there was quite a vogue for introducing new species of wildlife to Newfoundland, rainbow trout and brown trout were both introduced to St. John's. Both became well established, and provide excellent fishing in the limited area of their range.

The rainbows are landlocked, and confined to eighteen lakes in St. John's East, all within fifteen miles of the city. They are larger, sportier, more accessible, and harder to catch than brook trout.

The browns have a wider range, from lakes inside city limits to Conception Bay and Southern Shore rivers. In lakes they offer larger and more difficult trophies than the native trout. In streams they run to sea, and grow to enormous size. They are caught mainly in the estuaries at such places as Seal Cove, Manuels, Holyrood, and Witless Bay, all within thirty miles of St. John's.

Appendix III

Big-game hunting

Along the wild and mountainous south coast of Newfoundland, where the cliffs rise out of the sea in great pillars of grey granite and the rivers cascade through deep canyons into the bays and fjords, where eagles by the hundreds still circle in lonely pride, and the moose browse along the sand beaches, in those regions where men came late and did not linger long, the world's last great herd of woodland caribou is found.

This noble animal – the largest and handsomest of the reindeer – with antlers unmatched by any creature on earth, inhabits a narrowing patch of wilderness hemmed in by southern cliffs and northern forests.

Canoe routes through central Newfoundland traverse the caribou grounds. Roads cross them from north to south. Civilization presses in, remorselessly, from every side. In time it may have its way, and, except for herds on show in parks and reservations, the caribou may vanish. But meanwhile, just beyond the roads, in glacier country rich with rock and moss, on bushland and peat bog and lichen-covered barrens, from the Blue Hills of Coteau and the Annieopsquotch Mountains in the west to Wigwam Brook and Piper's Hole in the east, the caribou roam quietly, in family groups, in local clans, in thousand-headed herds, depending on the season.

Small herds of woodland caribou are still to be found on the barren lands of the Long Range, in the rough country north of the Topsails, and on the wild southern pasture of the Avalon Peninsula. But south and central Newfoundland are the only places where this animal may be hunted today with assurance of success. All the world-record heads have come from this region, and a few animals have been photographed there with heads far finer than any in the record books. I personally counted sixty points on the antlers of one stag.

I am a meat hunter, exclusively. Even if I shot a stag with a forty-point head (probably a season record) I would cut out the tongue, pour the brains into a jar, and throw the antlers into the nearest copse. I look upon trophy hunters with the same sort of intolerant contempt that trophy hunters have for meat hunters. But, on the subject of caribou, both classes of hunters are agreed: here is one of the world's finest trophy animals, and the finest of all meat animals, barring none.

Toward moose I have rather different feelings. Ever since the day back in 1952 when I had to get out of my car and throw stones at a moose to make it get out of the way I have had a certain amount of contempt for this plentiful, rather stupid, cow-like beast. Every year in Newfoundland many thousands of moose are shot for meat and for trophies, both by residents and by visiting hunters. Shooting them requires no skill, no courage, no knowledge of the wilderness. Except at the height of the hunting season, when they are driven a few miles back into the woods by the fusillade of shots ringing around their ears, they are scarcely wilder than Holsteins. They wander out into the fields and parks, and onto the golf courses, and sometimes even appear on downtown city streets.

Newfoundland has one of the world's healthiest and most prolific moose herds. For those who want either a caribou or a moose, or both, Newfoundland is certainly the place to hunt. I have talked to guides who, in more than a quarter of a century, have never known one of their hunters to go home without an animal.

The moose live and feed mainly on cut-overs and burns where they can get plenty of young forest growth to eat – bushes, shrubs, herbs, tips of fir and spruce trees, with grasses or lily pads for dessert. The huge logging industry that feeds the paper mills at Corner Brook and Grand Falls is constantly creating new moose pasture in all parts of Newfoundland.

Since they find it hard to travel in snow, and consequently hard to get enough food, moose often emerge from the winter looking thin and sickly. This impression is increased by their coats, which at this season are falling off in patches, and by their antlers, which are just starting to sprout anew after having been shed in the winter.

By midsummer the moose are sleek and fat once more, with healthy new coats and antlers forming 'in velvet'. By late summer the antlers are fully grown, and the moose begin rubbing off the velvet, using small trees on which to clean and polish their great, palmate branches of horn, often killing the trees outright in the process.

When hunting opens in September the moose are at the peak of condition. A few weeks later, at the beginning of the rut, the bulls become brave and belligerent, and start knocking the grilles off motor cars, particularly when the drivers of the cars try to chase them to see how fast they can run. Occasionally, a bull in rut is so full of hormones that he will even face a man. But the only person ever killed by a moose in Newfoundland was a hunter who made the mistake of attacking this immense animal with a .22-calibre rifle. He killed the moose, but not quite quickly enough; the moose managed to charge him, and collapse on top of him; they were found dead together.

Moose and caribou are not white-tailed deer. They are *big* game. Personally, I wouldn't hunt either animal with anything smaller than a .30-calibre rifle, and preferably with bullets of 160 grain or heavier, carrying plenty of knockdown power.

Moose are easy to hunt and easy to shoot. Many hunters regard the other major Newfoundland game animal, the woodland caribou, as exceedingly wild and hard to approach. A friend of mine who hunted caribou each year for almost a quarter of a century says that he always used a long-range rifle with a telescopic sight, and shot from ranges of 400 yards and more – like Ernest Hemingway in Africa. Caribou are certainly warier than moose, and they live on range that is much wilder and harder to reach, but I have never failed to get within 150 yards when making a shot, and I have often approached within twenty or thirty feet of them. I am well prepared to credit the story told me by an Indian who claims to have crept up on one lying on a bog and touched it with his hand.

One afternoon about a mile from Devil's Lake on the central Newfoundland plateau, as I was standing guard with a rifle over a wildlife photographer engaged in making a caribou film, we found ourselves out in the middle of a great peat bog while a small herd of seventy-six animals collected around us. They came wandering in, one and two at a time, from both ends of the bog, crossing Devil's River from the lake, and moving in Indian file out of the hills. They grazed and lay down to sleep all around us. The stags did a bit of mock fighting, for it was the mating season. After a while we could move around quietly without disturbing them. If they saw something moving they apparently supposed it to be another caribou.

Soon, however, the does – always much more alert than stags – sensed that there was something not quite right with us, became curious, and started clustering around, forming a semicircle with a radius of forty or fifty feet, ourselves at the centre, and an unoccupied stretch of marsh and bush behind us. The does stared at us out of large, solemn eyes, tossing their heads lightly. Some of them returned to nibbling the bog sedges, but more and more of them joined our audience, while the stags continued to doze or to court the remaining females in the background.

We never did put them to flight, but after a while – we by now much bolder, and moving about more freely – a large, dark, barren doe on our extreme right tossed her head more sharply than before and snorted slightly. All around her, other caribou lifted their heads and looked. She turned and began to pace slowly away toward the end of the bog. Just as slowly, the others began to follow. They went in an organized retreat, not running but walking, the fifteen stags and the sixty does and fawns and yearlings following their guide in an orderly march into the hills, among the gullies and patches of scrub spruce for the coming night.

I never did shoot an animal while 'riding shotgun' for the camera man, even though he often worked practically under the noses of stags in rut. Nevertheless, they have been known to charge people. This happens only when a stag has just been sparring with another stag, and the challenger is driven off. Anything the stag sees at such a moment he is likely to attack. I knew one man, in those circumstances, who picked up his gun and downed a charging stag at a range of fifteen feet, and another who claimed to have dodged the animal, leaped on its back, and killed it with a knife. In spite of these rare incidents, caribou are not belligerent or dangerous, and I have never heard of anyone being killed by one of them.

My most exciting encounter with a caribou – far more thrilling than any hunt – occurred one evening at a tiny pond near Louse Lake on the headwaters of Great Rattling Brook, a tributary of the Exploits River. The hunting season had not yet opened, and I was not carrying a gun. Just before dark I was stalking a stag that I had seen earlier in the day, never suspecting how close I had got to him, when he suddenly leaped up, almost from under my feet, and bolted. Every hunter stalks upwind as a matter of course, and there was a strong wind blowing in my face at the time. The stag had been flushed by sound, not scent, and he ran only a little distance before stopping and facing me, obviously uncertain what had startled him. I remained completely motionless until he began to feed, then moved cautiously, but every time I moved, even slightly, his head came up once more. This went on for about half an hour, until the stag, his curiosity conquering his fear, decided to investigate.

Ordinarily, a curious caribou would make a wide circle and approach his man from down-wind. But this one happened to be hemmed in by the lake on one side and a thick bank of brush on the other. He approached slowly, cautiously, ready to bolt at the slightest move, with many pauses en route, but finally he came right up to the small rock on which I was standing, stretched his neck toward me, and sniffed, just like a dog sniffing a stranger that he is meeting for the first time. It was undoubtedly the tensest moment of my life. It didn't last. In a split second the caribou identified the scent, and actually stood up on his hind legs as he wheeled and made for the woods, almost falling over backwards with fright. But even then he stopped and looked back, and, seeing that he was not pursued, faced me once more. I have wondered since whether he would have come back for another sniff had I waited long enough.

Though caribou are now more plentiful than they were in the early part of this century, they have never recovered from the merciless slaughter that began about a hundred years ago and continued down to the time of the First World War. As Newfoundland was opened up, first by railway and then by road, hunters flocked to the barrens, and killed without limit. Since caribou will not cross even a flimsy fence, the railwaymen left gaps in their snow fences for the use of the migrating herds. Hunters stationed themselves at these gaps and mowed down the animals as they came through. The carcasses piled up in heaps, and the railway ran special meat cars, railway employees buying the gutted animals on the spot and selling them to meat-cutters in St. John's. In addition, all trappers regularly killed three to four caribou each winter so long as the fur trade lasted, and caribou provided winter meat for most fishing and logging families in the north and west. Trophy hunters came from foreign places, not to shoot a single head, as they do now, but to see how many they could collect on a trip.

After decades of this, hunters began to notice that the caribou were no longer plentiful. They wondered what could be happening. Were the animals getting 'gun shy'? Could lynx and bears be killing them off? It took a long time even for government officials to conclude that they were simply being slaughtered ten times faster than they could breed. The slaughter was stopped in the nick of time, and a permanent closed season was imposed until the almost-extinct caribou increased to a few thousand once more.

You can drive to the caribou barrens in a car, and reach the wilder parts by canoe, in a small boat, or on foot. You can also fly to hunting lodges on the lakes of the central plateau, using small bush planes based at Gander or Grand Falls.

Seasons vary somewhat from year to year, and from one area to another. In general, caribou are hunted from mid September to the end of October, and moose from mid September to the end of December, or even later. Female as well as male animals are legal game in some areas and some seasons.

Black bears are hunted in the same regions as moose and caribou. You can buy licences for caribou, moose, bear, or all three. These animals are hunted successfully with bow and arrow, as well as with rifles, and some camps are operated exclusively for archers.

Rates, including transportation to hunting lodges, run from about $200 to about $800 per week, the higher rates being for combined caribou-moose-bear hunts.

Index

Where any entry receives major treatment, the major reference is given first, followed by the minor references.